UNIVERSITY STARTUPS AND SPIN-OFFS

GUIDE FOR ENTREPRENEURS IN ACADEMIA

Manuel Stagars

Apress®

University Startups and Spin-Offs: Guide for Entrepreneurs in Academia

Copyright © 2015 by **Manuel Stagars**

This work is subject to copyright. All rights are reserved by the Publisher, whether the whole or part of the material is concerned, specifically the rights of translation, reprinting, reuse of illustrations, recitation, broadcasting, reproduction on microfilms or in any other physical way, and transmission or information storage and retrieval, electronic adaptation, computer software, or by similar or dissimilar methodology now known or hereafter developed. Exempted from this legal reservation are brief excerpts in connection with reviews or scholarly analysis or material supplied specifically for the purpose of being entered and executed on a computer system, for exclusive use by the purchaser of the work. Duplication of this publication or parts thereof is permitted only under the provisions of the Copyright Law of the Publisher's location, in its current version, and permission for use must always be obtained from Springer. Permissions for use may be obtained through RightsLink at the Copyright Clearance Center. Violations are liable to prosecution under the respective Copyright Law.

ISBN-13 (pbk): 978-1-4842-0624-9

ISBN-13 (electronic): 978-1-4842-0623-2

Trademarked names, logos, and images may appear in this book. Rather than use a trademark symbol with every occurrence of a trademarked name, logo, or image we use the names, logos, and images only in an editorial fashion and to the benefit of the trademark owner, with no intention of infringement of the trademark.

The use in this publication of trade names, trademarks, service marks, and similar terms, even if they are not identified as such, is not to be taken as an expression of opinion as to whether or not they are subject to proprietary rights.

Business man/woman icons in front matter made by SimpleIcon (http://www.simpleicon.com) courtesy of www.flaticon.com under Creative Commons Attribution 2.0 Generic.

Government icon in front matter and icons in Chapter 1 made by Freepik (http://www.freepik.com) courtesy of www.flaticon.com under Creative Commons Attribution 2.0 Generic.

While the advice and information in this book are believed to be true and accurate at the date of publication, neither the authors nor the editors nor the publisher can accept any legal responsibility for any errors or omissions that may be made. The publisher makes no warranty, express or implied, with respect to the material contained herein.

> Managing Director: Welmoed Spahr
> Acquisitions Editor: Robert Hutchinson
> Developmental Editor: James Markham
> Editorial Board: Steve Anglin, Mark Beckner, Gary Cornell, Louise Corrigan, James DeWolf, Jonathan Gennick, Robert Hutchinson, Michelle Lowman, James Markham, Matthew Moodie, Jeff Olson, Jeffrey Pepper, Douglas Pundick, Ben Renow-Clarke, Gwenan Spearing, Matt Wade, Steve Weiss
> Coordinating Editor: Rita Fernando
> Copy Editor: Tiffany Taylor
> Compositor: SPi Global
> Indexer: SPi Global
> Cover Designer: Anna Ishchenko

Distributed to the book trade worldwide by Springer Science+Business Media New York, 233 Spring Street, 6th Floor, New York, NY 10013. Phone 1-800-SPRINGER, fax (201) 348-4505, e-mail orders-ny@springer-sbm.com, or visit www.springeronline.com. Apress Media, LLC is a California LLC and the sole member (owner) is Springer Science + Business Media Finance Inc (SSBM Finance Inc). SSBM Finance Inc is a Delaware corporation.

For information on translations, please e-mail rights@apress.com, or visit www.apress.com.

Apress and friends of ED books may be purchased in bulk for academic, corporate, or promotional use. eBook versions and licenses are also available for most titles. For more information, reference our Special Bulk Sales–eBook Licensing web page at www.apress.com/bulk-sales.

Any source code or other supplementary materials referenced by the author in this text is available to readers at www.apress.com. For detailed information about how to locate your book's source code, go to www.apress.com/source-code/.

Apress Business: The Unbiased Source of Business Information

Apress business books provide essential information and practical advice, each written for practitioners by recognized experts. Busy managers and professionals in all areas of the business world—and at all levels of technical sophistication—look to our books for the actionable ideas and tools they need to solve problems, update and enhance their professional skills, make their work lives easier, and capitalize on opportunity.

Whatever the topic on the business spectrum—entrepreneurship, finance, sales, marketing, management, regulation, information technology, among others—Apress has been praised for providing the objective information and unbiased advice you need to excel in your daily work life. Our authors have no axes to grind; they understand they have one job only—to deliver up-to-date, accurate information simply, concisely, and with deep insight that addresses the real needs of our readers.

It is increasingly hard to find information—whether in the news media, on the Internet, and now all too often in books—that is even-handed and has your best interests at heart. We therefore hope that you enjoy this book, which has been carefully crafted to meet our standards of quality and unbiased coverage.

We are always interested in your feedback or ideas for new titles. Perhaps you'd even like to write a book yourself. Whatever the case, reach out to us at editorial@apress.com and an editor will respond swiftly. Incidentally, at the back of this book, you will find a list of useful related titles. Please visit us at www.apress.com to sign up for newsletters and discounts on future purchases.

The Apress Business Team

For all startup entrepreneurs, wherever you are on your journey.

Contents

About the Author..ix
Acknowledgments xi
Preface...xiii
Introduction xv

Part I: **Strategies for University Startup Entrepreneurs** 1

Chapter 1: The Status Quo: How Do Startups Fit into Universities? ... 5
Chapter 2: The Lean Startup Changed Everything................. 15
Chapter 3: What Does It Mean to Be a Startup Entrepreneur? 29
Chapter 4: Engaging Others with Actionable Next Steps........... 55
Chapter 5: Benefits vs. Features 61
Chapter 6: Simple Strategies to Get Unstuck..................... 67
Chapter 7: Troubleshooting..................................... 77
Chapter 8: The Financial Model 81
Chapter 9: The Legal Setup of Your Startup..................... 93
Chapter 10: Meetings and Communication Skills 99
Chapter 11: Startup Grants: Can Government Programs Stimulate Entrepreneurship? 119
Chapter 12: Venture Capital and Angel Investors.................. 125
Chapter 13: Incubators and Accelerators 131
Chapter 14: Moving Past the Startup Stage....................... 137

Part II: **Strategies for Universities** 145

Chapter 15: How Do Universities Measure the Impact of Their Research? 151
Chapter 16: Why Are University Startups Not Taking Off? 157
Chapter 17: How Universities Can Support Their Startups Today.... 165

Chapter 18: Building a Bridge to the Market 171

Chapter 19: Platform Thinking for Startup Success 177

Chapter 20: More Platform Projects 187

Appendix A: Additional Considerations 203

Index 219

About the Author

Manuel Stagars is a serial entrepreneur, founder of seven companies, and business consultant. He has worked on over 200 client projects in the United States, Switzerland, Japan, and Singapore and has been supporting startups as an angel investor and consultant since 2007.

A graduate with honors from the London School of Economics (LSE International System), he holds certifications as a Chartered Financial Analyst (CFA), Chartered Alternative Investment Analyst (CAIA), and Energy Risk Professional (ERP). This enables him to blend creative entrepreneurship with contemporary macroeconomics and the perspective of an investor and venture capitalist.

www.manuelstagars.com

Acknowledgments

I am grateful to all the entrepreneurs who have shaped and tested the ideas in this book. Their feedback and experiences with launching startups have helped challenge and improve the approaches and recommendations you are about to read. Thanks to all the people who believed in my own startups over the years, whether by co-founding them with me, investing in them, buying their products, or otherwise guiding them through their launch phases.

I was fortunate to advise Singapore-ETH Centre (SEC) with my ideas, which Dr. Remo Burkhard made possible. I am grateful for his trust and his open-mindedness. Heartfelt thanks to his staff and the entire research and management team at SEC as well. I would also like to thank Dr. Ioannis Akkizidis for his outstanding remarks and guidance through the writing and editing process. Many thanks to Dr. Ting Dor Ngi from the National University of Singapore (NUS) for her excellent feedback and to Nati Sang for reviewing a very early draft of this book and improving it massively.

At Apress, a brilliant team turned these ideas into the book you are reading. I would like to thank Robert Hutchinson for believing in this project early on and the entire editorial board for supporting it. Many thanks to James Markham, Rita Fernando, Tiffany Taylor, Anna Ishchenko, and everybody else at Apress who contributed their knowledge and energy to make this happen.

Preface

Eighteen Years as a Startup Entrepreneur

When I embarked on the path of entrepreneurship 18 years ago, little did I know exactly where it would lead me and what surprises were in store along the way. Some of my ideas and projects failed dismally, but luckily, others were far more successful than I ever dreamed. I learned many lessons and combined them with some thoughts about launching startups out of universities. This is what this book is about.

My journey was far from elegant. Always thinking I would be a surgeon, I enrolled in medical school in my native Zurich/Switzerland. During the first year, it became clear that this was not for me, because my attention mostly focused on my private projects and experiments. After trying a few other fields, including psychology and sociology, I left university at age 21, slightly confused, with big plans about my own company and a bankroll in the high three digits. It was the dawn of the first Internet boom, and the winds were fortunate. Within a few short years, my little startup producing multimedia content for web pages had mushroomed into a respectable enterprise with several verticals and clients among the largest Swiss banks, insurance companies, airlines, hotels, automobile companies, and consumer brands. I profitably exited that business in 2001, six months before the NASDAQ crash had sunk in as a reality, and emigrated to Los Angeles, where the grass was greener (or so I thought).

Replicating the business model that had worked back home was my first attempt at American business, which gave me much insight into how well-protected and transparent the Swiss business environment had been. After producing a documentary film and founding several companies, a fun idea that had started as a side project eventually took flight and ended in a seven-figure joint venture deal with a large Japanese media company. So I moved to Tokyo. Simultaneously, a software startup I had co-founded in San Francisco received seed funding from a venture capital firm. Life was good. A strong believer in life-long learning, I enrolled in the international program at the London School of Economics and studied for three post-grad finance and private equity designations, all at the same time. Then the software business missed its milestones for next-round funding in the financial crisis of 2007/8. In the following years, I started a consulting practice in finance and economics, into which I integrated my diverse entrepreneurial experience.

Is entrepreneurship always fun? Of course not. Nevertheless, startup war stories are fun to tell. There is often more learning in a failure than in a success, however painful it is. For example, I remember an epic computer crash that resulted in the total loss of all the data and backups of an expensive client project that was ready for delivery. It had taken 6 months to complete, and the deadline was 24 hours away. With much rhetoric, it was possible to push it forward 2 days. This left me with exactly 72 hours to produce everything again from scratch. Fixing the defective hardware. Flying in some of the experts who had been working on the project. Explaining the crisis, which made them laugh and me cringe inside. And on top of all that, keeping everybody on the project happy while pulling a three-nighter myself. Then the day came to deliver the project to the wary client. I needed all the goodwill I could possibly get. The principal decision-maker wanted to take a seat, but an employee accidentally pulled the chair out from underneath him and he landed hard on the concrete floor. And I had thought the situation could not get any worse.

In fact, many entrepreneurs doubt the path they have embarked on when they speak in private. Not when the million-dollar buyout has just completed, but when things are not going so well. Entrepreneurship seems in many respects to be the path of most resistance. It is impossible to know all the answers to why and how it works. It took me about a decade to wrap my head around certain successes and failures and to understand why they had happened and what I could have handled better. However, when the stars align and a project takes off like a rocket, that makes it all worthwhile. Over time, it becomes much easier to cope with the volatility of entrepreneurship. After all, high waves hardly scare those who have seen them before.

Currently I advise several startups on strategy, business development, and financial innovation, integrating the perspective of the serial entrepreneur, economist, investor, and venture capitalist. One consulting project includes a research university in Singapore. Launching startups out of academia holds much promise for the future and is dear to my heart, and so this book came about.

For your journey to a successful startup, I wish you all the best. If I could do it, so can you. Just take that first step, and never look back.

—Manuel Stagars
Hong Kong, October 2014

Introduction

If you have ever been inside an MRI scanner, had a vaccination, flown in an airplane powered by rocket fuel, or used the seatbelt in your car, then you have experienced the benefits of university research. Thousands of products used every day have sprung to life out of university research labs. But in recent years, when it comes to leadership in innovation, universities have ceded the limelight to the private sector. Although much university research is still potentially useful, it rarely sees the light of day beyond publication in a scientific journal. Most of the patents held in university patent portfolios never earn a cent in revenue. Only a tiny minority of researchers will ever run their own company and apply the technologies they have so passionately invented. What does this disconnect stem from? Often from a lack of information about how to turn ideas into startups to make an impact.

Startup entrepreneurship is a learning experience that encompasses disciplines outside of your domain. It is a mindset, not a job. With that mindset, you should embrace the opportunity to integrate new skills into your life. You may discover a new talent you never knew you had. Starting a company sounds difficult, but the alternative, working in a corporation, is no cakewalk either. Few big corporations innovate. Climbing the ranks from the ground up often takes decades and is fraught with politics. Doing a good job and trying to be inventive will not help you to advance in the corporate environment. This leaves creative people frustrated. However, when joining a big corporation as an accomplished entrepreneur, your chances are much better. I know several founders who sold their startups to large companies. For them, entrepreneurship was the fast track to an executive position in a larger corporation.

Startup entrepreneurship is a huge advantage on your resume. You will gain diverse knowledge unlike that from any other project you have undertaken so far. After all, life is short. Wouldn't it make sense to explore all the possibilities before committing to a line of work in which you spend 60% of your waking hours? I encourage everyone to give entrepreneurship a try. The guidelines in this book will enrich your experience and give you the tools to make the most of your ideas. You will gain a wealth of diverse knowledge by launching a startup. When you work in your own company instead of somebody else's, you will learn the ropes of doing business and making an impact much faster (see Figure 1). This makes up for the long hours spent trying to get it off the ground. You will be able to draw on this throughout your life.

Introduction

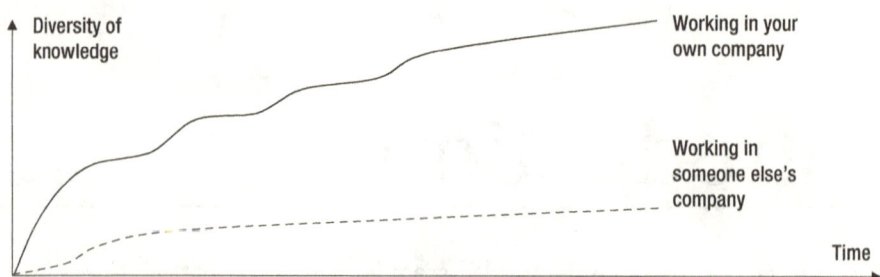

Figure 1. Diversity of knowledge from launching a startup

Who Is This Book For?

The first part of this book speaks directly to students and researchers who are interested in launching a startup or spin-off. In a nutshell, this is about showing founders how they can use the existing university system as a springboard for entrepreneurship, make the best of existing synergies, and sidestep all the ballast not conducive to startup success. The strategies are of course also useful for entrepreneurs venturing out on their own without an academic support system.

I do not examine the topic academically. Much has been written elsewhere about the commercialization of university patents and the complexities of public programs to stimulate entrepreneurship. It is also not my intent to suggest sweeping reforms to the education system to make it more entrepreneurial. But if you are studying, researching, or teaching at a university and are thinking about entrepreneurship, this book is for you. It contains practical advice that I find useful in launching a company, mostly based on my personal experience. All startups and entrepreneurs are unique, and I do not claim to have all the answers. Nevertheless, I introduce some unconventional ideas and approaches here that you may find useful in your own endeavors as an entrepreneur.

The second part of the book concentrates on universities. You may find yourself in a position where you wonder how the current system could better help foster startups and entrepreneurship. There are numerous opinions about how this should be done. However, a relatively conservative organization like a university cannot be turned on its head overnight with a sweeping reform. Yet there exists a growing desire among universities to redefine their relationship with the market and other external stakeholders. Making an impact with research beyond scientific publications occupies more and more mindshare. By understanding how the startup process works, universities can leverage their existing resources to help students and researchers launch companies with more impact.

Introduction

Many of those ideas and approaches run contrary to what your startup advisors will tell you. This book may advocate that you do the opposite of what you read in the university's official startup publication or in popular books about startups. It may even suggest that you forget what you just learned in a Guru workshop about entrepreneurship. Some of the ideas may seem overly opportunistic to you, especially if you have never been exposed to entrepreneurship before. Launching a startup is by definition opportunistic. If there is a chance, then take it. If there is none, then make one. Nobody will make your life work for you. You need to take matters into your own hands and take full responsibility for your destiny. This is one of the prevailing themes of this book.

What Will You Learn in This Book?

Launching a startup is not rocket science. Regardless, there are a few strategies and skills that founders must know to have a real chance at success. Putting together an entrepreneurship program at a university has much in common with launching a startup. So the strategies outlined in the first part of the book are just as useful for those who implement entrepreneurial programs in the curricula of universities. The overview in Figure 2 groups the book's chapters by topic.

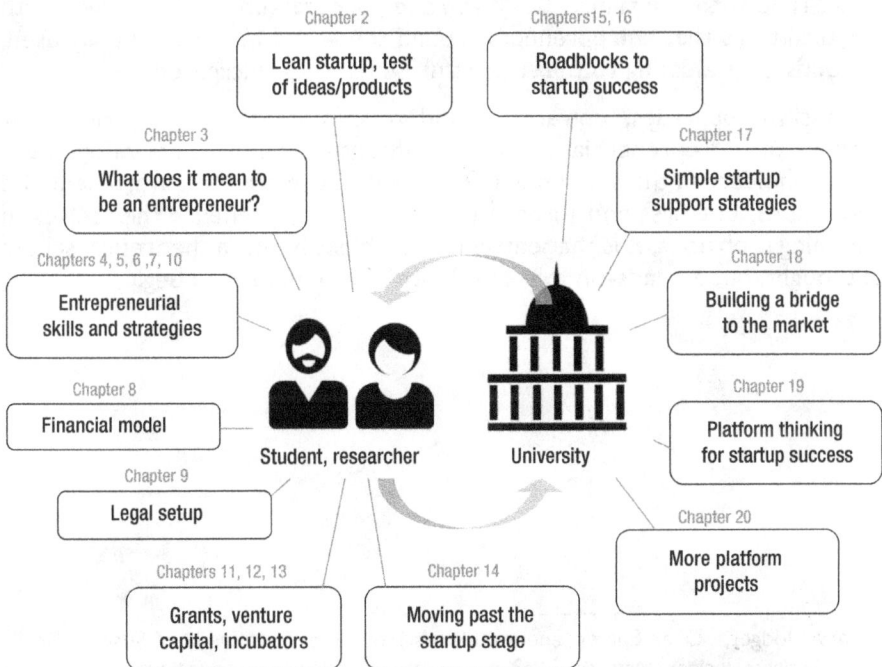

Figure 2. Chapters and topics

Introduction

While you read, I encourage you to keep an open mind. Look at entrepreneurship as a process—an ongoing learning experience. It is in many ways more a mindset than a job, which may confuse you at times. There will be much conflict ahead. Armed with some basic tools, you will come to understand what it means to launch a startup. You will be in a position to analyze your challenges, break them down into manageable parts, and move them toward solutions quickly. Even though the end goal of your startup may still be uncertain, you will have a guide that explains the next steps.

All this comes not from a theoretical source, but from a battle-hardened practitioner who has walked this walk before: seven times, to be exact, as of this writing. That being said, do not take any of this as gospel. This is simply a collection of concepts I find helpful in getting a company off the ground in a relatively short time, with limited resources.

I wish I had a sure-fire recipe to create a successful company, but I don't. Many turtles hatch, but few make it to the sea. Achieving startup success remains elusive. A whopping 93% of companies backed by Silicon Valley–based accelerator Y Combinator fail.[1] Mind you, these are the 2% of handpicked companies that were selected to enter a 90-day entrepreneurship crash course in the startup capital of the world. Startups fail despite the best efforts of an army of talented venture capitalists, consultants, and the entrepreneurs themselves, who often display incredible drive to make their company work. There is no shame in failure. But if you and your startup arm yourselves with practical tools that entrepreneurs around the world have successfully used, the odds of graduating to the successful 7% have just increased.

With slight upgrades, universities and their startups can improve their chances of entrepreneurial success significantly. This requires effort from all stakeholders in the startup equation—not just from the government and universities, but first and foremost from the entrepreneurs themselves. If one thing is obvious, it is that entrepreneurship is hardly a theoretical school of thought, but a hands-on exercise. With this in mind, let's begin.

---

[1] Henry Blodget, "Dear Entrepreneurs: Here's How Bad Your Odds of Success Really Are," *Business Insider*, May 28, 2013, www.businessinsider.com/startup-odds-of-success-2013-5.

PART

I

Strategies for University Startup Entrepreneurs

When did you choose to become an entrepreneur? In early childhood, or just yesterday? Or are you still on the fence? Whatever the case, you should have some idea about what it is like to start your own business before you take the plunge—an idea based on the entrepreneurial experience of someone who has done this before.

If you study or do research at a university, take a step back and observe your environment from 50,000 feet in the air. You see a fail-safe system where you acquire deep knowledge without much distraction. It does not matter whether the economy is in a boom or in a slump; learning always has priority. Now think about what this environment could do for you as a startup entrepreneur. You have a strong community, an excellent network, diversity of ideas and opinions, fully equipped workshops and labs, and tech support at your disposal—all for free. Your university may have a strong reputation. It may attract powerful external parties such as governments and corporations that want to be involved in one form or another. All these advantages are unique, and they exist only for students and researchers. In this walled garden, you can test and experiment. If you fail, there is almost no consequence. Companies seldom have such luxury. University startups have a leg up on anyone else. When you know how to use this environment to your benefit, you can compete with companies anywhere in the world from a strong base that supports you all the way. Why not give it a shot and make the most of your university experience?

Most of the time, your university or government will have some startup advice for you. This is the conventional advice that others have diligently followed: apply for this or that grant, participate in the business-plan competition, and get some MBA students from another faculty to create a business model for you. The startup consultant from the university or the government has never launched a startup, so how can they be experts to guide you toward success? Out of ignorance about what entrepreneurship really entails, startups give away much of the control over their destiny.

Part I of this book will empower you with actual, practical steps that you can apply today. Of course, this is no guarantee that your venture will succeed. Nevertheless, it is much better than having no clue about how to begin, in the process relying on non-entrepreneurs to call the shots for you. I have included a few episodes from my own startup journey. They have little in common with the success stories you would read in a Donald Trump book, but they paint a picture of what most entrepreneurs may go through to eventually turn their companies profitable. To make the point that successful startups are not created overnight, let me recount how my first company came to pass in a little more detail.

When I started out as an entrepreneur, I had the odds stacked firmly against me. Nobody from my family had ever started their own business. None of my friends had, either. Because I thought I wanted to be a medical doctor from a very young age, I never seriously looked at any other professions. Not only that, I never investigated what it really meant to be employed in a hospital. After the first year at medical school, I terminated my studies with the vague idea of doing something with the Internet and multimedia. All of my old friends from school reacted to the decision with disbelief and criticism. The same was the case with the new friends I had made during my freshman year. Nobody could quite understand why this guy was dissatisfied with what worked so well for them. Why did he decide to give it all up to try to do the impossible? My parents were obviously less than thrilled when they heard of my latest plans. They were not particularly supportive of this new direction, yet they had no other choice than to let me try.

Because I was not independently wealthy, I had to take on some humbling, menial jobs—just menial enough that I had enough time to develop my vision and skill set in my free time. The first was part-time work as an usher in a movie theatre. Occasionally some old classmates would see me vacuuming popcorn from the floor; they must have chuckled at the sight of the valedictorian of their class from the prestigious high school, the former medical student, who was now laboring side by side with shady characters, some of whom you would rather not face at night in a dark alley. This was a difficult time, no doubt. But in retrospect, it was an essential test of my dedication to make it work.

With the little money I had saved, I bought a desktop computer and picked up some programming on my own. After a brief stint at a copy shop (where I learned to use Adobe Photoshop), I took a part-time job at a TV station (where I learned about marketing and using multimedia software). A few more interludes followed, most of them hardly worth recounting. However, after about a year, I felt I had enough knowledge to launch my first startup. The Internet was just beginning to take off, and there was a fast-growing demand for flash web sites with audio and CD-ROMs with sound effects and narration. This is what I offered to produce as a service. I was 22 years old, with no experience, let alone a track record. As you might expect, I blundered my way through many embarrassing episodes. One of them was the brilliant idea of making a big marketing splash by sending 100 potential clients little boxes of chocolate with my business card inside. After a few days, I called the clients and asked whether I could come by for a meeting to show my services. It turned out to be an unusually hot summer. Someone at the post office must have parked their delivery truck in the roasting sun. You can imagine what those well-intentioned presents looked like when they arrived at the clients by mail. It was an expensive marketing stunt gone wrong.

Finally landing my first paid project put the gears in motion. The Internet was rocket fuel to the economy, so more projects followed in swift succession. All in all, I have to admit I was lucky that this first startup was successful. Many other entrepreneurs went under in the first dot.com crash. Their founders had come from much more privileged backgrounds than me. Some were MBAs; others were launching their second company with powerful joint venture partners and ample funding. Because none of that was available to me, I had to be creative and resourceful from day one. Had I relied on my surroundings and waited until someone took me under their wing to make things happen for me, I would not be writing this book today. Through trial and error, I found an approach that helped my company become profitable fast, with products that clients paid money for from the start. This trial phase is something I still draw from today. Some of the startup advice in this book is directly related to it.

Fortunately, it got easier over time. With more experience, I put less trust in those who insisted that starting a successful company without funding was impossible, perhaps because I knew that it could be accomplished. Not all my ventures were profitable, but the failures were just as valuable as the successes.

An iron will and common sense go a long way. Unfortunately, these are what I see lacking with many of today's startup entrepreneurs. A flood of recent business literature gives founders the impression that they have to study entrepreneurship before they can do it. Grant programs, government initiatives, and startup workshops saturate them with theory, taught by people who have never started a company themselves. Media stories about recently minted billionaire founders are selling the Hollywood version of entrepreneurship. Please do not buy into this hype.

Entrepreneurs have always existed, and to launch a thriving business is doable with little theory if you put your mind to it. It was possible before any government grants existed and before venture capital and seed accelerators arrived on the scene. You need the determination to succeed and a few simple strategies. Most important, you have to take action, sooner rather than later. The simplicity of entrepreneurship is its power. This power lies with the entrepreneur alone. As soon as you take matters into your own hands, you will start making real progress toward your own success story.

If you come from an entrepreneurial family, then you have a better chance of making it. But if not, what will you do? Not even try because nobody is helping you? Quietly agree with the opinion of the mainstream that startup success is a lottery or requires an MBA and millions of dollars in venture capital? If your university or government has programs available, then take full advantage of them. But do not let them distract you. If you get on the wrong trajectory early, reaching your destination will be a challenge.

A recurring theme of this book is taking matters into your own hands to move your startup forward step by step. On the way, take advantage of all the synergies you can get. Learn from your mistakes. Pick yourself up and keep walking. Take initiative, and never wait for opportunities to come to you. This is the defining characteristic of a successful entrepreneur.

CHAPTER 1

The Status Quo: How Do Startups Fit into Universities?

Students and researchers have always founded their own companies right out of universities. This is not new. Just as in any other venture, some of those companies thrive, while others falter. Some entrepreneurs have a natural talent for running a business, whereas others are less skilled. In recent years, there has been a huge surge of interest in entrepreneurship, both inside and outside universities. Researchers are beginning to realize that running their own company may be more adventurous and rewarding than a lifetime teaching position in higher education. Students converge on popular fields such as computer science to launch their own companies while working on their degree or after graduation. News stories abound about 20-year-olds turning into billionaires with virtual reality startups.[1]

---

[1] Alexei Oreskovic and Malathi Nayak, "Facebook to Buy Virtual Reality Goggles Maker for $2 Billion," *Reuters*, March 26, 2014, www.reuters.com/article/2014/03/25/us-facebook-acquisition-idUSBREA201WX20140325.

Entrepreneurship has attracted global buzz. However, when it comes to practical know-how about launching a startup, universities have much catching up to do. To fill the void, incubators and seed accelerators have sprung up as startup schools that offer crash courses in entrepreneurship, infrastructure, mentoring, and financial aid.

Before you jump in and learn about the practical guidelines for entrepreneurs, you first need to understand the place of startups in universities today. This chapter explains the components that enable startup success, how they interact with each other and how universities currently put them to use. It also outlines the launch sequence of academic startups and the roadblocks entrepreneurs encounter, Later in this book, we will look into some of the support systems available for startups, such as entrepreneurship programs, technology transfers, and startup grants. The discussion would be incomplete without deliberating on why some of these programs are useful and others less so. This chapter also introduces the main obstacles that stand in the way of setting up effective startup programs at universities, and common misconceptions about startup entrepreneurship in general. This groundwork sets the tone for the rest of this book. Without it, I feel entrepreneurs have only half the picture of what it means to launch a company. Examples for upgrading a university's startup program are in the second part of this book.

Universities Can Build the Optimal Startup Ecosystem

Universities are still the undisputed centers of excellence when it comes to knowledge and scientific research. But using their assets in the marketplace is not their strength, and, unfortunately, the impact of scientific research on the lives of people outside of academia is small. This is unnecessary, because universities occupy an important space at the intersection between science, business, and public policy. They connect many stakeholders from different domains in their daily activities. Some universities have a high pedigree and an international reputation that draw attention from financial investors and the media. They participate in summits such as the World Economic Forum (WEF), world city summits, and climate conferences. Universities often interact with multinational companies that sponsor their research. And the government is also on board as principal financier.

Despite the fact that opportunities for network building and cooperations are readily available to them, universities hardly use them enough for their own benefit. They actively communicate with many third parties, but the energy this creates often evaporates, unused. If universities channeled this energy, they could help create a robust ecosystem for startups, to the advantage of students and researchers interested in entrepreneurship. Such an ecosystem would prepare participants for the journey ahead and would eventually build a bridge between scientific research and millions of people who stand to gain from it in their everyday lives. It would anchor the university in the public image as a force for real-world impact. And it would motivate staff and professors to discover a deeper meaning in their work. Let's examine what such an ecosystem could look like.

Universities are platforms. Many different stakeholders exchange ideas and energy with universities daily, creating vast potential resources that are just sitting there, unused. As soon as universities focus and channel energy toward their startups, synergies emerge. Dynamic knowledge exchange, collaborations, constant feedback, and engaged discussions grow a ring of *network effects* around the institution (the large arrows in Figure 1-1).

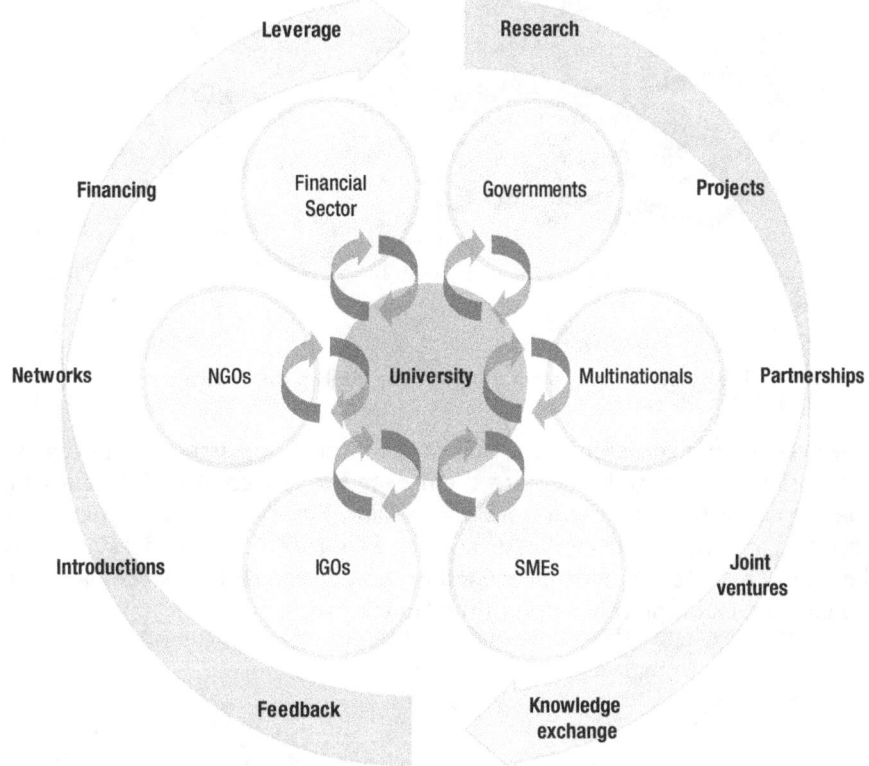

Figure 1-1. Ideal university ecosystem and resulting synergies

With the energy and momentum available on this supercharged platform, startups load their batteries and eventually lift off like helicopters. Figure 1-2 shows what the ideal situation looks like. A university with a strong entrepreneurial ecosystem is the ideal launch pad for startups founded by students and researchers. Most universities have all the components to build it right in their backyard. They just need to remove the blockages that prevent the ecosystem from growing. Academia is a natural magnet for smart people and interested external stakeholders. As soon as their energy is channeled toward a common goal, startups in this environment draw on much stronger resources than the private sector alone can provide.

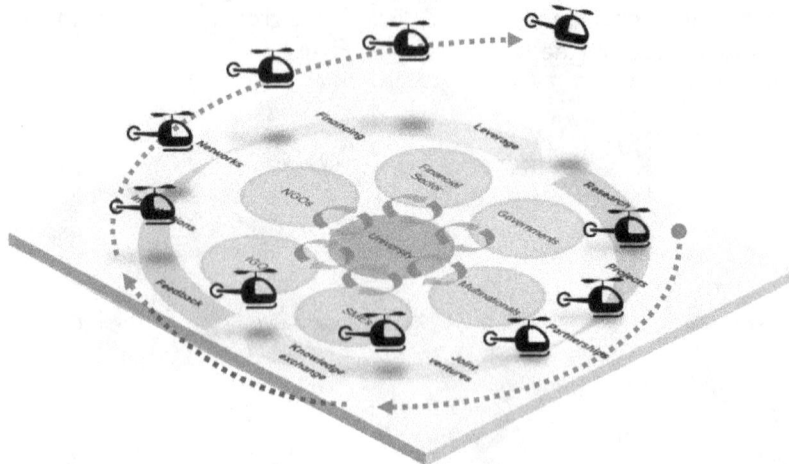

Figure 1-2. The university ecosystem turns into the ideal startup launch pad

However, such ecosystems are still nascent or nonexistent. A few global hotspots have managed to create them over the last couple of decades, but one can count them on the fingers of one hand. At present, most synergies lie dormant, and startup launch pads are not fully formed. To understand what this does to university entrepreneurship, look at Figure 1-3, which illustrates the current, incomplete version of the launch pad.

University Startups and Spin-Offs

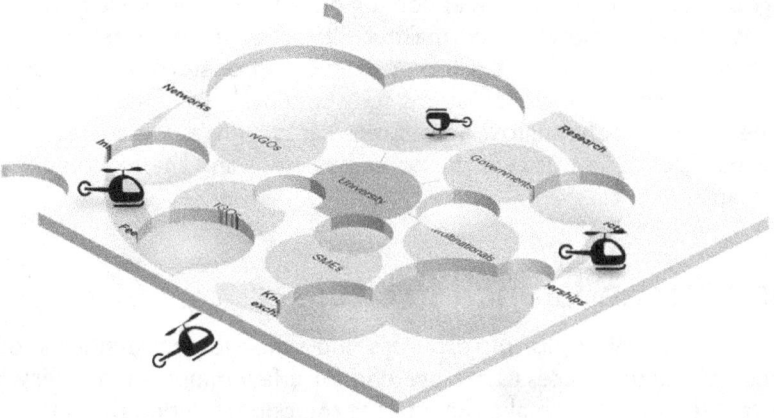

Figure 1-3. Startups on the incomplete launch pad

The status quo looks much less inviting. A weak entrepreneurial ecosystem leads to a weak startup launch pad. The ring of network effects around the university is interrupted, and no ecosystem can grow. Synergistic interaction with third parties is almost entirely missing, which leads to roadblocks and gaps in the structure. Far fewer startups are possible on an incomplete platform. That is obvious, because there simply is not enough room and energy for them to thrive. Serious pitfalls can hamper startups at any stage of their evolution. Looking at it from this perspective, it is evident why so few successful startups come from academia.

Why don't universities repair their incomplete startup launch pads? They would first have to grow stronger entrepreneurial ecosystems, and the need to do that is not yet dire enough. In many universities, the opinion prevails that entrepreneurship workshops, business plan competitions, and grant funding will fix the underlying structural problems. However, without a fundamental shift in the way academics and institutions approach entrepreneurship, current efforts will bring mostly cosmetic improvements that only go so far. This is unfortunate. As education becomes increasingly globalized, it will be critical for universities to adopt entrepreneurial thinking and have something to show for it. It will no longer be sufficient to point to key performance indicators (KPIs) that show a certain number of spin-off companies or patent applications per year. Uncomfortable questions about the measurable impact of such startups will surface. This may not happen immediately, but the day will come. Academia will have a lot of catching up to do then.

Chapter 1 | The Status Quo: How Do Startups Fit into Universities?

The good news is that many ideas coming out of universities are groundbreaking. They have the potential to make a difference in the lives of millions of people. With a mind shift, it will be possible to transform the status quo at universities into thriving ecosystems for startups. It will take much effort to put the gears in motion. How universities can do this is the subject of part 2 of this book. Let's first discuss the necessary steps and the roadblocks on the way to startup success.

The Startup Launch Process

With their natural wealth of resources and synergies, universities should be hotbeds of startup success. Let's pretend for a few minutes that everything is perfect and universities make the most of the opportunities available to them. Figure 1-4 shows the ideal launch sequence for startups.

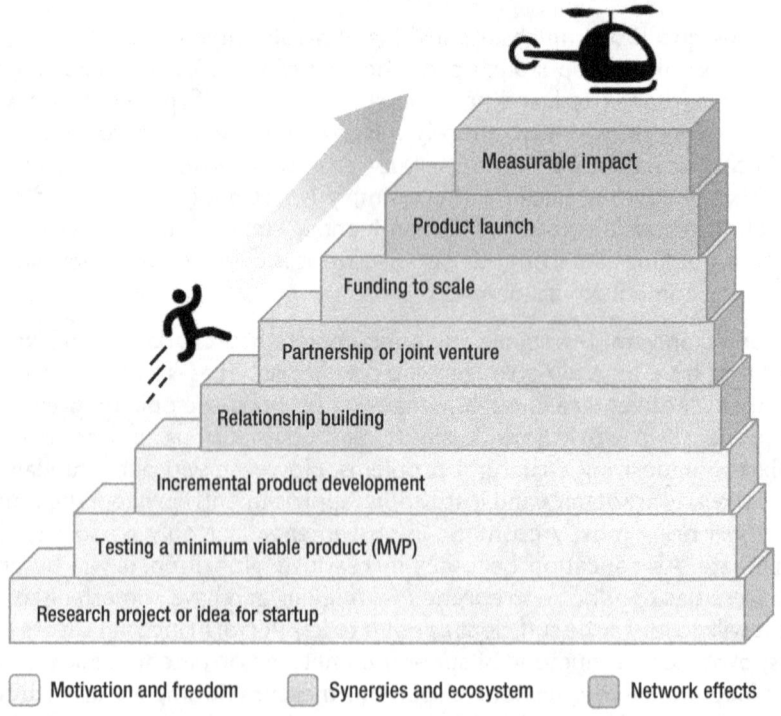

Figure 1-4. Ideal startup launch sequence

The underlying forces that enable startup success are as follows:

- *Motivation and freedom*: Students and researchers have a strong motivation and the freedom to follow through on their ideas for startups.
- *Synergies and ecosystem*: The university has cleared roadblocks to synergies and has allowed an entrepreneurial ecosystem to grow. Startups draw massive energy from that.
- *Network effects*: Once enough synergies are in place, network effects kick in. Launching additional startups becomes increasingly easy, and startups stand a better chance of making an impact in the market.

If these forces are in place, the stage is set for startups to take off. How universities may develop these forces is the subject of the second part of this book. For the time being, let's assume they exist already. In the ideal environment, all that students and researchers need is a practical approach to entrepreneurship. Unless they mismanage their venture in the launch process, they automatically achieve the right trajectory.

To illustrate how the launch sequence works, let's start with a research project at a university. Assume the team had an idea about a potential commercial product and decides to launch a startup. Empowered to do so, they first test their assumptions. Without testing, the startup would be flying blind. Serious entrepreneurs cannot afford to do that; they need to know if their intended product meets a demand in the market. If enough people are ready and willing to pay money for the product, then there is a business. The startup can charge ahead full-steam and develop the product incrementally. The founders test and re-test their upgrades often with potential customers in the market. In parallel, they begin building relationships with third parties. These may be companies in the same field or other experienced entrepreneurs who have already launched successful startups. The financial sector and wealthy individuals should also be part of entrepreneurs' networks. The startup engages them all for frequent feedback on their progress and a dynamic exchange of ideas.

Because the founders communicate effectively and professionally, they have a clear understanding of who to approach. They also understand the benefits they provide to third parties. With actionable next steps, they keep them involved and direct all the energy they can into the development of their product. Because stakeholders outside of the university see a value in what the startup produces, they inspire the founders with ideas. When the product has evolved to the point that the startup can launch it in the market, the team brings their connections to venture capital firms to the table. The entrepreneurs can scale rapidly when they need to. Their product serves an existing need in the market, and their business model is strong enough to drive a profitable company. Because they always had an ear to the ground, the launch is a success. The startup transformed university research into a useful product that improves the lives of people. It has a measurable impact on the real world.

Universities and their entrepreneurs should continue to strive for this ideal process. As you already learned, universities *can* build powerful ecosystems for startups. Once they have achieved that, reality will be closer to the ideal scenario we just described.

Let's now take off the rose-colored glasses. Unfortunately, the reality for startups at universities is less than ideal. The experience for entrepreneurs can often feel similar to the illustration in Figure 1-5.

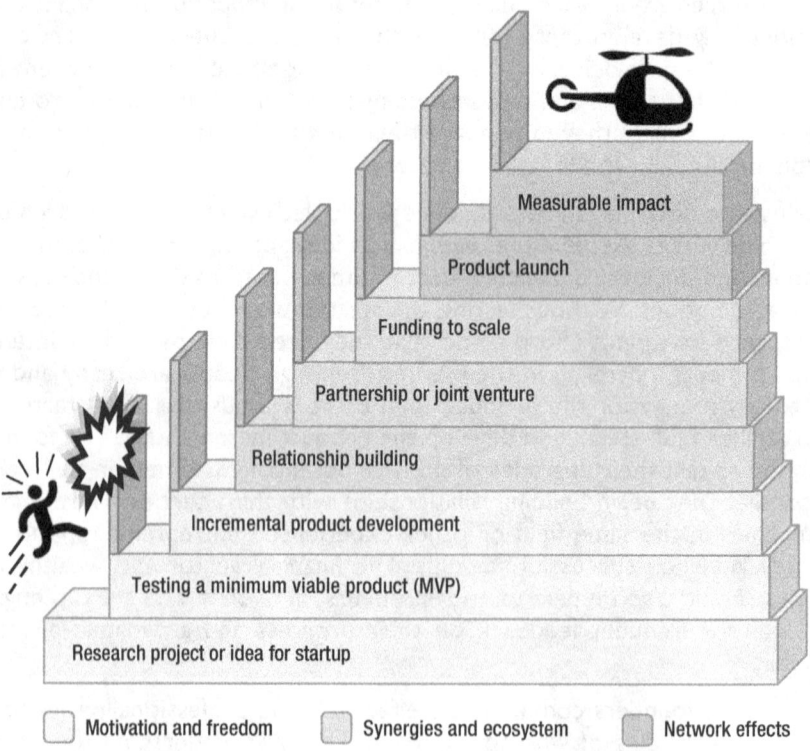

Figure 1-5. Startup launch sequence with roadblocks

Numerous roadblocks prevent startups from moving from one step to the next. Entrepreneurs cannot skip any of the steps of the launch sequence—they are all necessary to build a solid foundation for the startup. Some of the hurdles are external: they exist within universities that are unprepared to give startups what they need. Synergies, the ecosystem, and network effects may be missing. Other hurdles are internal: students and researchers may not know how to advance from one level to the next. They linger in analysis paralysis or lack constructive strategies to express and develop their ideas. They often struggle to define their own value for third parties, let alone engage them in a mutual knowledge exchange. As a result, their networks are not strong enough to help them reach escape velocity. Despite good ideas, many startups are trapped on the ground level. They never launch a useful product, so they fail to attract a joint venture partner or venture capital. Such startups and spin-off companies do show up in the university's KPIs, but their measurable impact is zero.

So what is there to do? It will take a while for universities to get their ecosystems up to speed. In the meantime, it is up to the entrepreneurs to overcome the roadblocks. More often than not, the prevailing thought is that more money fixes all problems. But instead of paying the roadblocks to go away, startup entrepreneurs need to know *practical strategies* to overcome them (see Figure 1-6).

Chapter 1 | The Status Quo: How Do Startups Fit into Universities?

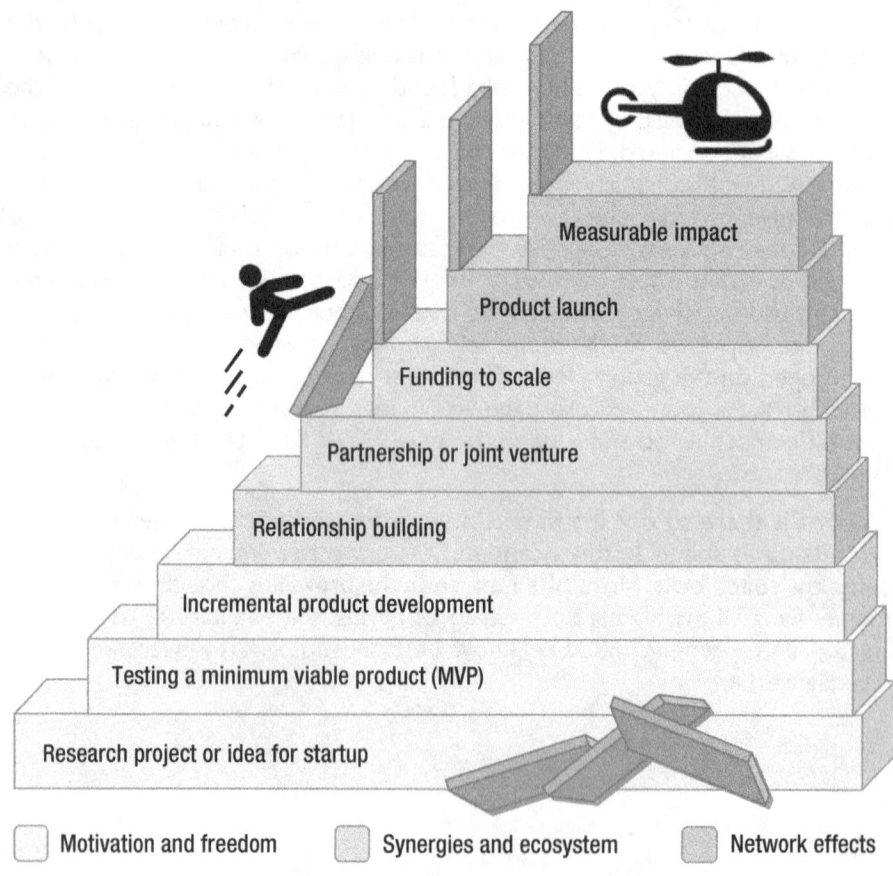

Figure 1-6. Overcoming roadblocks with practical strategies

In a less-than-perfect world, students and researchers must take matters into their own hands. Whenever they encounter roadblocks, they should know how to kick them away with the right karate moves. With entrepreneurial thinking at their disposal, they develop products with the lean method. They learn how to articulate their business ideas to third parties outside of the university. This gives them a clear understanding of their value proposition and helps identify the right partners, which helps them to build strong networks with established companies and the financial sector.

When they have to fend for themselves, startups may advance more slowly than in the ideal launch sequence, but they do so steadily nevertheless. They move forward step by step and eventually take off on their own terms. By developing their own powers, entrepreneurs can thrive in today's less-than-perfect ecosystem. What these powers are and how to acquire them is up next in this book.

CHAPTER 2

The Lean Startup Changed Everything

When Eric Ries published his book *The Lean Startup* in 2011, he brought about a paradigm shift in business modeling.[1] Only a few of the ideas in the book were groundbreaking or new, but many people were seeing them outlined neatly and logically for the first time. According to the Lean Startup method, "build, measure, learn" is at the heart of entrepreneurship. This means testing, measuring, changing, and retesting several hypotheses before a product launch. Real potential clients give feedback on minimum viable products (MVPs), which helps tailor the product or service to the market in small steps. Learning and experimenting therefore trump planning and politics. Businesses focus on product development close to their customers to improve their impact from day one. Hallelujah!

When the book came out, I was recovering from a venture that had started out promisingly. Flush with seed investment in the mid-six figures, the company I cofounded in San Francisco was about to revolutionize the trading of copyrights, trademarks, and patents on a digital platform. Offices in the Mission District were rented. A board 12 members strong, including executives from

---

[1] Eric Ries, *The Lean Startup* (New York: Crown Publishing Group, 2011).

eBay, was summoned. A fancy code shop full of developers was hired to program the platform. Hours were spent in conference calls, with phone-ins from different continents. Things were looking up, until the financial crisis in 2007/8 came around. The second round of financing fell through, and the startup collapsed under its heavy overhead without having launched a single line of code. This was the opposite of a lean startup, and it is painful to remember all the silliness. We wasted much time, not to mention the investment of the venture capital firm. Lucky for us, they understood that bad things happen to good people, which softened unwinding the mess a great deal. Having such lenient investors was by no means a foregone conclusion.

According to the Lean Startup method, we should have approached the business differently. Instead of trying to build a new universe to revolutionize the licensing market with a big bang, we should have thought about our MVP first. If we had coded it ourselves, we could have tested it daily with actual potential users and clients. We probably would have learned that the original idea was much too large and doomed to fail and that we should focus on a smaller niche from the beginning. We could have found the most profitable niche through further testing. With clear signals for or against the need for such a platform and a much stronger idea of what the code should look like we could have engaged professional developers to finish the beta for launch. Going about the project this way would have required only 10% of the investment, with much more learning and insight along the way. Instead we were flying blind based solely on our own rigid assumptions, which we even vehemently defended to investors and advisors.

Before the Lean Startup method became widely adopted, most business founders focused primarily on launching the perfect product and much less on feedback from the market. Long brainstorming sessions about the perfect strategy replaced simply trying something and seeing what happened. Entrepreneurs founding a company today should figure out how to run it lean to make the best use of their resources.

The Lean Startup method is not only for tech startups. Multinationals like General Motors use it for their in-house R&D as well. Steve Blank goes as far as calling it a new strategy for the 21st century that goes hand in hand with other changes like democratization of knowledge and capital, low startup costs, mobility, globalization, and convergence.[2]

There are various schools of thought about launching a company. For university startups, I find the Lean Startup method ideal. This chapter explains how to apply it with two examples. But let's first understand the main underlying principles.

---

[2]Steve Blank, "Why the Lean Start-Up Changes Everything," *Harvard Business Review* (May 2013).

Incremental Product Development

Under the old paradigm, most university startups think they have to brainstorm extensively to arrive at the perfect product. After meticulous planning, they build it behind locked doors and finally launch it in the market with a big splash. This is expensive and risky and also impractical. There is a more intuitive approach to develop products, which the Lean Startup method refers to as *incremental product development*. This is how it works: you first create an MVP based on your assumptions about what the market could be willing to accept. This is obviously not the full-featured version of your ideal product, but the opposite. The simplest, least-expensive product you can produce quickly with the sole purpose of getting feedback from real potential clients is your MVP 1. Now you continually improve your product, called *pivoting* in Lean Startup jargon. You test the next assumption with MVP 2—for example, when you have fixed the flaws in MVP 1 and made it more complex with added features. Along the way, the product becomes better and better, and it is always approved by the market. At some point, you feel it has developed into a robust commercial version that enough clients are willing to pay money for. Only then do you launch your first actual product (the final MVP) in the market. Even after launch, product development still continues. You keep collecting information about how you could improve the product in an upgrade or the next version. Figure 2-1 illustrates this process.

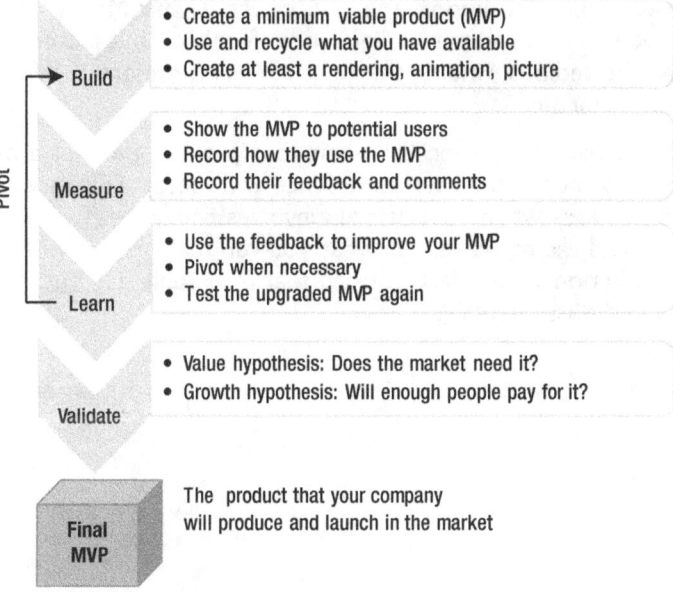

Figure 2-1. Minimum viable product (MVP) testing with "Build, measure, learn"

For each MVP, you need to test two hypotheses: the *value hypothesis* (whether anybody in the market wants it) and the *growth hypothesis* (whether there is sufficient demand in the market to have a business). This boils down to, "Do people want our product?" and "Will enough of them pay for it?" Often, both hypothesis tests can occur at the same time. MVP testing is about experimenting and recording your findings—not in the lab, but in the real market with real potential clients. By leaving the building, you shift the question from "Can we build it?" to "Should we build it?" If your market gives you the thumbs up, then you have a business, and the startup is ready for takeoff. Otherwise, keep experimenting with other MVPs.

Most university startups, even those with repeated grant funding, have never conducted such tests and are not going to do so anytime soon. This is unfortunate, because in a global marketplace you cannot afford to fly blind. You are up against millions of highly motivated incremental product testers who are validating hypotheses on a daily basis to get a head start. Spending time writing grant proposals will put you at a disadvantage.

Simplify, Then Simplify Again

The idea of testing MVPs sounds intuitive—that is, until you try to apply it in your own startup. It can be surprisingly hard to come up with a quick product that can be tested easily. Not only that, but you need to be able to implement that feedback rapidly to improve your product. If your MVP is too complex or expensive to build, you may collect some feedback, but incremental development will be tedious. Finding the right MVP is therefore the first order of business for a startup.

As a software company, especially when your product involves a mobile app, you can quickly mock up a user experience with design software or even on paper. It is less easy when your startup involves hardware. The MVP is never what you would *like* to make, but what you *can* make today with little funding and no additional materials. Toward that end, Table 2-1 outlines a simple process to find possible MVPs.

Table 2-1. Table to Arrive at Minimum Viable Products (MVPs)

	Description	Material Needed	Other Things Needed	Cost
What would we like to make?				$100,000 or more
What is a simpler version of that?				
What is a simpler version of that?				
What is an even simpler version?		Recycling what is already there	Nothing	$0
What does it look like?	An image or screenshot	Nothing	Nothing	$0

The goal of this exercise is to find an MVP that you can create quickly with the materials you already have. Go down the list until you cannot simplify any more. As a rule, the most-reduced product is always just a picture of what you want to make. This may sound trite, but many startups think their technology is too complex to create an MVP. You may have an animation, a screenshot, or any other visual representation of your product. Get feedback on this first, using a checklist like that in Figure 2-2. Then you can step up and test a physical MVP. Ideally it should cost you nothing, because you can easily put it together yourself. You should be able to produce this MVP in a few days.

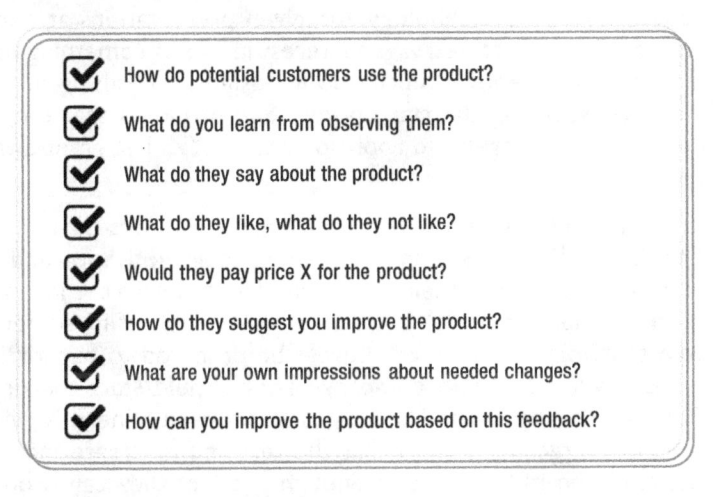

- ☑ How do potential customers use the product?
- ☑ What do you learn from observing them?
- ☑ What do they say about the product?
- ☑ What do they like, what do they not like?
- ☑ Would they pay price X for the product?
- ☑ How do they suggest you improve the product?
- ☑ What are your own impressions about needed changes?
- ☑ How can you improve the product based on this feedback?

Figure 2-2. Checklist for MVP testing

Entrepreneurs generally like to start with the *maximum* viable product in mind. To scale that down to the minimum is easier said than done. Researchers in particular feel like frauds unless their product is flawless. In startup entrepreneurship, this is impractical. Pivoting a buggy product wins the day. Have you thought hard, but you cannot come up with any ideas to simplify the MVP? Engage your team in a brainstorming session. Perhaps also invite the accountant and the guy who does IT support at your university. Those without domain knowledge sometimes have unexpected suggestions that help you strip down your MVP. You will have difficulty to gather timely information in the market if your product is too complex. The worst outcome is to perfectly carry out a plan that results in a product nobody wants. Better to make the simplest prototype you can think of and show it to potential consumers today.

The Lean Startup in Action, 1: Battery Startup

Imagine the following fictitious example. Three PhDs named Adam, Ben, and Christine are working on their postdoc, researching a new smartphone battery technology. Not only is their battery biodegradable, it also fully recharges in ten minutes. Two years of diligent research have yielded promising results, and the postdoc is nearing its end. One evening, over beers, the team talks about their future, and someone makes a joke about starting their own battery firm. Hours later the trio is still brainstorming about how to do that, and it becomes obvious the entrepreneurial bug has bitten them. The idea sounds even better the next morning. But where to begin? They have published several papers about the technology and given presentations at congresses. Industry leaders have expressed vague interest in "doing something together," but none of the team knows much about business or raising funds. Their scientific advisor supports the startup idea. She proposes that they write a business plan, make a budget, and apply for grant XYZ. The grant-award date is 12 months away.

Instead of getting sidetracked in writing a lengthy business plan and a grant proposal, the team should first gain clarity about their motivation and product. They should start confirming their idea while they still have the infrastructure of the university available. Is the battery (or a variation of it) something the market wants? If so, what price will buyers be prepared to pay for it? Does the team really want to run a company? They should start thinking about their MVP. Instead of the finished battery for the smartphone, this will be perhaps a larger rechargeable battery that the team could create more quickly. In the best case, the MVP is a good-enough product they can produce in a small series for market testing without much effort. Before they produce the MVP, the team should leave the lab and speak with manufacturers and wholesale and retail customers about the product. Would they carry it in their stores or make their distribution channels available? Will they pay price X?

What about price Y? The first MVP could be an advertisement in which the battery is available only on paper for preorder. In love and war, all is fair. Another simple MVP could be a campaign on a crowdfunding platform such as Kickstarter. The goal is to get real-life data from potential clients fast, without spending much time and money.

Once you start thinking about possible test cases, you will come up with many. The key is to engage your thinking along this path and get busy—not in the bubble of the lab, but in the real market.

Back to the battery startup. Within a month of the first hypothesis test, one of the team, Adam, has thrown the towel and left for his native land where a position on a tenure track beckons. Good for him. Now it is up to Ben and Christine. They have found that the biodegradable, rechargeable battery they imagined is too expensive to make. However, if they forget about making it rechargeable, they can offer it competitively. But then it will no longer work in a smartphone. Interviews and responses to the mock advertisement have shown that a deep market exists for biodegradable batteries. The simplest battery they can produce is a car battery. Tests with potential buyers have validated both the value hypothesis and the growth hypothesis: people want a biodegradable car battery and are willing to pay for it.

Let's recap. The team wanted to produce a smartphone battery, but it became obvious that they needed to simplify their MVP. The original idea involved complex manufacturing, device dependence, and other roadblocks that can only be overcome with scale. As a result, they had to think about other applications of batteries, such as AAA, 4.5 volt, CR, and car batteries. Whichever of these was the simplest for them to make, they chose as their MVP. Tests of the car battery in the market showed that there were willing buyers for such a product. Thus, with a car battery, they have a product that satisfied the value hypothesis and the growth hypothesis. With this, they have a valid business idea and can move forward.

The startup duo can now decide whether they still want to embark on the venture. If they do, they may approach a leading battery manufacturer and offer to enter a joint venture to further improve, test, and finally mass-produce the battery. If this happens, they will not need to raise funding because their joint venture will be a subsidiary of the battery manufacturer, in which both Ben and Christine will own equity. The university will often also own a small stake in spin-off companies, which is only fair.

To engage the battery manufacturer, Ben and Christine had to first confirm their idea. They had to find out the original product they planned was impractical and too expensive to produce. Only through testing in the real market could they match their technology with existing demand. Because they were running lean, they developed a useful product inexpensively. Had they not done that, someone else would have had to figure out the right product based on their technology. This is often unattractive for joint venture partners, who have enough on their minds with their own problems. Yet if you can prove to them that a profitable market for your validated product exists, their risk is much lower. They only need to finalize the product and can then integrate it in their sales and distribution channels.

This is an idealized story, of course. But note that no business plan was at the heart of this team's success. Many assumptions about the project changed, which would have resulted in pointless updates to a business plan that nobody will ever read. And no grant proposal was submitted. Had the team done that, they would have robbed themselves of momentum, valuable data, and deeper insights about the nature of the market. This eventually laid the foundation for the future of the business. As a bonus, they learned that one of the cofounders was uncomfortable with startup life and preferred a 9-to-5 job. Sorting this out later down the road would have been a messy affair.

Because lean product development is inexpensive, startups have strategies at their disposal to test ideas and assumptions right away. From the beginning, they have one foot firmly planted in the market, collecting feedback and incrementally developing products. The founders immediately see what startup entrepreneurship entails and can decide if they are cut out for it or not. Gaining momentum as early as possible is extremely valuable. The lean startup will always have a leg up against those who sit at their desks, formulating perfect business plans even before they test their product ideas in the market.

The Lean Startup in Action, 2: Electric Scooter Startup

Let's look at another fictitious example of MVP testing. In this case, a prototype exists that incorporates several individual technologies. This is frequent with university startups.

Assume that in his PhD, Simon has built an electric scooter that he wants to bring to the market with a startup. The scooter has a slick design with several innovations in the technology of the wheels and the closed body. Other features include a newly developed accelerator, regenerative braking, and a quick-charging battery. Simon believes the retail price of the scooter should be around $2,000. A prototype of the scooter exists in the lab, but he is unsure what to do as the first step to commercialize the idea. How should he go about all this with the Lean Startup method?

First, Simon should test the value hypothesis with potential buyers of the scooter. Do they want what he built in the lab? If the scooter drives safely, he could test the prototype right out of the gate. However, this is not his MVP. What will Simon do if he finds that test drivers do not like the prototype?

Is there something wrong with the wheels, the body, the accelerator, or the brakes? There are too many moving parts, which will prevent him from gathering meaningful feedback, and he will be no wiser than when he started. Instead he should simplify the MVP and break down the tests into several steps.

Simon can start by testing any of the scooter's components, but he should focus on the one that is easiest to test. Is it the battery, the wheel design, the electronics, certain features of the build, or something else? He should find the MVP, with emphasis on *minimum*. If he is testing the wheel design, then he can take an existing scooter and just add his wheels. He has already tested them in the lab to see how much traction they have and how many hours they last with normal use. Now he has to leave the building and invite some potential customers for a ride to see what happens. Do they prefer his wheels, or are they indifferent? Simon should measure how his MVP scooter fares compared to a normal model. He may learn that customers love the wheel design, because it provides a new kind of driving experience. If this is the case, he could commercialize the wheels alone and approach a manufacturer. Right from the beginning, Simon's startup has a product with the potential to generate revenue. If he was still brainstorming about how to build the perfect untested prototype, he might never have known that a marketable product was lying around in the lab, unused.

Simon has tested the wheels. Test riders felt that they are "more fun" than traditional wheels, because they are easier to navigate with. He records this and moves on to the next MVP. To find out how close to the market his original prototype is, he adds parts of his scooter to the MVP one by one and tests how long the market still accepts it as a product. The next component of the scooter is the accelerator. Simon adds it to MVP 1 and arrives at MVP 2 (wheels and accelerator). He tests it in the center of town, where most potential buyers of the scooter are. One day, it begins to rain unexpectedly, and the accelerator stops working. He never knew of this flaw, because up to this point, he only tried it in the university's air-conditioned hangar. He can now find out what the problem is, improve the accelerator, and test it again.

Then Simon moves on to the brakes. Afterward he tests the closed body. The original prototype of the body turns out to be impractical for most potential users. So Simon mocks up changes with CAD software and shows the renderings to potential customers, just to see what they say. He adapts and improves the design until the market gives him the thumbs up.

He moves along like this until he has tested all the different features of his prototype. The wheels and the accelerator deliver a new driving experience, but the fast-charging battery adds too much weight, which slows down the scooter. He learns which individual parts—the wheels and the accelerator—satisfy the value hypothesis of the market. So, Simon could start with them alone as his first products. Had he tested his prototype in one go, he would have gotten either a positive or a negative response and would not have known where to start with improvements. Based on his findings in MVP testing (illustrated in Figure 2-3), he can now commercialize the individual components and build a scooter the market wants.

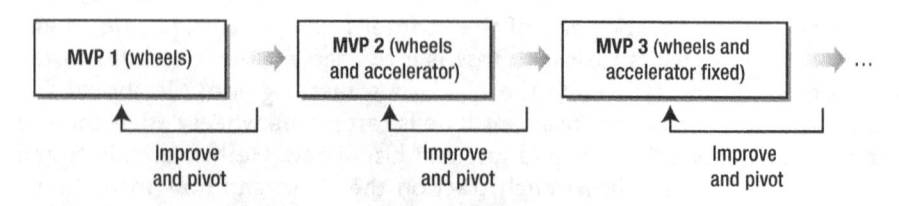

```
┌──────────────┐     ┌──────────────────┐     ┌──────────────────┐
│ MVP 1 (wheels)│ ──> │ MVP 2 (wheels    │ ──> │ MVP 3 (wheels and│ ──> ...
│              │     │ and accelerator) │     │ accelerator fixed)│
└──────────────┘     └──────────────────┘     └──────────────────┘
       ▲                     ▲                         ▲
    Improve              Improve                    Improve
   and pivot            and pivot                  and pivot
```

Figure 2-3. MVP testing of the electric scooter

Simon confirmed several value hypotheses. How about the growth hypothesis? Will people pay $2,000 for the scooter? If some testers already want to buy the scooter, then yes. Otherwise, Simon can speak with potential customers about pricing and find out this way. He may learn that adding the closed body leads to most of the cost, so he has a bigger market if he produces a conventional, open scooter. In either case, Simon has first-hand intelligence about his market and his customers' preferences.

To have a viable startup, both the value hypothesis and the growth hypothesis need to check out. When they do, a startup is infinitely more advanced than one that is still brainstorming. If Simon is not exhausted yet and wants to pursue entrepreneurship with his startup, then he is in the game, up and running.

A Startup Coach Can Be Valuable

In the real world, the process of creating and testing MVPs is easier said than done. Doing so often requires experience and unconventional thinking that may not be native to the founding team. It is therefore helpful to engage a startup coach for the research team in the early stages, when the idea seems daunting and many insecurities about the path ahead exist. Universities are often open to engaging external advisors for startups. Of course, this should not be theoretical advice or yet another weekend workshop in startup entrepreneurship. An MBA or economics student from another faculty who will work on the case as part of their master's thesis also is not enough. The team needs a dedicated, experienced entrepreneur who will enjoy working with them for several weeks in the lab to address their challenges.

Research shows that it is often very effective to learn a new skill by seeing an expert doing it and then repeating it.[3] This approach trumps theoretical advice any time, as well as self-directed learning by doing. If startups have access to a seasoned entrepreneur who works with them one-on-one, this can make all the difference. It can accelerate the learning curve by two or even three times while avoiding many early common pitfalls and distractions. If the team has built their own network and reached out to other entrepreneurs, they may suggest someone they see fit as their advisor. A startup coach should obviously have firsthand entrepreneurial experience, but domain knowledge is unnecessary. The whole point of working with a coach is to get an outsider's view and a fresh perspective on the team's challenges. Domain knowledge exists already on the team in the form of the founders. The added value of the startup coach lies more in management: getting the startup out of the building and into the market as soon as possible.

Do You Need a Business Plan?

A business plan in the classic sense is a thing of the past. It is largely a thought experiment with little merit once a business has gotten underway. Some entrepreneurs admit that but insist the business plan can be a guideline to keep them on track and their thinking focused. To me, it is the other way around: once you start, you need to be as flexible as possible to pivot and incrementally change your products and services. A rigid 50-page document will only hinder you in that regard. I have never written a business plan for any of my businesses in almost 20 years. Launching a startup is an exercise not in thinking, but in doing. The practice of requiring a written document before taking any action is against the nature of entrepreneurship. Flexibility and time to market are much more important than perfect planning and consideration of eventualities. A business plan stands in the way of getting started.

Of course, you still need to think about your startup in a systematic manner before taking the plunge. This is important, but you need to do it with an open mind. A relatively new approach is the *business model canvas*, which is basically a business plan condensed onto one page.[4] It does away with the need for speculation about potential revenue down the road and focuses on a

---

[3]Robert Greene, *Mastery* (New York: Viking, 2012).
[4]Alexander Osterwalder and Yves Pigneur, *Business Model Generation: A Handbook for Visionaries, Game Changers, and Challengers* (Hoboken, NJ: Wiley, 2010).

few specific key questions about the business and its market. An updated version of the business model canvas has been proposed by author Ash Maurya.[5] His *lean canvas* is what I use for the startups I work with (see Figure 2-4). Although the original canvas is good to analyze a business, the lean canvas helps entrepreneurs get started quickly. I also find it more useful when I need to discuss the business with third parties.

	Product			Market	
Problem Top 3 problems	**Solution** Top 3 features	**Unique value proposition** Single, clear, compelling message that states why you are different and worth paying attention to		**Unfair advantage** Not easily copied or bought	**Customer segments** Target customers
	Key metrics Key activities you measure			**Channels** Path to customers	
Cost structure Customer acquisition cost, Distribution cost, Hosting, People, Etc.			**Revenue streams** Revenue model, Life time value, Revenue, Gross margin		

Figure 2-4. Lean canvas, adapted from the Business Model Canvas (www.businessmodelgeneration.com), licensed under the Creative Commons Attribution-Share Alike 3.0 Un-ported License

When filling out the canvas, make a different one for different assumptions. For example, if your startup is in Singapore, you should show how it applies to the local market, to the wider market in Southeast Asia, and to all of Asia including China. Analyze different scenarios for your startup on different canvases. If you speak with different third parties, make a canvas for each of them. The problems, solutions, unique value propositions, distribution channels, customers, costs, and pricing models will vary from market to market. This is a good exercise to understand the platform you are playing on.

---

[5]Ash Maurya, *Running Lean: Iterate from Plan A to a Plan that Works* (Sebastopol, CA: O'Reilly, 2013).

When you begin, you will quickly find that all this looks simple but is far from intuitive. Prepare yourself for the fact that your first canvasses will rarely survive much scrutiny and will need an update soon. This is fine, because the canvas is the opposite of a business plan set in stone; it is a fluid document you use to organize your startup and put the different puzzle pieces together over time. Treat the canvas as a work in progress, and carry it around with you. Update it as needed, when new findings emerge from market feedback or you feel a pivot is necessary. The lean canvas and the financial model, which we will visit later are both the cornerstones of your toolkit to present your startup to the world.

CHAPTER 3

What Does It Mean to Be a Startup Entrepreneur?

Thanks to the movie *The Social Network*, we now all know what startup entrepreneurship is like.[1] Late night hackathons in the house in Silicon Valley, half-empty pizza boxes and shot glasses everywhere, groupies, parties. We lost a few friends on the way, but there is still the billion dollar paycheck at the end of the road. It would be nice if this were true. Unfortunately, it is not—unless you are Mark Zuckerberg. Entrepreneurship is fun, but rarely the sort of fun shown in the movies. More the fun of solving a complicated chess problem. Or the fun of writing a beautiful mathematical equation. Or combining many agents who seemed unconnected into a springboard for your product.

At this point, I encourage you to stop for a minute and think about your motivations for startup entrepreneurship. Are you seriously dedicated to making this work? Or is the startup more of a convenient strategy to stay a little longer at your research institute after your postdoc has run its course?

---

[1] *The Social Network*, directed by David Fincher (2010; Columbia Pictures).

Chapter 3 | What Does It Mean to Be a Startup Entrepreneur?

Do you just want to find out what it is like to dabble in entrepreneurship, with no plan to see the whole affair through? Ask yourself the inconvenient questions at the beginning. Be aware that unless you have a strong motivation, it will be hard to enjoy the fruits of your labor, in terms of both experience and success. I believe that everybody has entrepreneurship in them. That's why I encourage you to give it an honest try.

Entrepreneurship is taking place on a global stage today. Right this second, millions of startup entrepreneurs are thinking about how they can take market share from somebody else. They are hungry, scratching and clawing their way into the market with little or no capital. They are fueled by Top Ramen, sleeping three hours a night in their parents' basement (at age 35), with no other choice than to make their startup work. You need to know that launching a successful startup is no cakewalk. It also has little to do with a lottery that you can play passively and hope to win the jackpot. Honestly check your own motives and those of your team before you charge forward. This chapter is not meant to dissuade you from entrepreneurship, but you should understand what you are getting into before you dedicate time and resources to this rewarding but demanding challenge.

You may have guessed it by now—there is no quick fix to launch a startup. There is also no secret sauce that only the chosen few have. Viewed from a distance, entrepreneurship is just a persistent movement toward a certain goal. The road is winding, and you only see the short distance right ahead of you. By taking one step after the next and adjusting your course, you will eventually achieve the goal. That's it. This chapter discusses some defining characteristics of entrepreneurship and some loosely defined ground rules that distinguish entrepreneurs from non-entrepreneurs. Some of those may be unexpected because they are different from commonly accepted business advice. They come primarily from my personal observation and experience, with no claim to be contextually exhaustive. Think of this chapter as a conversation with someone who shares his personal viewpoints about the mindset required to become an entrepreneur.

More Management Than Creativity

Contrary to public opinion, entrepreneurship is nothing like going to the casino and betting everything on red 13. It is more perspiration and management than fun and games. Creativity is important, but long stretches of running a company have little to do with that. In other words, startup success lies less in creative planning and brainstorming and more in *doing* and taking action. Many nights are spent diligently managing delicate issues, evaluating data, and troubleshooting. Researchers have an advantage, because they are familiar with meticulous documentation, statistical testing, and reporting their findings. This can be a considerable asset over the college dropout who has a great idea but few tools and no patience to work with data. Startup entrepreneurship has a great deal to do with tinkering. Getting it right the first time is nearly impossible. Make sure you have the energy and flexibility to adjust your course when you see that improvements are necessary.

Here is another popular view of entrepreneurship. A team has decided to launch a startup. Before they can do so, they need to brainstorm for months about the perfect product. Finally they hit on a brilliant idea, which they carry out over the following months by endlessly laboring in their top-secret lab. They get feedback from MBAs who help them create the perfect business plan and marketing plan. With the perfect product and the perfect plan to push it into the market, they are prepared to conquer the world.

I certainly thought this is how it works until I launched my first startup. However, it is an outdated notion of product development, which arose in the paradigm of mass production that held true during your parents' lifetime. Today's model is *lean* production, which Chapter 4 explores in more detail. As a startup, you need to first come up with the simplest test product imaginable to see how potential buyers react to it. We explored how to do this in the previous chapter. You can build your MVP in a few days, with little brainstorming and planning. When you get positive signals, you continue and improve the product. If the signals are negative, you change course, tinker with the product, or invent a new one. You do this until you have proof that enough people in the market need your product and will pay for it. Then you are ready to launch it. Because you tested it in every upgrade cycle, you already know which market segments want your product. Advertising and marketing costs are minimal and draw on pull factors, not push factors. This requires diligent market testing, recording data, managing progress, and keeping track of your overall goal. With creativity alone, this is impossible.

Many additional aspects of startups need management. For example, angry clients, or the lack of clients altogether. A neglected spouse. Concerned parents. These require management skills and perhaps some creativity, but mostly they just need to be handled. When there is a founding team, even more politics and psychology enter the mix. Perhaps one co-founder has lost faith in the startup and wants to exit, but still wants to share in future gains of the invention he helped pioneer. If no paperwork exists, then this can quickly become a sticky issue. Or you may receive a cease-and-desist letter from a lawyer in a far-off land, stating that you are infringing on patents X, Y, and Z and are hereby notified to immediately stop any and all business activity and contact her firm to negotiate damage compensation. Dealing with such issues is most unwelcome, delicate, and a huge time waster. You can only master them if you draw from a well of strength, fueled by your own conviction that you are on the right path. Per aspera ad astra.[2]

---

[2]Latin phrase, loosely translated "A rough road leads to the stars."

Succeed Turtle-Style, Not Kamikaze-Style

Discipline and self-motivation are extremely important for entrepreneurs. Forget about the cliché of the entrepreneur who is finally his own boss, spends most of the time on the golf course, and wanders into the office once in a while to make certain profits are still rolling in. The other cliché of the workaholic who only got her startup off the ground by working 24/7 also is inaccurate. Both of these are extremes—the real-world experience lands somewhere in the middle. Although it sounds good to work hard and play hard, this is rarely helpful in the long term for entrepreneurs. It is better to adopt a disciplined, slightly boring lifestyle to get things done. Putting one foot after the other every single day will take you to the finish line faster than quick sprints with much exhaustion in between. Binge behavior, even if it is good behavior, such as staying up all night to solve a problem, is rarely helpful in the long run. Discipline yourself to adopt healthy, sustainable habits. If you are older than 30, you know that staying up until 6 am three times in a row will take a toll on you. You will achieve your milestones faster if you warm up to the idea of getting to the finish line turtle-style, not kamikaze-style.

Willpower vs. Self-Confidence

What about self-confidence? Isn't that also vital? It is true that those who have good self-esteem are more likely to act on their beliefs than those without. But research has shown that pep talks in the style of "You can do it" mostly improve a person's ego instead of their performance.[3] On the other hand, if you develop long-term willpower, you are much more likely to achieve success. This is also essential for universities and their advisors. Little good will it do their startup performance if they hire motivational coaches or engage an expert to give a talk once in a while to fire up the students. Sure, an interesting afternoon will be had by all. But the effect on the bottom line will be questionable. It's better to help startups by providing practical support such as a hands-on startup coach or longer-term advisor who is living proof of the entrepreneurial attitude required to succeed.

Time Management

Time management is another important skill. Most successful entrepreneurs are always working, when they are working. Get the most out of the time you have available, especially if you can benefit from the well-equipped research laboratory or other infrastructure at your university. Make sure you use it

---

[3]Roy Baumeister and John Tierny, *Willpower: Rediscovering the Greatest Human Strength* (New York: Penguin Press, 2011).

thoroughly while you're at it. Being an entrepreneur occupies a different paradigm than being a student or staff at a university. The sense of urgency that a startup introduces is often foreign to the daily business of research institutions, which mostly run on their own time. When you launch your startup lean, time will take on an entirely new meaning for you. It is critical to keep your momentum going, so you cannot afford to waste any of it. Stop procrastinating. Stop wasting time. Stop spending time with those who do. This may mandate some radical strategies, because not everybody at a university is goal oriented and on a timeline.

Dealing with disruption is a good skill to learn. First, avoid disrupting your own flow. Of course, stay off Twitter and Facebook when you need to get something done. Avoid compulsively checking your e-mail or other messaging platform. Always being connected is addictive. It is also damaging your concentration. If you wish to improve your time management, turn off all toys that may ping you any second. Answer your phone just one hour in the afternoon, and make this known on your voice-mail. The same applies to your e-mail. You may even want to block out time on your calendar for replying to messages. I know this all sounds extreme and strange. If you have enough time during the day, a few instant messages here and there will seldom make much impact. But if you are on a mission and are strapped for time, then these habits are the first that have to go. Shut them off for one day and see what happens—this frees up a surprising amount of concentrated time.

There are also many distractions beyond your control. In each office or university department, there are always those with too much time on their hands who will begin a conversation with you and then ramble on endlessly until stopped. They are rarely willfully wasting your time but are simply unaware that for entrepreneurs, time is money. If someone has made it a habit for a decade or more to stop others in their tracks and tell them about the latest thing that happened to so and so, then this behavior will be difficult to shake. However, entrepreneurs should beware of those who interrupt their flow. After each interruption, even an innocent text message ping, it takes about ten minutes to get back to the level of focus you had prior to the interruption.[4] If you are already in a conversation with someone via messaging or e-mail and engage in a purely administrative task at the same time, the impact of the disruption will be smaller. But if you are in deep thought about your strategy, brainstorming a thorny issue, or just getting in the flow with some good ideas coming, then even a harmless smiley face sent to your phone can have devastating effects. You will lose your train of thought and may never regain it.

---

[4]Gloria Mark, Victor M. Gonzalez, and Justin Harris, "No Task Left Behind? Examining the Nature of Fragmented Work," *Proceedings of the SIGCHI Conference: on Human Factors in Computing Systems, Portland, OR*, April 2–7, 2005 (New York: Association for Computing Machinery, 2005).

Chapter 3 | What Does It Mean to Be a Startup Entrepreneur?

Assume you get six unexpected text messages a day: one each hour. In addition to the time you spend responding to these messages, they will cost you about 1 full hour of fully focused work during the day—7 hours per week, about 30 hours per month. Think about all the brainstorming and MVP testing you could complete in that time. Now, what if you get a total of 60 messages per day, including text, e-mails, and instant messages, each of which you address immediately? You may get some routine work done, but your focus and concentration will be subpar most of the time. That may be fine if nobody competes with you, but entrepreneurship demands as much concentration as practicing martial arts. Postpone interruptions until your free time, and avoid all of them during your work hours.

In addition, I strongly recommend that you go on a low-information diet from time to time, as recommended by author Tim Ferriss.[5] Unplug yourself from all media, including news, TV, blogs, e-mails, messaging, phone calls, and so forth. Celebrate selective ignorance for a week, and you will find you have all the time you need to accomplish what you thought was impossible. You can easily do this while working on your startup. Just announce to everyone via voicemail and e-mail autoresponder that you will be unavailable for the next seven days. Most people will think you are on leave and will postpone their questions until you return. Meanwhile, some pressing issues lose their urgency or turn out to be unimportant, and you will never know they existed. When you return to the plugged-in world after this one-week media fast, you will see how stressful all the disruption going on in most people's lives is. It will take you a while to adapt—but before you know it, the Matrix will have you back. If you need more time in your life, remove the things that waste it. It is as simple as that.

I recently worked with a startup team on the lean canvas. Some good ideas were flowing until about an hour into the session, when somebody appeared and asked for "just five minutes" of one of the founders' time. The discussion took place in the room where we were working, so this distupted the whole group. There was some confusion about a certain unknown webmaster, who might have failed to update some content on a web site about a project. Finding this webmaster proved difficult, so speculation started about who he was and where he might be at present. Perhaps he was on holiday? Or perhaps he had left for his home country? Or perhaps it was the entrepreneur himself, but he couldn't remember? Or perhaps ... This took fully ten minutes, with no conclusion to the matter. I sat there, flabbergasted. Why couldn't this have waited until later? Clearly, the interrupter had no plans to willfully disturb our session, and I love her dearly. Yet the effect was devastating. After this

---

[5]Timothy Ferriss, *The 4-Hour Workweek: Escape 9-5, Live Anywhere, and Join the New Rich* (New York: Crown Publishers, 2007).

incident, the group never achieved the previous focus and flow. This was a pity, because such consulting sessions are rare, and they are exactly what bring entrepreneurs forward. Five more minutes of focused attention can make all the difference: they can result in a breakthrough about the business model or a solution to a certain problem. When you need to focus, hide where people cannot find you. Make it a rule to turn off all phones, and ban tablets or laptops on which people may otherwise read their instant messages or book a flight while you are trying to work.

It is difficult to avoid all interruptions, but you should try to minimize them. When others interrupt you with unimportant requests or gossip, the following strategies by author Dan Kennedy have worked quite well for me[6]:

> Someone: "Have you got a minute?"
>
> You: "Sorry, but I'm extremely busy today. We can meet at 4:45 pm for 15 minutes and tackle everything on your list at one time."

Or even better:

> Someone: "I need to discuss something with you."
>
> You: "I am extremely busy right now and can only deal with tasks that are either a nine or ten on a scale of one to ten. Is this a nine or ten?"

Stop Being Late

An often-overlooked component of time management is punctuality. Although it may be OK among students to be academically late, business people, bankers, and other entrepreneurs value their time above all else. As the saying goes, "Those who cannot be punctual cannot be trusted in other ways either." Nobody will inform you that you should be on time more often—they will just categorize you as someone who is habitually late and untrustworthy. Or even worse, they will not meet you again and will never do business with you. Avoid this at all costs. Being late is rude (both in business and private matters).

When I lived in Los Angeles, one of my neighbors was a retired rock-star guitar player from a famous 1980s band. For 20 years, he had toured the world, flown around in private jets, and lived the good life. Just as with entrepreneurship, his lifestyle actually had very little in common with the Hollywood version of stardom as all chaos and mayhem. Celebrities have a tight schedule and must show up on time. They can only do this with iron discipline and serious planning. Whenever I met with this neighbor for coffee, he would suggest an

---

[6]Dan S. Kennedy, *No B.S. Time Management for Entrepreneurs: The Ultimate No Holds Barred, Kick Butt, Take No Prisoners, Guide to Time Productivity & Sanity* (Irvine, CA: Entrepreneur Press, 2004).

odd time like 9:10 am or 3:25 pm. It later occurred to me that he was running on a schedule partitioned in slices of five and ten minutes: 9:10 am meant 9:10 am, not 9:15 am. In those five minutes he could have done something else, and time is money. Do you think someone like this would give you another meeting if you were 15 minutes late? There is no need to be that extreme, but you get the point. Make it a rule to be extra punctual to all meetings and gatherings.

Bootstrapping

Startup entrepreneurs should be experts in bootstrapping. As mentioned before, I think the best way to ruin a startup is to give it a lot of money. This may sound illogical, but I have seen it happen firsthand with my own projects. The ones that eventually turned profitable always limped along on limited private finances for a longer time than I would have liked, then slowly turned profitable, and then accelerated along the "hockey stick" (see Figure 3-1). Because the changes are exponential, it is impossible to spot them at the beginning. Over time, as they compound, growth reaches the upward sloping part of the hockey stick and explodes.

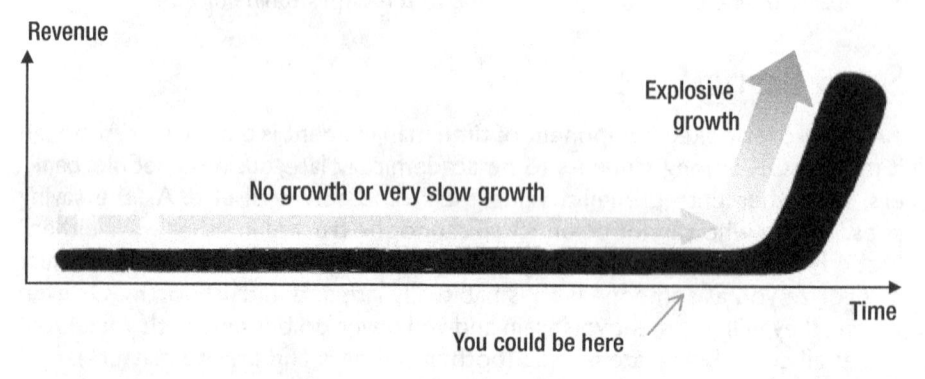

Figure 3-1. The hockey stick

The flat part is necessary in order to iron out the business model, market approach, and financial model. Last but not least, you gain clarity about whether you and your co-founders wish to continue this venture. The groundwork for your future business success starts in the tough times of the flat hockey stick. The accelerating part is when you experience the fun and payoff. Without the flat part, long-term success will be impossible. If your goal is just about making a quick buck, then entrepreneurship is the wrong avenue. You need to learn important lessons about your venture and about yourself first. These insights will last you a lifetime.

The learning experience that comes with entrepreneurship is another reason having wealthy parents or early funding is a disadvantage for the bootstrapping entrepreneur. It steals the thunder of being inventive and robs you of the ability to make do with little or no means. A successful serial entrepreneur I know had an incredible drive in his first self-funded venture, launching product after product in a 24-hour release cycle. After selling the first startup in the low nine-figures, he embarked on his next tech venture, which immediately attracted multimillion-dollar venture capital. But instead of losing sleep fretting together with the team about ideas for the next MVP, he phoned in from the racetrack (he had taken up sports-car racing) and only showed up at the office once a week. The entrepreneurial fire was obviously gone. The venture did OK, but it was a mere shadow of the first company. Early funding puts you right in this second category. You lose your edge over all the hungry entrepreneurs who must make it work on a shoestring. If you are really interested in learning the ropes of entrepreneurship, there is no way around experiencing the long, flat part of the hockey stick.

Ideally, you should wrap the initial stage of your startup into an existing engagement, such as an ongoing research commitment or postdoc. It is best to start with hypothesis testing without having to scramble for a roof over your head. Most universities are open to letting their research teams start a business with their ideas, and they even encourage them to do so. If you are straightforward about your plans, others will support you. Make sure the university is on board with your idea. Then use its infrastructure 24/7.

Make a Good First Impression

I cannot stress enough how important good manners and being presentable are in business. Startup entrepreneurs play in the league of the business world rather than the academic world. They should therefore adopt the style that will brand them as businesspeople. Yes, Mark Zuckerberg wears flip-flops and a bathrobe for meetings with venture capital firms, but he is probably the lone exception. Extremely few entrepreneurs have been able to engage other companies, investors, and venture capitalists by dressing down and celebrating the student image. Of course, nobody asks you to wear a suit and tie to your lab. But how about a polo shirt instead of a t-shirt? That simple shift alone can make a huge difference. You can still wear tennis shoes, but they should be clean, without holes. By all means, wear something comfortable, but please do not show up in your pajamas. If you dislike wearing a business suit, fine. Wear dark jeans or khakis and a dress shirt. Or a longer skirt and a blouse. Please, leave the athletic pants and the Adidas flip-flops at home. You never know when unexpected visitors will drop by, and you never know who they may be. They may be distant descendants of the royal family, looking to invest in a university startup. You never know when a government delegation may tour the building, and you will have the opportunity to give a little presentation about your current development. Not only will you make a better impression, but you will feel more on par with the people you present to. When you feel underdressed, you lack the confidence to inspire others.

A brief word about language. For some reason, in some parts of the world, it has become fashionable to use obscene language in everyday conversation as if there was nothing to it. If you are an entrepreneur, this is not for you, because you wish to be taken seriously by the business and investor community. You may think this advice is overly conservative and patronizing. However, the majority of businesspeople and those in decision-making positions at venture capital firms will appreciate it if you refrain from using gutter language. They may use this or that word once in a while themselves, but their language is generally cultivated.

The tricky part about language is that you may think you can adjust easily to different settings depending on who you are talking to. Unfortunately, this is not true. As soon as you establish some rapport with other people, you will drop your guard. If you normally use profanities, they will roll off your tongue without you noticing it. Just as with being late, nobody will tell you to please watch your language. But they may subconsciously feel that your startup still needs more development, or that they preferred another entrepreneur who made a more professional impression. Give third parties as few reasons as possible to reject you. One of them is proper language. No need to emulate Prince Charles but f-words and any derogatory language have no place in business.

I once introduced a friend in Los Angeles to an attorney I had worked with previously. I thought she might be interested in an invention my friend was working on. So I set up a lunch for the three of us to see if there was some common ground. Having known my friend for a while, I had somewhat gotten used to his rough language and liberal use of f-bombs. Naively, I assumed that he would control himself in a business meeting. Was I ever mistaken. F-bombs were flying in the chic cafe in Venice Beach, over seared ahi tuna salad and sugar-free ice tea. F- this, and f- that, this f---ing m-----f---r, what a f---ing idiot, and so on. He talked himself into a frenzy. In his view, people were out to get him, and they should all be f----d. This was obviously the first and last time I introduced this guy to anyone. Not only was his behavior blatantly rude, but he also sabotaged himself—and it reflected terribly on me. You cannot tell a grown man in front of others to watch his language. After he left, I had to profusely apologize to the lawyer from Beverly Hills, who commented that the guy was quite intense, in her own words. That introduction led nowhere. My friend failed to get his project off the ground. And the next one. And the one after that. It's a pity, because some of his ideas were good and could have taken off. By all means, do not be that guy.

In addition to avoiding gutter language, you should avoid speaking negatively about others. Think twice before you talk down about your competitors in their absence. In fact, never speak ill of anyone, except to their face. Recounting the calamities that have happened to you is also unattractive. Avoid stories about how you were sick over the weekend and spent most of it in the bathroom. Put yourself in the other person's shoes: would you like to spend time with someone who mainly speaks about things you would rather never have happen to you? Or would you prefer someone with an upbeat outlook on life who sees the opportunity in everything? By no means am I advocating that you fashion yourself into a careless Pollyanna. But there exists a magical balance between being a realist and having a positive outlook. Start observing the impact it has on you when someone won't stop telling you about their problems and mishaps. It creates a climate of negativity that drags everything down. It's better to see the bright side of things and avoid dark topics. This makes a better impression on others, especially in your first meeting.

Doing Business Abroad

If your university has a campus in a foreign country, then you may already be familiar with the idiosyncrasies that different cultures bring with them. Asian cultures in particular often stump the American or European visitor with their many intricacies. As a student, consequences of severe mishaps may be minimal; but for an entrepreneur, a misstep can break your venture. Business culture is rigid in some countries, whereas it is relaxed in others. Become familiar with the business etiquette of your locale. As a foreigner, nobody calls on you to do everything right. If it seems as though you genuinely care, then you are in the green and small mistakes will matter less. There are numerous books about conducting business abroad. Read one about the country where you are a guest. Even if you think you already know everything, the dos and don'ts may surprise you.

A key custom is the act of greeting. Each country has its own protocol. Some religions may forbid a man to shake a woman's hand. People may dislike it if you hug them cordially. But others will find it strange if you refuse to participate in the ritual of three kisses on their cheeks. Familiarize yourself with the greeting protocol if you engage with partners from a foreign culture. It is usually easy enough to ask someone before the meeting about how things will unfold. You can then copy what others do. It has always been a good practice to wait on a handshake until the other party extends their hand. If they don't, then you do whatever they do: either bow or nod.

The same goes for food. You will rarely have an important business lunch or dinner where table etiquette is so exotic that you are at your wit's end. Most lunch meetings are informal. But occasionally you may unexpectedly find yourself at a banquet. If this happens, copy what everybody else is doing. If you are being served food, then let that happen, without refusing any of it. Nobody expects you to eat everything that is put before you, but rejecting food is seen as very impolite in many cultures.

A few years ago, a company of mine entered in a joint venture with a Japanese company. When the business relationship was forming, the Japanese partner flew my firm from Los Angeles to Tokyo for a week to hammer out the legal agreements. One of the partners in the American business, let's call him J, had a tattoo of the Chinese character "love" on his forearm. This may have been cute in Los Angeles, but in Japan, only Yakuza and other delinquents bear tattoos. Foreigners are often unaware that a tattoo reflects badly on the person in Japan. In the Japanese view, tattoos violate the body, and they are a reflection of low self-esteem. In a negotiation, you obviously need to make the best impression possible and come from a position of strength. To negotiate with Japanese businesspeople is tricky enough, to say it mildly. The last thing you want is the other party perceiving you as flawed and weak. I advised J of that and suggested he wear a long-sleeved business shirt to cover the tattoo. Knowing he had a stubborn personality, I doubled up and sent him an article from a book that explained the problem. With that, I considered the issue closed. Fast-forward two weeks. We are seated in the conference room in Tokyo: three people from my company on one side of the table, five older Japanese businessmen on the other side of the table. Negotiations are not going well. The Japanese repeatedly say, "Just sign the contract!" That contract contains blatant flaws and is a long way from I want for my business. But most important, J's tattoo is shining brightly for everyone to see. Not only that, but his cowboy boots and the rolled-up sleeves of his flannel shirt give the impression that he comes right from the farm in Ohio. He certainly made his point that nobody can tell him what to do with his tattoo or what to wear. Yet how can a settled Japanese businessperson in a tailored suit consider a person looking like a farmhand an equal partner in a joint venture? I certainly am no micro manager. But dressing properly for a business meeting is a basic requirement when negotiating a contract. After much wrestling, the deal eventually came to pass, in the least elegant way possible. The business later turned sour, and I exited before it tanked. I am not blaming that on J. However, the foundation for a strong future of that joint venture was missing. It could have started in that first meeting, had the other party taken us seriously.

This concludes the crash course in manners. Read a book about business etiquette, and you will be all right.

A Mindset, Not a Job

Entrepreneurship is much more a mindset than a job. It is about finding openings and possibility where others don't. If you look at the world through the entrepreneur's eyes, you will suddenly see many opportunities that you previously missed. Opportunities to get feedback from others to assist you in moving your idea forward. Opportunities for partnerships that open new platforms for you. And opportunities to save money wherever you can. You can be entrepreneurial in any line of work, not just as a startup founder.

The main point is that an entrepreneur needs to switch from being a consumer to being a producer. What does that mean? Producers have new ideas, come up with innovative solutions, and launch products and services that consumers cannot live without. Consumers benefit from these ideas: they need the new solutions and buy the products or services the producers offer. Of course, everybody is both a producer and a consumer at the same time. On balance, however, an entrepreneur should be more producer than consumer. This is a tricky topic, and by no means is this a value judgment. But it is important to understand that startup entrepreneurship shifts you from the consumer side to the producer side. This is intuitively clear, because a startup produces a product or service for the benefit of clients in the market. You provide a product or service instead of consuming one.

This shift is fundamental and will eventually seep into other areas of your life. You can no longer take the easy way out, but have to meet challenges with leadership. Instead of blaming others for a botched job at your company, you must now take on full responsibility, because there is no one else to point fingers at. Instead of trying to carry out a task, you must deliver, whatever it takes. Instead of partying the whole weekend and calling in sick on Monday, you must be a professional, always ready to pull the trigger when a lucky chance presents itself. It may be inconvenient, but if it helps get your startup off the ground, you should jump on it.

As an entrepreneur, you are always on. Most people are no startup entrepreneurs and are firmly rooted on the consumer side, so making the switch is difficult. Why do you keep talking about business when everybody else is trying to forget the day at the office after five o'clock rolls around? When you see your startup as a mission, then there are no business hours. It takes willpower and determination to stay the course. Otherwise, you may miss an opportunity that could potentially launch your venture into the stratosphere. To adopt an entrepreneurial mindset, it is of course very helpful to surround yourself with other entrepreneurs. These are your peers, from whom you can learn by osmosis. When you have access to a supportive group of businesspeople, then over time you will see how they do things and approach certain situations and learn what it takes to get your startup off the ground.

Get Out of Your Comfort Zone

As an entrepreneur, you must learn to be open about life and its opportunities. These often present themselves in the least likely places. What do you do if a project is only somewhat in line with what you can or want to deliver, but it has the potential to get you closer to a company you would like to enter a joint venture with? By all means, take on the project, even if doing so is a little uncomfortable at first.

One day, a casual acquaintance from a business workshop called my company in Switzerland and asked me to put together some documentation for a certain sound system for a store his architecture firm was working on. This had little to do with the core business of my company, but sound systems are a hobby of mine. I did some research, called a manufacturer to order a catalog, and then sent everything to the architect. With this documentation, he went to meet his client. Rather unexpectedly, I then received a phone call with a request to calculate the exact cost of the system. So, I made another call to the manufacturer and created a table in Excel. I thought of this as nothing but a favor to another businessman. A week or so later, the architect called me excitedly and congratulated me on landing the project. What project, I wondered? It turned out that his firm was remodeling the stores of a mini-supermarket chain, which wanted to install sound systems in each store. Because the documentation I had put together looked professional, he was under the impression that I was a dealer of these sound systems. His client approved of using the system I had researched and wanted to order it from my company. Well … sure, we could deliver that! All I had to do was ask the wholesaler to drop-ship a system to each location. Local electricians then carried out the installation under the architect's supervision. My company's markup on each system was $1,000. There were 500 stores in total. Feel free to do the math.

When I met this architect, did I know that he would turn out to be an important business contact who would eventually secure a substantial project for my company? Far from it. I had never thought about collaborations with architects, but I was curious to find out about his projects in the workshop where we met. The conversation went well, so we exchanged business cards. At networking events, you can always learn something new and meet people you would rarely otherwise be exposed to. Networking events are more than a free buffet and a chance to pick up girls. When you launch a startup, you have graduated to adulthood and should see networking events in a new light. I know, it can be uncomfortable to introduce yourself to strangers. Making small talk is also not my forte. Nevertheless, if you make it a habit to get out of your comfort zone regularly, you will acquire an important skill for success. Your university may put on some sort of catered event for a delegation from industry or the government. Instead of loading up your plate and then huddling around a table with your fellow researchers, do something different this time. Look for a table with just a few people, and introduce yourself. Ask what brings them to the event, and find out what they are doing. Exchange business cards. Tell them about your startup and the current insights you've had or the challenges you are struggling with. Ask for their feedback and whether they may know someone interested in your technology. Make outrageous demands. Do they perhaps know an investor or a joint venture partner for your startup? Or would they be willing to assist you with testing your MVP? See what happens. You never know what will come out of these encounters.

Building a strong network is important for the future of your startup. You may meet someone in a few months who could benefit from a casual connection you made last week at a networking event. Once you have connected with enough people, you can begin linking them up with your existing network. This is fun to do and will do more than benefit those you introduce to each other. When you need somebody's help, you may also tap into their network. Before you know it, you are part of an active exchange of contacts and ideas. And all this happens because you leave your comfort zone once in a while.

Read and Improve

Most successful entrepreneurs are voracious readers. They constantly read books, publications, and the news to keep on top of what is happening in the world. This concerns topics beyond existing domain knowledge, about which I assume you are already an expert. Knowledge is power, and startup entrepreneurs need all the power they can get. You need to expand your horizon with knowledge from outside your field of vision. In addition to absorbing all the information you can to solve your current challenges, also read books that have no obvious application to the situation. If you need to find a solution to an issue with a certain material, then do the required reading along with a biography about Nicola Tesla. Far-flung ideas may cross-pollinate the problem-solving process, and they may originate in the least expected places. If you read one sentence somewhere that holds the answer to a pressing problem, your life may change forever. You cannot expect to have that one sentence presented to you on a silver platter. To distill the wisdom that is useful for you, you need process large amounts of information yourself.

It is surprising how few books people read after their college years. Even some smart people proudly announce they have read the last book a decade ago. Sure, they may browse the news online, scan some RSS subscriptions, and academic publications here and there, but systematic reading with the goal of massive knowledge acquisition is rare. Not among the successful entrepreneurial elite, though, who practice it as a daily habit. By the way, I am not talking about reading novels, but nonfiction books. Imagine you read one such book each week. That would be 52 books in a year. Quite a sizable library. I doubt most people read 52 books in their entire life. Here is a knowledge advantage you can gain in a single year. With speed-reading techniques you can read two or even three books per week. That amounts to a whopping 156 books by the end of the year and 1,560 books after 10 years.

The reason I prefer books to other written material is that you enter a conversation with the author. It takes about one year to write a complete book. Considerable research and knowledge condensation go into the process. The author recounts many experiences for your learning pleasure. When you read a book, you absorb a whole year of somebody's work. With speed reading, you can assimilate in one year what 156 people took an entire year of their life to compile. This 156X multiplier is incredible leverage.

Whenever I read a book or a research paper, I make a summary. It consists of bullet points and some of the most important drawings or graphs from the book. At the end of the summary, I do some quick brainstorming about how the ideas from the book are applicable to my current circumstances. I strongly encourage you to do the same. Even though it is extra work, you will benefit hugely from having summaries of what you have read. It enables you to review your reading later and quickly look up the most important ideas. Who has ever read a 400-page book twice, or three times? I revisit most of my summaries at least once a month so they stay fresh in my mind, ready for use when I need ideas. When you have your own summaries, you can also share them with others. Exchange summaries with like-minded individuals. When you progress along your entrepreneurial journey, you will be surprised to learn that many successful entrepreneurs are doing exactly this and have done it for years. Only the relatively passive mainstream prefers watching TV to knowledge acquisition.

To become excellent, you should avoid all things that make you mainstream. When you are picking up new, positive habits, they rarely seem to make a big difference at first. But over time, when your efforts compound, you will pull away increasingly quickly. After several years of knowledge acquisition, there will be a huge gap between you and the mainstream and a much smaller gap between you and successful entrepreneurs. To achieve success, you need to do the things that successful people do. Reading a lot and putting that information in context with your situation is just one of them.

Then there is the subject of self-improvement. I know, you may think this is soft and only applicable for esoteric types. But all successful people engage in one form or another of self-improvement. Perhaps adopting a new positive habit, like getting up at 5:30 am every day. Or learning a new language just for fun. Or improving their working memory with N-back programs. They do little things each day that push them a bit. Self-improvement is much more than meditation and yoga. If you go to the gym regularly, that's a form of self-improvement. If you deny yourself that second piece of cake, that's another form of self-improvement. And if you read a book every day for 30 minutes, that's also self-improvement. This has little to do with seeking enlightenment, but with adopting positive habits. When those habits have become part of your day like brushing your teeth or taking a shower, they have the power to help you achieve your goals without even thinking about them.

So how can you get in the habit of reading more to accelerate your learning? Begin by scheduling daily reading sessions. Make a regular, recurring appointment at some time during the day to read a nonfiction book for 30 minutes. Or put the item on your daily to-do list. It is in your own best interest to follow through on this commitment.

Get Used to Big Numbers

When you manage a business, you must begin getting used to bigger numbers. What does that mean? Well, if your profit margin on each product sold is $100 and your potential market size is 1 million, then that will amount to $100 million in profit. Can you imagine such a number? Yes? Good. Feel free to skip this chapter. But you may feel slightly queasy when talking about capitalist concepts like profit, margin, and sales revenue. You may think $1 million is an enormous amount of money. If anyone asks you about your revenue target in five years, you may feel uncomfortable if it is more than $5 million. If this is the case, you are not alone. Startup entrepreneurs rarely come from a background where they received early education about money. The financial literacy of most people around the world is limited. If there is more month at the end of the money, then they notice that they have overspent; otherwise, budget planning has no mindshare.

Financial intelligence has nothing to do with IQ. The smartest people can make terrible financial decisions. And some people who have never gone to school have amassed fortunes. Nobody expects you to become a financial planner or financial analyst, but you should at least get comfortable with bigger numbers. When you deal with corporations, you will notice that they have another definition of revenue and cost. Hundreds of millions may be cheap for a corporation, compared to their other overhead.

Once upon a time, a company of mine was working on a project for an airline. Our contribution was small, but the entire project, handled by a large consulting firm, cost several million dollars. We thought our part should be worth $30,000, because it only involved a limited engagement for a week or so. The big meeting took place on the top floor of the client's corporate headquarters, right next to the airport. The decision maker and his staff sat around the conference table in tailored suits and silk ties. When the time came to approve the budget, he addressed me and asked, "So, about your budget item here. This is in addition to your other $30,000, am I correct?" Somebody must have made a mistake and entered our fee twice in the overall budget. Honest as I am, I cleared up the confusion, only to notice a hint of disappointment on the face of the airline man. Oh, I see. It's that cheap ... I am sure those were his thoughts. To me, $30,000 hardly seemed little at all. However, the airline man would not have blinked had that fee been twice as big. It might even have been OK to charge $100,000.

Budget items need to make sense in relation to other items. If all the other items are $100,000 or more, then yours should be in a similar range. If the overall budget is several million, then adjust accordingly. But wait a minute, you say. You would charge a company twice the cost that another company paid, just because their budget is higher? Yes, absolutely. Your markup should adjust to the capability of the market. Price is a result of the ability and willingness to pay and has little to do with the manufacturing cost of the product or service. This is called *price differentiation* in economics. It is what hotels do all the time. Booking directly on their site may cost 50% more than booking on a discount web site. It is the same room—the only difference is the margin a particular customer is willing to pay. What if you sell a product with a fixed price? Then you will always have a dominant market to which you tailor your margin. If you cannot sell your inventory, that's when you begin reducing the price and your margin. As a rule, choose a market that can pay a high price for your product or service. Marketing to them and delivering the product takes the same effort as catering to a low-cost market. As a startup, you should attempt to extract the highest price you can. To do this, you have to think in large numbers.

Many startups project their future revenues way too low. If you believe you will hit $3 million in sales in the third year, then you are thinking too small. Look for markets and business models that will allow you to make $100 million, $500 million, $1 billion. This market size is interesting for joint venture partners and investors. Do a little research about other companies. Speak with some investors. Read books about how venture capitalists think. Watch the movie *Wall Street*.[7] Direct your thinking toward larger numbers, and seek out projects that can help your startup gain momentum. If you provide a service and a project pays just $1,000, seriously think about whether you should go ahead or decline it. If it puts you in the same room with people who could help you land bigger projects in the future, that may be a reason to take a bath on the first project and then engage the client toward larger projects. If you can wrap some MVP testing into the project, that may be another reason to accept a low-paid assignment. But steer clear of making this a habit. If you keep doing small projects, then you will always be the small-projects company. Clients will rarely consider you for larger projects, because you have pigeonholed yourself into the inexpensive category. Your work should never be inexpensive or cheap. Abandon clients who think it should be. Nobody wins when you set the sights too low for your startup.

---

[7]*Wall Street*, directed by Oliver Stone (20th Century Fox, 1987).

80% Specialist, 20% Generalist

How often have you heard the following phrase? "Only do what you are an expert in, and outsource all the rest." This is a common pattern for businesspeople, but it misses the point of what startup entrepreneurship is all about. Sure, you should avoid wasting time with tasks that someone else can do much better, faster, and for a lower price. Should Tiger Woods mow his own lawn?[8] He spends a lot of time walking around on grass and may therefore have profound knowledge about the dimensions of a golf course. Tiger would most likely be more efficient with a lawnmower than a normal gardener, but his opportunity cost is much too high to be doing that. In the time it takes him to mow the lawn, he could earn a million dollars doing a photo shoot.

Despite the economic concept of opportunity cost explained with this classic textbook example, you need to know how to pull yourself out of a sticky situation or deadline when there is no help around the corner. Therefore, being ignorant about anything outside your expert domain is a bad strategy for a startup entrepreneur.

Recently, I was working on a project where we had five days to prepare a 40-page printed and bound brochure for an investment proposal. A decision maker on another continent needed this information, so the deadline was firm, and the presentation determined the future of the project. This may not sound like much. But since that project had started, about 100 folders with countless articles, diagrams, summaries, and PowerPoint presentations had been accumulated on three people's hard drives and Dropboxes. The founders now needed to revisit everything and pick out the most important bits. The brochure had to measure up to others whose teams had spent six months getting everything right. If you have ever put together an annual report, then you know that this usually takes much longer than a week. We had five days to condense all the information, write an executive summary, and make a professional layout in Adobe InDesign. A printer would then bind three copies of the brochure, which had to look glossy and flawless. Somebody knew a graphic designer who was available on such short notice, who flew in to do the layout. Straight off the plane, she raced to the office on Thursday morning, where we put her in front of a PowerBook that was preloaded with all the assets and had the layout software already running. The deadline for the printer was Friday noon, 26 hours away. Let the fun begin.

Many unforeseen issues arose. The first was the keyboard of the computer. Because the designer was used to a foreign layout, she found our PowerBook with the QWERTY layout very confusing. Luckily she had her own machine with her, so all the assets were hurriedly copied to her hard disk. In the

---

[8]N. Gregory Mankiw, *Principles of Economics* (Independence, KY: Cengage Learning, 2008).

transfer to her laptop, which had a different software version and was missing some fonts, settings in the file were changed. The layout template looked completely different from what we imagined. That was the moment when it became apparent that the designer was much less proficient in working with the layout software than expected. Sure, she had done motion design and stunning Photoshop and Illustrator work, but laying out a brochure was a first. With 20 hours to go until the deadline, it dawned on us that this would be anything but smooth sailing.

On Friday morning at 11 am (one hour before the deadline), the file was still unfinished. Working around the clock, the designer was in no shape to spot errors and typos. One of the founders sort of knew his way around the layout program, so he troubleshot the most blatant issues right in the printing company's office. With everybody hunched around the computer screen, pointing out a missing image credit here or a wrong description for a graph there, the file finally went to print. Five hours later, we picked up the bound brochures. They looked like a million bucks and were soon on their way to Europe. The goal was accomplished, just in the nick of time. Nobody who saw the final product would ever know that it was up in the air until the last second and only came together thanks to lucky circumstances.

Do you believe this would have worked out if the founders had concentrated on the high-value task of concepts and product development, and let the designer deal with the supposedly low-value task of the layout job? For the entrepreneur, the high-value task is getting the job done, whatever it takes. In this case, it meant knowing how to use that layout software and staying up to motivate the designer to keep the pace. Finishing what must be done takes the mindset of a generalist, and entrepreneurs must put on more than one hat. From this viewpoint, the notion of outsourcing everything but the tasks with the highest payoff is terrible advice for a startup. If you care about nothing else than your one area of expertise, you will be at a disadvantage when things veer off course, as they often do.

It is difficult to identify which tasks are of high or low value in the first place. Is touch-typing low or high value? I have seen too many C-level executives desperately trying to knock out a 100-word letter with two fingers when their speech recognition software refused to work. How about basic web design and using WordPress? When an important potential joint venture partner asks you to forward your online documentation to her team, it may be impossible to hire someone to set up a web site for you in an hour. Make sure you know your way around more than one thing. Diverse skills can help you directly and can create considerable goodwill for you when you get others out of a tight spot. This is why constant learning and reading are so important. Become 80% specialist and 20% generalist. You will rarely need your generalist knowledge every day, but it may come in handy when you expect it least.

How to Learn Something New

Did you learn something new in the last month? A few words of a new language, juggling, or how to stay under water for more than 60 seconds? Life is learning, so the saying goes. If you think learning stops after your graduate degree, then you are missing many opportunities right in front of you. Curiosity and an open mind are indispensable for entrepreneurs. You should make it a habit to acquire new skills at all times. This benefits you personally—plus you never know when you can help somebody out of a bind with a skill you possess.

A splendid example of an easy-to-learn skill is touch-typing. Most people believe this is unimportant, because they can always hack their way through a paper using two fingers. Speech-to-text software is also often used, and it makes the keyboard unnecessary. As long as the software works, that is. When you can type fast without errors, you can translate your thoughts into the computer at such speed that a new world of possibilities opens up for you. You can blog about your company and your progress, write manuals or reports about MVP testing you did, or write a book about your trials and tribulations as an entrepreneur. If typing is a dreaded activity you would rather outsource, then you will subconsciously try to avoid anything that has to do with it. If rapid new skill acquisition sounds intriguing to you, and you still type with two fingers, then I recommend you put touch-typing on the top of your list.

Wait a minute, you say. What about the 10,000-hour rule? Author Malcolm Gladwell found that experts in their domain practiced an average of 10,000 hours until they achieved world-class levels. Studying prodigies like Bill Gates, Tiger Woods, famous musicians, and chess grandmasters, Gladwell found that none of them were geniuses when they started out. Only after about ten years of single-minded, deliberate practice of their chosen skills did their hard work pay off. Ten years equate to about 10,000 productive hours. The rule states that mastery in any field requires 10,000 hours of practice.[9]

Research has shown that success comes down to deliberate practice much more than innate talent. Even prodigies like Wolfgang Amadeus Mozart produced dismal works in their early years. Only after diligent study were they able to reach the status the world knows them for.[10] With this in mind, it seems as though you could never learn anything new that you would not be mediocre at. Who has ten years available to engage in single-minded study of just one skill? At the same time, many people learn languages well into adulthood. They pick up a complex game like golf long before they put in 10,000 hours. There is no need to compete with Tiger Woods on the golf course or with Mozart on the piano—just play well enough to have fun.

---

[9]Malcolm Gladwell, *Outliers: The Story of Success* (New York: Little, Brown and Co., 2008).
[10]Geoffrey Colvin, *Talent Is Overrated: What Really Separates World-Class Performers from Everybody Else* (New York: Portfolio, 2008).

Author Josh Kaufman found that a minimum of 20 hours of concentrated, deliberate practice is necessary to feel the first improvements when learning a new skill.[11] By putting aside 1 hour each evening for 20 days for deliberate practice, you can improve any skill you set your mind to. The word *deliberate* is important. Just reading about a subject does not count. Nor does attending a seminar about it. A passive activity is not deliberate practice and does not qualify toward those 20 hours. Most of us forget what practice means after childhood. If you learned to play an instrument well, then you know what deliberate practice means: endless repetitions of the most difficult part of a piece of music, under the watchful eyes of a teacher who criticizes your every mistake.

Applying this kind of practice to new skills is key to becoming good at them. When you can manage that, you will be able to pick up a new skill with acceptable results within 20 hours. You will be able to show some ability, but you will hardly be a master who can compete with the best of the best. For most of us, this is unnecessary. Being good enough at a skill to avoid frustration is all we want.

I recently learned touch-typing while I was in Vietnam. I had my own typing system before, using more than two fingers; but without looking at the keyboard, I failed to produce satisfactory results. Replacing this haphazard system with professional ten-finger touch-typing was as simple as blocking out one hour each evening for typing practice for 20 days. Using software to learn typing, I can now produce 70 words per minute with few errors. Sure, this is a far cry from the world record of 216 words per minute. However, it is plenty to write this book without frustration and exhaustion. Touch-typing is the ideal first skill to learn in 20 hours. I recommend you look into it.

Begin getting into the habit of practicing new skills regularly. As you saw in the specialist/generalist discussion, there are various useful skills that startup entrepreneurs should know. These reach beyond intellectual or computer skills. Also pick up fun skills like riding a unicycle or kickboxing. Make it a habit to be enterprising and curious, instead of passive and withdrawn. Be interested, to be interesting. Just like the knowledge you will gain from reading extensively, your newfound powers will accumulate over time and build on each other. That takes a while, so you need to start early to reap the benefits later. You need to practice several years to be an overnight success.

---

[11]Josh Kaufman, *The First 20 Hours: How to Learn Anything—Fast* (New York: Portfolio/Penguin, 2013).

Who to Turn to for Advice

Entrepreneurship can be a confusing and lonely affair, especially when your environment consists of people with a strong need for safety and predictability. These may be your professors, fellow students and researchers, parents, friends, and significant others. Asking non-entrepreneurs for their opinion about your startup and advice to solve certain problems can be frustrating. Not only do they lack the experience to actually help you, but there is also the risk that they will (subconsciously) try to dissuade you from your plans. They have never started their own company and probably have nobody in their circle who has, so they are hardly the right people to call for advice. Of course, please keep your old friends. Enjoy their company and have a good time with them, but look for qualified startup and business advice elsewhere.

The same goes for the experts in commercialization at your university, the technology transfer or licensing office (TTO or TLO). By definition, they are thinking about patents when it comes to commercializing research. If your startup has no patentable assets, they will be at their wits' end. In the rarest cases, will they admit that. They may point you toward the grant track and government agency XYZ, which has been set up to guide young entrepreneurs in the "correct" direction. Someone at the TLO may have taken a crash course in entrepreneurship at a seminar. However, because that is purely theoretical, you may as well read a book—you will know just as much. Good intentions are at the root of most of the current support programs, but startups that take off have seldom gone through these conventional channels. If it was that easy and predictable, there would be many more successful companies coming out of academia and government programs, don't you think?

When you meet venture capitalists and other investors, inquire about their practical experience and their track record before you ask them for entrepreneurship and business advice. Have they ever started their own company? Has the company achieved profitability? No and no? Then think for yourself why you should trust their advice. It is perfectly OK to ask direct questions like these. When a venture capitalist becomes serious about investing in your company, they will grill you about anything and everything. As a rule of thumb, ask yourself why people are doing whatever they do. If they could run their own successful company, they probably had better options than working somewhere 9–5.

Successful entrepreneurs are much better qualified to guide you than anyone else. Seek out other successful startup founders in your city or country and become friends with them. Use the Internet to connect if there are no networking events or meetups in your city. Make it a point to upgrade your personal network. Exchanging ideas with other startup founders and established entrepreneurs is stimulating and inspiring for you and your team. Most entrepreneurs, myself included, are happy to give advice if they feel the person asking for it has drive and motivation. They recognize earlier versions of themselves in people who ask them questions. Openly approach other entrepreneurs and ask if they can give you feedback on your ideas. Most of the time they will accept, and a new friendship may be in the making.

Why Even Bother?

By now, you may have decided that launching a startup is interesting but too invasive in your life and hardly worth the hassle. Perhaps you hoped you could somehow start a new business on the side without much effort. Why bother, if it is so grueling and uncertain? Why not simply take on a cushy position at a university? After all, that is what everybody else is doing, so it cannot be that bad.

Sure, the temptation to give up is there. When things are on the rocks, it will become even stronger. Regardless, be aware that real change always originates from a determined entrepreneurial mind. Entrepreneurship is pretty much the only way for anyone to have a chance to change the world. Working as a researcher may lead to groundbreaking insights, but rarely do they find their way into the lives and hearts of people. Teaching at a university may instill certain knowledge in motivated students, but it is by starting your own company that you can make a real impact. Not everybody has to reach for the sky and try to make their mark. It is perfectly OK for most people to work a normal job, enjoy the weekends with their friends and family, and lead a quiet, comfortable life. There is nothing wrong with that.

However, you may lie awake some nights with the gnawing feeling there should be more to your life. You notice the lack of a deeper mission and purpose. You feel you are on a treadmill, failing to live up to your potential. You wonder if you are making enough use of your talents and your energy. Your work at the university never leaves the ivory tower and has no impact in people's lives outside academia. Later you fall asleep. The next morning, you have largely forgotten those silly thoughts, which you blame on insomnia and stress. But they return—regularly, and at shorter intervals. What to do in this situation is unclear to you, because the necessary changes seem so sweeping and impossible that you better forget about them. Does this sound at all familiar?

Not everybody asks these questions, but chances are you do, because you have picked up this book and are still reading it. If you feel you should make better use of your talents, then launching your own company may be the answer for you. Your deep understanding of a certain technology can find its way into a useful product with the power to transform lives. How about giving your mind the platform to express itself fully and make an impact in the world at the same time?

There is a whimsical Japanese movie by Akira Kurosawa, called *Ikiru* ("To Live").[12] The protagonist, Watanabe, has spent the last few decades in a government agency where he has advanced to the respected position of section chief. His work consists of little more than stamping papers and shuffling project proposals from one desk to the next until they disappear into a drawer. One day he receives devastating news: he has stomach cancer. He will die within the next six months. Watanabe wakes up to the fact that he has done nothing important with his life up to this day. He sets out on a search for meaning and makes it his mission to see through at least one project: a proposal to turn a festering sewage pond into a park. This proposal has been repeatedly submitted by residents who suffer from the sewage pond near their homes, but it is sent from section to section, and the government does not intend to take action. But this is no longer how Watanabe does his job. He scratches and claws his way through the bureaucracy, through a thicket of complacency and corruption, up to the highest positions. Most of his colleagues think he is crazy and will never prevail. Against all odds and through sheer will, Watanabe makes it work. He eventually dies a happy man in the park he helped create.

A friend of mine recently confessed that she thought there was nothing left to discover. All the important and fun adventures had taken place already. The discovery of new continents, the flight to the Moon, were all checked off the list. Of course, she would quit her job as a stockbroker and become an entrepreneur, if she could only find a satisfactory field for her startup to venture into. Clearly, this person had set her sights on the Hollywood version of entrepreneurship.

Most people think the status quo is how things are and should be for eternity. When the world was flat, there was no need to sail past a certain point in the ocean. Yet somebody did and induced a paradigm shift that set a whole new ideology in motion. None of these discoveries were fun and games. The voyages of Christopher Columbus took many years of preparation, tedious politics, and fundraising alone. Not only did the monarchs to whom he sent his plans to discover the western route to India believe them to be impractical, but they also doubted Columbus could possibly succeed. Many had tried before, so why should it work this time? When he finally secured permission and funding for his expedition, the dangerous part of the endeavor began. Three days into his first journey in 1492, the rudder of his vessel broke—a potential act of sabotage. Then his crew allegedly grew so homesick that they threatened to sail back to Spain. It was unclear whether the indigenous people Columbus might encounter would be friendly toward foreign visitors. Had Columbus's primary motivation been the fun and potential honor of the project, he would have given up after the first few weeks.

---

[12]*Ikiru* (生きる, "To Live"), directed by Akira Kurosawa (Toho Studios, 1953).

Fun and prestige are weak motivations to launch a startup. You should feel a burning desire to explore, learn, and make an impact in the lives of people who find your startup's product or service useful. This is often little more than a feeling deep down that this idea could potentially be big. When you have this feeling, I encourage you to follow it, using the list in Figure 3-2 as a guideline. You can rationalize for as long as you want whether the idea will be successful. But if you have an inexplicable drive to make it work, chances are high that it will. Setting the wheels in motion without much deliberating is the best policy. Overcome analysis paralysis, and boldly step forward. The recommendations in this book will allow you to do just that.

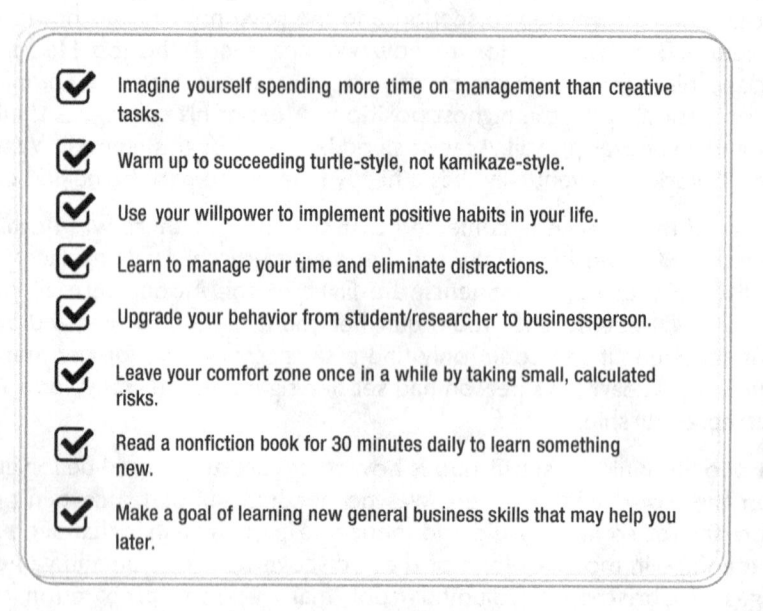

- ☑ Imagine yourself spending more time on management than creative tasks.
- ☑ Warm up to succeeding turtle-style, not kamikaze-style.
- ☑ Use your willpower to implement positive habits in your life.
- ☑ Learn to manage your time and eliminate distractions.
- ☑ Upgrade your behavior from student/researcher to businessperson.
- ☑ Leave your comfort zone once in a while by taking small, calculated risks.
- ☑ Read a nonfiction book for 30 minutes daily to learn something new.
- ☑ Make a goal of learning new general business skills that may help you later.

Figure 3-2. Checklist for a startup entrepreneur mindset

CHAPTER 4

Engaging Others with Actionable Next Steps

How many times has this happened to you? A businessperson you meet at a networking event finds your research project interesting and wants to learn more about it. You exchange cards and set up a meeting in the coming week. The person comes to your lab, signs the NDA, and approvingly nods at your technology, which you present in much detail. When the hour is up, your guest thanks you for the time and suggests keeping in touch, especially when you have advanced the technology more and it is closer to implementation. The person then departs, never to be heard from again. You assume this person was not all that interested after all and chalk it up as one more pointless meeting.

In reality, you failed to engage the visitor properly. You were most likely unclear about what you wanted from the interaction in the first place. You showed your work, but you missed the chance to gain insight into the business of your visitor and the person's challenges, expansion plans, or product innovations. When making a new contact, most people never research who that person really is, let alone read up on their present and past job history or personal interests. Every person has a valuable network, and when you meet someone, you can get access to their network. It may not be the initial contact you do business with, but rather someone on the edge of that person's network. Entrepreneurs must know how to use others to advance their cause. This is a cornerstone of entrepreneurship.

In your dealings with those outside your university, you should begin thinking about engaging them with actionable next steps. They may be government agencies, financiers, insurance companies, businesspeople, successful entrepreneurs, or others. At a large public university I worked with, several banks scheduled visits to show the impressive infrastructure of the world-renowned institution to their C-level staff and wealthy clients. After the first few tours, the managing director decided to stop the visits with the argument that his facility was not a zoo. With this only half-joking statement, he and his staff got rid of the annoying visitors, but they threw out the baby with the bathwater. Imagine what a good relationship with banks and their wealthy clients could have done for the university's startups. Many other universities and public companies act the same way every day. Few people know how to engage others with actionable next steps to gain leverage.

By means of "build, measure, learn," you already know that frequent market testing is required in order to get feedback about your products and services so you can incrementally improve them. You can use interactions with the real world for the same purpose. Instead of giving visitors a feature-laden lecture, why not engage them in a fun experiment that helps your startup collect data about its product or service? Why not ask them questions to learn more about their opinions and interests? It is often possible to turn the situation around and derive a constructive learning session from engagements that at first seem dull and boring.

Know What You Want

You have gained clarity about your startup, your process, some of your first MVPs, and other insights. Now you have a good picture of who to engage for the cause of your startup. In the world of the startup entrepreneur, everybody becomes a potential MVP tester, client, partner, or advisor. Is someone telling you about their children at a networking event? If your startup works on an electric scooter, ask them to bring the kids to the lab to test how it feels to be the underage copilot. Are you programming software for traffic flow, and someone mentions that they know an operator at the transport authority? Ask them to set up a meeting so you can MVP test your prototype. Even if your MVP is still under construction when you set the meeting, whip up something overnight. Has a bank announced a visit to show high-net-worth individuals (HNWIs) around the campus? Design a questionnaire for them relating to your project, and make sure you're the center of attention during the visit. Does a government agency want to see in action some of your university's technology that holds promise for the future? Engage them in the discussion, and get as much feedback as you can. Don't resort to simply giving them the old shtick of your academic, top-down presentation, leaving them with nothing to act on after the visit. Engage them wherever you can. Collect their business cards, ask for referrals to other agencies, and ask for one-on-one sessions to gain a better understanding of their problems. You will learn invaluable lessons this way.

All this may sound grossly opportunistic and slightly crazy. It is not, when you begin thinking like a startup entrepreneur who has to make do with whatever presents itself. You will learn that you can be quite aggressive with your ideas and questions before anyone turns you down. As a startup entrepreneur, the world is your MVP testing lab.

The One-Page Proposal

A more formal approach to engaging people with actionable next steps is the one-page proposal, as described by author Patrick Riley.[1] It spells out a target or goal, background information about your request, financial details, status quo, and next actions. Thinking in terms of one-page proposals is a helpful exercise to approach business with others. If you know exactly what you want, you can test how serious the other party is about collaborating with you. It is in your interest as an entrepreneur to find those who can help you get your venture off the ground and avoid wasting time with those who cannot or will not.

Here are the individual elements of the one-page proposal:

- Title
- Target
- Secondary targets
- Rationale (the pitch)
- Financial
- Status
- Action
- Name and date

Let's go through each of them, one by one.

Title

Obviously, this is what your proposal is about. Make sure the title fits on one line. Make it bold, a few points bigger than the other type. "Proposal of XYZ for [company] to investigate potential for joint venture" is a workable title.

---

[1] Patrick Riley, *The One-Page Proposal: How to Get Your Business Pitch onto One Persuasive Page* (New York: HarperBusiness, 2002).

Target

The target is what you want—the outcome of what you propose. For example, "Merging synergies with XYZ, complementing product line Z, establishing cost leadership in market X".

Secondary Targets

These are other effects of the outcome you propose: increasing market share over competitors, a first-of-its-kind project or product, opening the door to a new customer group, and so on. List three secondary targets in bullet form.

Rationale

This section is slightly longer—one or two paragraphs. It outlines your background, some history, how you got started, what you are seeking to do, and some biographical information about the founders and their expertise.

Financial

If you ask for money, or if any other cost is involved (for example, to put on a special event or conference), list what you need. You can also break down the cost of components or anything else that may be relevant to finances in the proposal.

Status

Describe the project's status quo. For instance, "The concept phase of project X is complete, and the project is ready to go. Prototype X is 80% complete and expected to be ready for testing next week".

Action

This is the call to action to the other party. For example, "For company XYZ to internally discuss possibilities of a joint venture, then to schedule a follow-up meeting for clarification and questions about the road ahead."

Name and Date

Print the proposal, and sign and date it at the bottom. This is important and introduces some urgency. All your contact data, including e-mail and phone numbers, goes in the footer of the page.

An Example Proposal

This may all sound abstract. To clarify, Figure 4-1 shows a sample proposal by a fictitious research startup for a joint venture.

FORMING A JOINT VENTURE BETWEEN SEISMIC SOFTWARE AND SENSORX
A joint venture with SensorX to create a commercial software package to predict earthquakes

<u>TARGET</u>: To test and create the product and launch it through SensorX' distribution channels.

- Addressing clear market need of governments and municipalities
- Approaching a large market in Japan from SensorX' customer base
- Using positive momentum of current policy, consolidation in the sector

The recent earthquake in Indonesia showed yet again how unprepared most governments and municipalities are when it comes to the prediction of tremors. The loss to the country's GDP in this last case is again in the billions of dollars. Therefore, their willingness to upgrade the existing systems is high and opens up a market opportunity.

Our company Seismic Software has patented several algorithms that have shown to be superior to existing commercial software in extensive lab tests over the last 24 months. This is achieved by ...

More background of the technology.

SensorX as the market leader in sensor technology is an optimal joint venture partner. Our software is already integrated and optimized for their sensors. A closer collaboration could help SensorX make the jump to a full-service company providing native software along with their existing products.

To launch the product a 50/50 joint venture with SensorX is proposed. Our core team will provide access to our IP and existing code, while SensorX will provide management and support services for the company and take over marketing, sales, and distribution.

<u>FINANCIAL</u>: To finalize the product costs approx. $1 million, mainly for screening and in-depth testing of the software in real application. Operation and support over ten years costs approx. $20 million. We predict a world market of approximately $100 million in revenue over the next ten years. This product could be the first in a series of follow-ups. Plans exist to expand the product line to other market verticals such as monitoring for asteroid impacts and several applications in national defense.

<u>STATUS</u>: Seismic Software has set up the strategic development plan and is ready to implement. All IP is cleared for use in the joint venture and the code documented so collaboration could start immediately.

<u>ACTION</u>: For SensorX to commit to a joint venture to propel the project forward and formalize agreements with Seismic Software by Q3 2014.

Professor X
Professor X, March 13, 20XX

© All rights reserved Seismic Software 20XX. Contact: +90 888 88 88, profx@university.com

---

Figure 4-1. Sample of a one-page proposal

In general, proposals are more convincing when you deliver them in person instead of via e-mail. Make an appointment, and say that you would like to schedule a meeting to talk about a proposal for a project. Then go to the appointment and take the printed proposal with you, neatly stored in a clear folder. If the recipient insists that you send it, or if they are located in another

Chapter 4 | Engaging Others with Actionable Next Steps

country, still steer clear of sending a pdf via e-mail. Print it on good paper stock, sign it, and send it to the company via FedEx, addressed to the office of the CEO. This is too significant to be sitting in an e-mail inbox, next to unimportant spam. Make your proposals special.

It may look short and simple, but such a document can take a week to complete. Remember that this is a one-pager, not a one-and-a-half pager. Keep it to one page not only because it is more accessible and elegant, but also because it forces you to strip all the bulk from your presentation and express it concisely. The font size should be at least 10 or 11, and the page should not look cramped.

Getting used to asking directly what you want takes a little while. At first sight it often seems too straightforward, especially to those in academia, where interactions are informal but hesitant. In business, people appreciate your getting to the point and putting your cards on the table. Working with written, actionable proposals shows that you are sincere in your undertaking. Even when you meet potential partners informally, you will sharpen your thinking toward engaging them in your process, rather than just providing entertainment or a good show in the lab.

Prepare a few proposals for mundane things, as practice. Perhaps even write one for the managing director of the university where you conduct your research, proposing certain actions to help you with your startup. Get into the habit of presenting the proposal, and learn as you go.

To begin engaging others with actionable next steps, use the checklist in Figure 4-2.

☑ Have a clear idea of who your potential clients are.

☑ Think of ways to get them to give feedback on your minimum viable product.

☑ When you have a meeting, have a clear list of goals.

☑ Prepare a one-page proposal today.

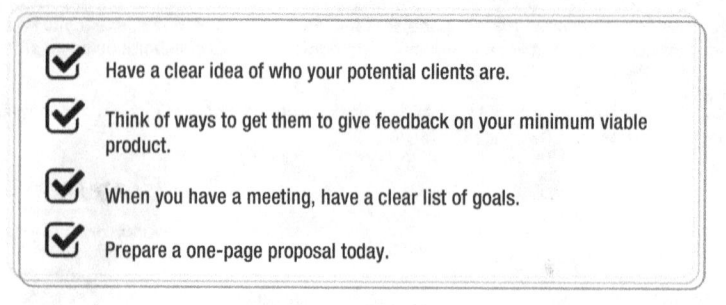

Figure 4-2. Checklist for actionable next steps

CHAPTER 5

Benefits vs. Features

A venture capitalist has read about your technology and has shown interest in learning more about your startup. When he and his associate come to the lab, you show them the research you have carried out in the last year. With your 200-slide strong PowerPoint presentation, you explain the features of the different technologies. This includes how you have improved on them by doing X, Y, and Z; an extensive list of software you used; and why most of it is no good to measure data with the precision you need. You show the statistical data that proves with confidence that this and that ratio have changed. Data from other tests is still waiting for processing, but once it is available, you can work on improving this and that ratio by so and so many percent. The venture capitalist and his associate both nod and say they find your work very interesting. They promise to stay in touch, and they leave. Since that day, you have not heard from them, and your e-mails to them remain unanswered.

Such an interaction is most frustrating. Yet it is clear why it happens: researchers are by nature deeply involved in a topic. They are experts in the *features* of a technology, how they interact, and how they have improved. On the other hand, consumers only care about the *benefits* of a technology. As Peter Drucker says, you don't buy a product, but what that product does for you. This thinking is relatively alien to scientists, yet it is vital when making the jump into the free market. It no longer works to just present a technology and then let the other party figure out how to draw a benefit from it, let alone create a product. Academic entrepreneurs must make this step clear when speaking with non-academics.

Chapter 5 | Benefits vs. Features

The SPIN Technique

Author Neil Rackham devised a simple process called SPIN to move the discussion from features toward benefits.[1] SPIN is an acronym for

- Situation
- Problem
- Implication
- Need-payoff

With this in mind, you can shift the discussion with external parties from a feature-laden presentation to an actual dialogue, where you match the benefits of a technology with the needs of the other party.

To do this, let's recap the fictitious example from the Lean Startup method: Simon has been building an electric scooter and now wants to take it to market with a startup. He is trying to confirm the growth hypothesis (will people buy the product?). His scooter costs around $2,000, which is above the price of similar models on the market. Features of the scooter include a futuristic design with several innovations (mainly the technology of the wheels), a closed body, new accelerator technology, and regenerative braking. Let's see how Simon could conduct an interview to discover whether the market would buy this product. He has identified a potential buyer and asks her a few questions.

Simon: Hi, and thanks for coming to this interview. This here is our scooter. It has a cool design with numerous innovations. The wheels are 15% lighter than comparable wheels. The same goes for the closed body. Because it consists of carbon fiber, the scooter has the identical weight of other scooters with an open body in the mid range. Crash tests have shown that our closed body reduces driver injuries by at least 50% when a car hits you full frontal. The accelerator is also a novelty. We managed to optimize the air/fuel mix with a special jet that we patented. The technology is very exciting; I can show you how it works in more detail if you want. The scooter also has regenerative braking, which extends the battery charge by 9.5%.

Potential buyer: OK.

Simon: Would you buy it?

Potential buyer: Well, what does it cost?

Simon: About $2,000.

---

[1] Neil Rackham, *SPIN Selling* (New York: McGraw-Hill, 1988).

University Startups and Spin-Offs 63

Potential buyer: Wow, that is beyond my price range. But it sure looks interesting. Well, thanks for showing it to me. Keep up the good work. All the best with your project!

Did Simon learn anything about the market in this interview? No—nothing at all. He only concluded that the potential buyer will not buy the scooter. Was his growth hypothesis validated? No, because the buyer said the scooter was too expensive for her. This may be the case, but this answer had a lot to do with how Simon bombarded her with the features of the scooter. Buyers never think in features but in benefits, and the only one that Simon mentioned (50% fewer injuries in a full-frontal crash) hardly registered with the buyer. This interview was a complete waste of time, largely because Simon neglected to ask the potential buyer about her real needs. Let's rewind and see what Simon could have done better.

Simon: Hi, and thanks for coming to this interview. Please tell me how you currently commute to work.

Potential buyer: I mainly take a bicycle.

Simon: OK. Every day, even when it rains?

Potential buyer: No, if it rains I take the MRT (a rapid commuter train in Singapore).

Simon: How does taking the MRT compare with the bicycle for you?

Potential buyer: The MRT is a drag. I live quite far from the station, and my office is also a 15-minute walk away from the next stop. This takes me about three times as long as taking the bicycle.

Simon: Have you tried wearing a raincoat on the bicycle when it rains? Or have you tried any other way to still be able to use the bicycle?

Potential buyer: Of course, I have tried everything! The thing is, I usually have my son with me, who sits in front in a child seat. I have to drop him off at kindergarten on the way and get him on the way home. When it rains, this is very cumbersome, and it is easier if we take the MRT.

Simon: OK, I see. So how often a week do you have to take the MRT then?

Potential buyer: About once or twice.

Simon: And how much time do you lose?

Potential buyer: About an hour per day. But it's not only that. If there is no rain in the morning, I take the bicycle. But when the rain starts in the evening on my way back home, I am soaked, and so is the work I take home, and my child. The weather has become unpredictable lately. I have considered taking the MRT each day, but that would cost me 5 hours per week in commuting time, 20 hours per month. What a waste!

Chapter 5 | Benefits vs. Features

Simon: What about a car?

Potential buyer: No way. I can't be seen in a vehicle that destroys the planet.

Simon: I meant an electric car.

Potential buyer: Yes, but those things don't work reliably yet. And they are ugly. And they cost a fortune.

Simon: Would you consider a different vehicle, perhaps a scooter or electric bicycle that had an enclosure to shield against the rain?

Potential buyer: I never thought about that … Yes, that may be an alternative. But what about reliability and cost?

Simon: We're working on a scooter that is very reliable and not that expensive. There are two seats, and it has an enclosed body. This would protect you and your son from the rain and is very safe.

Potential buyer: Interesting … What does it cost?

Simon: About $2,000.

Potential buyer. Wow, that is beyond my price range.

Simon: Yes, it's not cheap. But before, you said you would be wasting 20 hours per month by taking the MRT. That is 240 hours per year. If your time is worth at least $8 per hour, the scooter pays for itself in one year.

Potential buyer: When you look at it this way, you're right. Can I take a test drive?

Do you see how this works? Simon fully engaged the potential buyer. He let her talk about the situation and frame the problem. Then he let her discover that she should do something to address that problem. Finally, Simon brought up the scooter as a natural solution. In the previous example, when Simon told the potential buyer about all the features—regenerative braking, innovative design, and the accelerator—he left her to figure out the benefit for herself. When he used SPIN, the benefit became obvious. The herself buyer gave all the arguments that the scooter could indeed be a solution. Without any sleaze or hard sell, Simon presented the scooter as the answer to her problem. Unless the buyer strongly dislikes the test drive, chances are high Simon sold his first unit.

Let's analyze the interview in more detail:

- The potential buyer's *situation and problem* is that she cannot use her preferred mode of transport when it rains.
- The *implication* is that she is losing time because she has to use the MRT. If she let's this slide, she keeps on wasting 20 hours each month on commuting.

- The *payoff* of Simon's solution is that she can save time while still keeping her carbon footprint low and her finances intact.

Her actual need is not regenerative braking and fancy design, but a safe and reliable way to transport herself and her child around the city in any weather. These are benefits of the scooter, not features.

Simon was also smart to frame the discussion about the price in a different light. Because the potential buyer will make more than $8 per hour at her job, in just one year the scooter will have paid for itself because it saves over 240 hours annually. This is a solid benefit, and it seems that this buyer may confirm the growth hypothesis. The only thing that changed was how Simon approached the interview, and it made all the difference.

These answers gave Simon a good picture of how this particular buyer thinks and what is important to her. In any event, he has learned a lot in this interview. He can use the feedback he collected from this potential buyer in the next interview, and he can come up with a product that matches the needs of his market.

Listen and Learn

When you shape discussions with the SPIN mindset, people will tell you about their needs. You will learn whether your product meets them. If it does, great. If not, then you can adjust the product or find a different market. Had Simon asked the potential buyer directly about her needs, she might have given him a different answer than what he found out. Most people are unclear about what they want, so asking them directly rarely gives you the correct answers. It's better to read between the lines and find out for yourself. Then test whether your findings are correct.

Once you have framed the discussion around the value that your product can bring to clients, then all you need to do is show your ability to deliver that value. If they trust that you are competent, they will want to make a deal. The last step is simply getting the commitment to move forward from the other party. That's the whole secret of making a sale.

Validating the growth hypothesis is similar to making a sale. Unless you have clearly established the benefits of the product, trying to show your competency will fall on deaf ears. Unless people see you as competent, they will never buy. This is the difference between validating the hypothesis and not doing so. There is nothing more annoying than a salesman who drones on about their product or company, while the client is oblivious. Getting commitment is impossible if the other party has no need for the benefit of your product. If that's the case, why should they make a deal with you? But it is perfectly possible that you can help a client to discover his need to address a lingering problem. This is where SPIN comes in to guide you. Practice to break your communications into several steps. It gives you a proper framework to validate your growth hypotheses and sell your products or services.

Make it a habit to think in terms of benefits in your startup. When engaging in discussion with others, begin by asking questions about their situations, their problems, and the implications of these problems, and then think of how your technology could help. This is an effective strategy to frame the dialogue around benefits, away from academic facts and technology features.

When you leave the building and engage with others while testing your MVPs, you will find that you can gain much insight from listening and watching. If you guide the discussion toward needs and benefits, as shown in the interview and outlined in Figure 5-1, people will voluntarily tell you the best reasons why your product is valuable. It is then just a matter of keeping the dialogue going and taking notes. Practice asking questions rather than beaming down information. Practice listening and collecting feedback about your business model, financial model, product, or any other ideas.

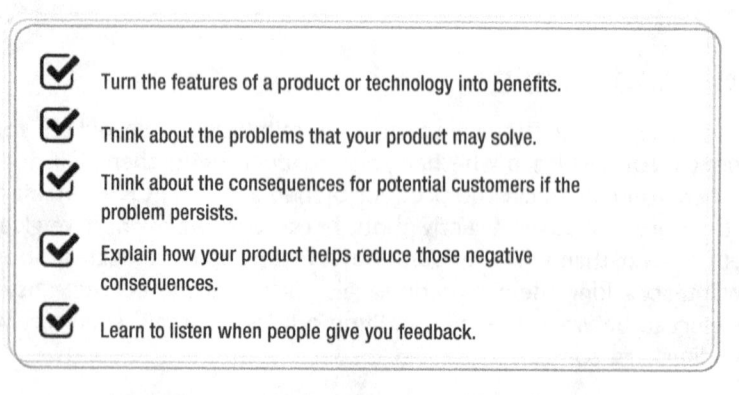

- ☑ Turn the features of a product or technology into benefits.
- ☑ Think about the problems that your product may solve.
- ☑ Think about the consequences for potential customers if the problem persists.
- ☑ Explain how your product helps reduce those negative consequences.
- ☑ Learn to listen when people give you feedback.

Figure 5-1. Checklist for benefits vs. features

CHAPTER 6

Simple Strategies to Get Unstuck

Jumping off the cliff into the unknown murky waters of entrepreneurship can be frightening. You have exposed yourself by proposing a bold idea and offered yourself up to criticism from those who follow a more conventional path. Because you have no successful entrepreneurs in your circle of friends who could guide you, it is your responsibility to master each challenge on your own. What do you do when your product is too expensive for the market, but you already stripped it down to the bare minimum? How should you react when a joint-venture partner calls with an offer that is too good to refuse but will take your company on a new, unfamiliar path?

Because it is impossible to have a detailed manual for every challenge, it is better for entrepreneurs to learn a few strategies that help them tackle a wide array of situations. With those in your toolkit, you will be ready to master situations on your own. You should always be able to come up with several solutions to a challenge by yourself. When you rely on outside counsel to solve problems for you too often, you need to step up your game. It's better to ask others what they think about your own ideas and hear their feedback than expecting them to do the work for you.

This chapter presents a few simple strategies that can help startups get an extra boost when they are stuck. These approaches are split into two main categories: those that help you take action and those that help you think.

They build on each other. You may already be familiar with some of them; others may sound new. As always, see which ones you find useful, not only to get unstuck, but to achieve better results in your startup in general.

Strategies to Take Action

Another analysis, another SWOT, another research paper, another workshop, or another brainstorming session will rarely help you get your startup off the ground. Usually, what is lacking is taking action. Have you tested your prototype in the market yet? Do you believe you need funding before you do so? And how will you get funding—by writing a clever grant proposal? The current practice of entrepreneurship at universities centers on analysis: thinking about fictitious products and how the market may or may not respond to them. The most important step of carrying out ambitious visions is missing in the curriculum. As a result, most students and researchers experience entrepreneurship in a bubble. There is no shortage of innovation policy that mandates the government should do this and that, and that universities should hold workshops and programs to promote more startup activity. In such a cocoon, entrepreneurs feel little pressure to make things happen for themselves. University entrepreneurship is in many ways still a theoretical exercise and much less a practical one. This is a pity, because it makes it OK for startups to spend time writing proposals and brainstorming instead of leaving the building and collecting accurate market intelligence about their assumptions.

As long as this continues, university startups will not be in the game. And not being in the game is worse than not being good enough. When I propose to software startup teams that they create a mockup frontend for their nonexistent software as the first order of business, they often discount this as "BS." They think they first need to complete the full backend programming over several months. Yet who knows if what they are coding will hit a nerve in the market? If it does, who knows if there will be enough clients who will buy the product? They can only find out by testing their hypotheses. If the product is software and there is no backend yet, you can create a faux user experience in a mockup program and fake the backend. This is the only way to get timely feedback on ideas.

As expected, such suggestions raise eyebrows at university startups. They go against everything a self-respecting scientist stands for. Scientific research by nature goes deep into an issue, and releasing half-baked ideas can have dire consequences. When results of academic research stand ready to be published, panels of experts review them and either approve or reject them. If a publication is turned down, then it is back to the drawing board. More research is carried out, and the paper is resubmitted. In startup land, it is quite the opposite. You had an idea this morning in the shower. By lunch, you have mocked up a minimum viable product (MVP) that you test with real potential clients in the afternoon. Come suppertime, you know whether your idea has legs. MVPs are shallow, buggy, unfinished, and have very little to do with your final product. But if the market gives signals that it would like to see more and is ready to pay for it, then you can tinker with the product and test it again until it reaches the stage where you believe it can launch.

Imagine an iceberg with a small visible tip above the waterline and a huge invisible part in the water (see Figure 6-1). The researcher first builds the huge invisible part. This symbolizes the research and data collected over many years, sometimes decades. If researchers decide to launch a startup, they build the small visible part on top of the large block of ice at the very end of the process. This small visible part represents the product that sells in the market. Startup entrepreneurs approach the issue from the other side. First they create the visible part and make it look as if there is a huge invisible part in the water. Only when the market flocks to the imaginary iceberg does the entrepreneur build out the entire block of ice under the water.

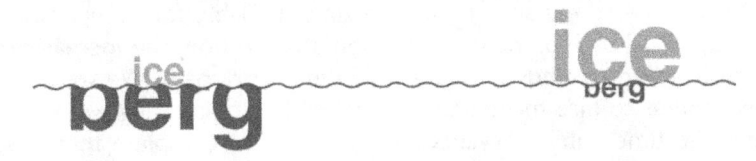

Figure 6-1. Difference in business approach between researchers (left) and entrepreneurs (right)

Scientists think that their product is the logical extension of all the research they have undertaken so far. This would be the ideal case, but they may have to adjust their expectations about what the market wants. They will have to tweak their product or come up with a different one. When the market speaks, all meticulous planning goes out the window. It is only through taking action that this process begins. How can entrepreneurs force themselves to take more action? Following are some strategies that have worked well for my startups.

One Action per Day

Avoid getting caught up in analysis paralysis. Most likely, you do not need more information, you need more action. Make it a point to take one action each day that moves your startup forward. Is it picking up the phone and setting up a lunch meeting with that potential industry partner you recently met at a networking event? Or is it finishing the one missing part of the MVP to test with a group of prospects? Draw up a list of such actions, and then spread them over the week. Pick one per day, and by the end of the week you will have completed seven. Instead of actions, you can also write down goals; this is entirely up to you.

Forcing yourself to take one action each day helps to take your mind off analysis and shift it into action. Avoid overloading yourself with tasks on one day. Spread them evenly over a longer period of time. When you have completed your daily tasks, resist the temptation to add more tasks to your list for the day. Instead, reward yourself for following through. Over time, you will form a habit of continually moving your projects forward in frequent small steps. This is much more helpful than only focusing on giant leaps, which are notoriously difficult to complete.

The Deadline Is Your Friend

Set deadlines for specific tasks, and publicly announce them. Set up interviews for your MVP tests before you have finished your MVPs. Promise to deliver reports by the end of the week that do not exist yet. Such commitments force you toward action. More often than not, you will finish your deliverables in a short time under such pressure. *Parkinson's Law* puts this empirical finding in words: "Work expands to fill the time available for completion" (see Figure 6-2).[1] Author Northcote Parkinson studied how the increasing number of civil servants stands in relation to their workload. We would expect the government to hire more staff to deal with its increasing workload. This increases the time public servants have available to complete their tasks, so they should get more done in a given amount of time. But the opposite is the case: when they have more staff and therefore more time available, it takes government employees far longer to complete their work.[2]

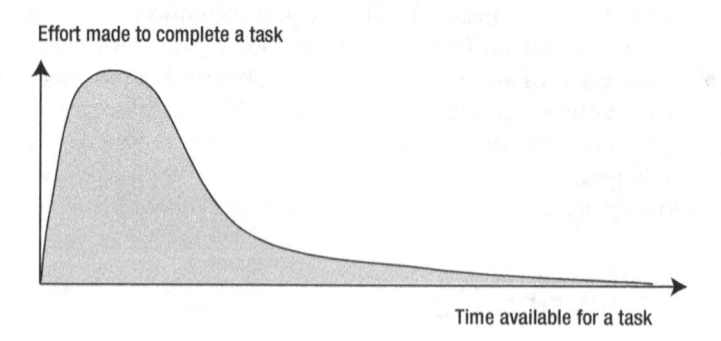

Figure 6-2. Parkinson's Law

---

[1] C. Northcote Parkinson, *Parkinson's Law, and Other Studies in Administration* (Boston: Houghton Mifflin, 1957).
[2] Ibid.

I often work with timers and alarm clocks. A specific task—for example, writing a report about the meetings that took place during the month—gets 90 minutes. I cannot go over time, but I also cannot do anything else during these 90 minutes. Author Roy Baumeister calls this the *Nothing Alternative*.[3] The strategy is powerful to focus your attention on one thing and one thing only. Looking at the timer counting down is a compelling reminder to complete the task instead of letting it drag on. Try it the next time you are writing a report. The traditional way, this can take several days. With the Nothing Alternative, you will surprise yourself when you complete the report in a few hours, or perhaps even in 45 minutes.

Once I asked a contractor when I could expect the finished product from him. "It is finished when it is finished," he replied. Obviously, this guy had no clue how to speed up his work. Parkinson's Law allowed the task to mushroom because he had set no deadline. This was greatly to his disadvantage because he was paid a fixed fee for his work, regardless of whether he completed it today or in a month. If you are a startup entrepreneur, this approach is not for you. Set clear deadlines, make them short, make them public, and stick to them.

Mastermind Groups

Sitting in your office or lab, surrounded by sceptics of free markets or those who have firmly subscribed to the security of 9-5 employment, will hardly stimulate you to make moves as an entrepreneur. Frequent contact with other entrepreneurs who are in the same boat as you can encourage you to get off your chair. Get their advice and feedback about how they tackle certain issues. See the way they are doing things, and copy it. Get together and discuss the specific actions you have taken this week and where they led your team. Discuss your successes and mishaps, and learn how others address the same challenges.

Going at it alone is much more difficult than approaching entrepreneurship in a group of like-minded individuals. They can inspire a healthy competition where they will call you out if you keep deliberating instead of testing in the market. Ensure that you have action-oriented people around you. A good network can have a major impact, not only on shifting your focus toward taking action, but in all stages of entrepreneurship.

Author Napoleon Hill created Mastermind Groups over 75 years ago.[4] How do masterminds work? A group of like-minded people meet regularly to talk about specific challenges. They provide advice, share connections, and

---

[3] Roy F. Baumeister and John Tierny, *Willpower: Rediscovering the Greatest Human Strength* (New York: Penguin, 2011).
[4] Napoleon Hill, *Think and Grow Rich* (Meriden, CT: The Ralston Society, 1937).

collaborate when appropriate. This practice is comparable to peer-to-peer mentoring. Mastermind groups are often invite-only. If no group exists in your environment, simply set up your own. Invite other startup entrepreneurs from your university to your new mastermind. Connect with entrepreneurs on the Internet or LinkedIn. Contact industry interest groups and ask them to introduce established businesspeople to you. It is essential that all members of the group are on the same wavelength. Do not include people who have only theoretical knowledge or no experience. Treat your mastermind group as an exclusive club. Not only will you add powerful contacts to your network, but the opportunities to learn firsthand from others and get in the habit of thinking big are worth the effort.

Strategies to Think

Despite what you just learned about taking action, there are of course many occasions that require you to plan and analyze the facts before jumping in. I have said that writing a business plan is unnecessary when you are running your startup lean. But this does not imply that you should never write down a word about how you plan for your business to unfold. The analysis part is important, but it should never overtake and dominate the action part. If you remember that, then the following strategies will help you tackle certain challenges in your startup from a fresh angle.

Mind Storming: The Twenty Idea Method

Author Earl Nightingale originally put forward the *Twenty Idea Method*.[5] In a somewhat spiritual context, he noted that when a person engages in "mind storming," the person's consciousness expands and taps into ideas that were previously out of reach. In essence, the Twenty Idea Method comes down to putting together a list of possible solutions to a challenge you are struggling with. However, instead of just writing down 3 or 4 ideas, you force yourself to find 20 ideas in a short amount of time. The final few are often those that yield surprising insight. Repeating this practice each day for a week will help you come up with astounding solutions to problems that are unavailable if you simply try to deal with them rationally. I find this method excellent for coming up with unconventional ideas. If your entire team brainstorms together, you will have an efficient process to look at problems in a new light. How does it work? Let's look at a basic example.

---

[5] Earl Nightingale, *Lead the Field* (Wheeling, IL: Simon & Schuster Audio/Nightingale-Conant, 1986).

Let's say you are struggling with your business model. You have a patent that you could let the technology licensing office (TLO) deal with on your behalf, but you want to start your own company with your intellectual property. As a business, should you sell a service, a product, or a license to manufacture the product? What are possible applications of the IP? This is a classic case for mind storming. Take out a blank piece of paper. Use pen and paper instead of a laptop, tablet, or phone—the process of writing down the 20 solutions has to be fast, so writing by hand is best. Something magical happens if you write with a pen on paper. Fiddling with a keyboard will only interfere. At the top of the piece of paper, write down the problem. In your case, this is: "What is a good business model for company X?" On the left side of the page, write the numbers 1 to 20. If there is not enough space, halve the page with a vertical line and split the numbers into two columns of 10. All the ideas should be on one page so you can always see them during the mind-storming process.

The trick is to rush yourself through this exercise. Take no more than 5 minutes to complete all 20 solutions. Set up a timer for this purpose. You begin with solution 1, which will be the most obvious one that comes to mind first. Perhaps you discussed this idea repeatedly with your co-founders, so it is nothing new. Regardless, write it down. Then advance to number 2. Same here. Number 3. And so on. Around number 10, the obvious ideas will run out. This is where the magic begins to happen. Whatever comes to mind from here on, write it down quickly. Some ideas may seem silly, but this is OK. Keep going until you have come up with 20 ideas. Then review them, and choose the three that you like best. They may be hybrid ideas, cobbled together from several different ideas. Elaborate further on those three, and find out in more detail whether they are feasible and how they apply to your startup situation.

Mind storming can be on your daily agenda for a while. You will be surprised by the strange ideas you and your team can produce. It can help to involve an outsider without domain knowledge when mind storming. Outsiders often see a problem from a completely different angle and may bring an unexpected viewpoint to your process.

Think on Paper

Never begin the day until you have finished it on paper, wrote business philosopher Jim Rohn. In a seminar on business strategy in the 21st century, he detailed his suggested practice of making several lists to guide you through the day, the week, the month, and the entire year.[6] After all, a successful week consists of successful days, a successful month of successful weeks, and a successful year of successful months. If you have a written outline of what you

---

[6]Jim Rohn, *The Weekend Seminar* (Lake Dallas, TX: Jim Rohn International, 1999).

wish to achieve each day, you will have a higher chance of staying on course. There is far less danger of losing focus when unexpected distractions come up. You do not have to go to extremes and obey your day planner without any autonomous thinking or spontaneity. However, writing your thoughts and tasks on to-do lists is a good idea.

In addition to doing daily planning, make other short lists for everything that is important. Writing it down clears your mind and frees up brain power for other tasks. If you call someone about business, make a brief outline of what you would like to talk about and what the next steps are. If you go to a meeting, make a list of the items you want solved and how they will be addressed with the next steps. You can discard these lists immediately after you have completed them. They simply serve the purpose of organizing and structuring your ideas before you discuss them with other people.

I often make a list in the evening on which I write down things to do the next day. I also have a weekly list with three larger goals or milestones for the week. If there are still items on the daily to-do list in the evening, I make a concerted effort to complete them or move them to the next day. This is OK as long as it still allows reaching the three weekly milestones. Another list I have is the *not*-to-do list.[7] These are actions to avoid, mostly time wasters and distractions. This list is a great reminder to put up next to your computer. Experiment with what works well for you. There is no one-size-fits-all recipe for thinking on paper.

Mind Maps

You have probably heard of mind maps, popularized by author Tony Buzan.[8] You may already be an avid mind mapper, or you may hardly use them at all. I find them helpful at times to summarize processes or books and bring them into a larger context. For brainstorming, however, I rarely use mind maps. For that purpose, I prefer the linear format of the Twenty Idea Method. Mind maps work better for me as a context tool. Figure 6-3 shows a mind map of the book *The Innovator's DNA*.[9]

---

[7] Dan S. Kennedy, *No B.S. Time Management for Entrepreneurs* (Irvine, CA: Entrepreneur Press, 2004).
[8] Tony Buzan, *The Mind Map Book* (New York: The Penguin Group, 1993).
[9] Jeff Dyer, Hal Gregersen, and Clayton M. Christensen, *The Innovator's DNA: Mastering the Five Skills of Disruptive Innovators* (Boston: Harvard Business Press, 2011).

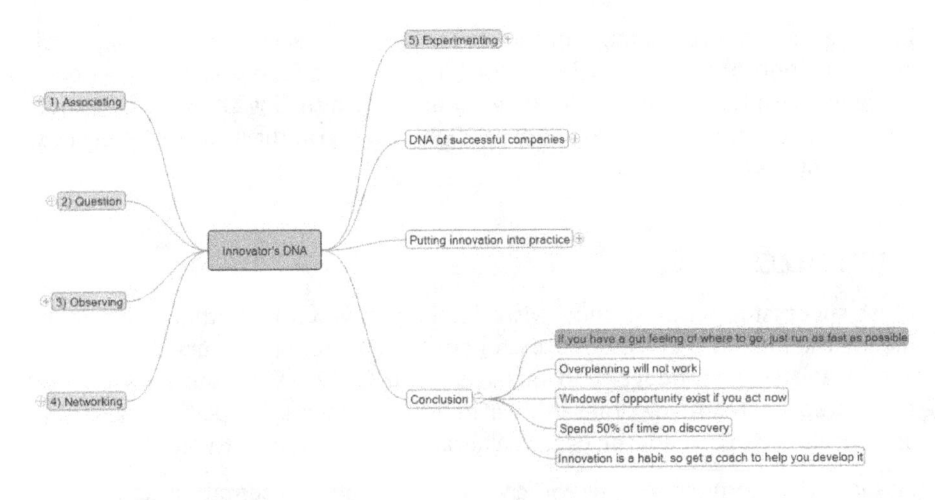

Figure 6-3. Mind map of the book The Innovator's DNA

Everybody has their own mind-mapping technique. I organize mind maps of books by chapters. Each of the chapters contains other nodes that I can expand with a click. Such a summary can be intuitive and straightforward for presenting the book's highlights to others.

Mind mapping is not for everyone, though. Some people find it cumbersome and prefer to write summaries with bullet points. I use both, depending on my mood. Try it to see whether it works for you. Plenty of free software is available that allows you to experiment with mind mapping and determine its usefulness for you. You can of course also use old-fashioned paper, but I prefer software for mind mapping because it permits painless archiving and retrieval even years later. The digital format also makes it easy to share mind maps with others.

Just Ten More Minutes

This is not a strategy by itself; it is more an add-on to give you a quick boost. When you are exhausted and have about had it with a task or problem, make it a point to spend just ten more minutes on it before you wrap up. Set a timer or alarm, and then give it all you've got. This will focus your thinking and assure you that after ten minutes, you can let it go.

It is surprising what this approach can do for you. There are projects where close to 80% of my good ideas happened in these last ten minutes. Try it, and see if it works for you.

Limiting the time remaining can also motivate your team. For example, if you are at the end of a two-hour brainstorming session that has failed to produce any good results, instead of finishing up and rescheduling the entire session, just give it ten more minutes. If you buckle down, you may think of your best ideas right then and there.

Visualize

Most successful people I know visualize in one way or another. This simply means thinking in pictures. Successful golfers and tennis players do it. So do actors and singers, hedge-fund managers and CEOs. They see an action or event step by step many times in their mind and imagine the perfect execution and result. If Roger Federer uses visualization, why shouldn't you?

Assume that tomorrow you will give an important presentation about your research startup to a government delegation. As the team lead, you will have the honor of introducing the project in a five-minute speech that explains how your technology is useful in infrastructure planning. For a week, you have chiseled your speech, memorized it, practiced it in front of the mirror, and annoyed your friends and family with its details. Now, on the eve of the critical day, you lie awake in bed and fret about all that could possibly go wrong. Should you have prepared differently? Should you rewrite the entire speech again? It will hardly do anything for you to say the speech out loud from memory one more time. There is also nobody left to give you further feedback on it. It is your responsibility now to make it work.

In a situation like this, visualization can instill great confidence and calm. Make sure nobody disturbs you for a while. Close your eyes, and imagine walking up to the podium. You tap the microphone, welcome the audience, and give a speech that would have made John F. Kennedy envious. There is a standing ovation at the end, and the government delegation commissions a large project from your startup on the spot. You go celebrate with a magnum bottle of champagne, and then ... The rest is for you to imagine. You see how this works: imagine the perfect outcome for about five minutes with great intensity. If you are nervous right before the speech, briefly visualizing everything going perfectly can also help you calm down. It may feel silly the first few times, but visualization has helped countless successful people master sticky situations with bravado.

Many more productivity and time-management techniques exist in the literature. The ones outlined in this chapter are among those that I use daily. Of course, I am not proposing that you practice them compulsively in every situation. But when you are stuck, they may help get you and your team moving forward again.

CHAPTER 7

Troubleshooting

Inevitably, there will be times when everything seems to go wrong in your startup. It is 2 AM, your third MVP still pleases hardly anyone, and you ran out of ideas a long time ago. Troubles are brewing on your team: they doubt your abilities as the CEO and think they should get real jobs and forget about this crazy entrepreneurship idea. The university is breathing down your neck to vacate its premises, and your personal bankroll is reduced to triple digits. The joint venture you aimed for has fallen through, while a competitor from another university has gotten exactly the terms you wanted with the company you targeted.

There are low points on every entrepreneur's journey—you cannot escape them. What matters most is the way you deal with them. Bumps in the road can always occur, but no problem is too large to straighten out.

Wherever there is trouble, growth is just around the corner. "Calm you shall keep and carry on you must," as Grand Master Yoda reminds us. The problems I just mentioned are not all that grave. Nobody has been seriously wounded by your product. Everyone is still alive. Stressed and grumpy, but alive.

Whenever there are conflicts, you should write them down on paper, so you get them out of your head. Never to go to bed before writing down your problems. Once they are on paper, you can organize them by importance and cross out the ones that are less significant. Solutions may arise as soon as you begin writing.

At your wit's end with the MVP? Look at your results. Make it a priority for the entire team to do nothing else until you have found a solid, testable case. Hold brainstorming sessions. Ask others for advice—even your competitors. Going for a walk or playing sports can help take your mind off an issue. An extended bike ride can generate many ideas. Give yourself a few hours to let your subconscious do the job for you.

The team lost faith in you? Get them together in a meeting and discuss the matter. What could you do better? What could they do better? Do they want to exit the startup? Perhaps you can find a compromise where everybody stays on board until a certain date and decides then. Until that date, everybody does their best to make the company work. Compromises are much better than a potential calamity that could break loose any second. It is simply a matter of addressing the issue and dealing with it like adults. In a quiet moment, ask yourself: What is the worst case that could happen in this situation? Imagine what that would mean for you, and begin living with the idea that it may become reality. Once you accept the worst possible outcome, you will no longer unreasonably defend a losing position. You will think much more clearly when attacking the problem head on.

What if the university keeps asking when you will get your own office? Make a deal with the university, and promise to deliver X until a specified date rolls around. Perhaps you can rally other stakeholders in the university who will let you use another, smaller office on a more permanent basis.

Money is running low? Bootstrap. Make Top Ramen the cornerstone of your diet. One way to have more money is to spend less. Otherwise, find a part-time job to restock your war chest.

Joint venture plans fell apart? Look for other candidates. When something fails, it may turn out to be a blessing down the road. Keep an open mind, and actively find new opportunities.

As an entrepreneur, you are a maverick who cannot please everybody. It may sound harsh, but you need to surround yourself with people who are on the same wavelength. You need a good, encouraging network and other entrepreneurs around you to keep you going. When a maverick made his or her mark, everyone is proud. Unless you ruffle a few feathers, it will be hard to find a way out of the mainstream and achieve success on your own terms.

Prioritize

When issues arise in your startup, avoid letting them linger. Step forward and address them. Open communication is key here, but refuse to hold yourself up with minor issues. Address the most important problems first, and some of the smaller ones may turn out to be less urgent. With "build, measure, learn," you have a powerful toolkit that teaches constant incremental improvement. Use this for your MVP and also for your general skills as a startup entrepreneur. If an idea fails to work, try something else. Keep moving constantly.

In general, thinking on paper is a great ally for problem-solving. You may make an old-fashioned list or draw a mind map to address certain issues. When you see problems laid out in front of you on paper, they become manageable. You can bring them into context with each other. You may brainstorm how to address them or what will happen if you let them linger. Get into the habit of carrying pen and paper around with you. This is valuable not only for problem-solving, but for all other facets of entrepreneurship as well.

An Outsider's View

Sometimes it can be useful to enlist outside help. If your startup is only two weeks old and you already find yourself at the brink of disaster, then there may be matters that need more thorough investigation. A startup coach may help you solve them. When all else fails, you have the option of hiring a so-called *interim CEO* to see the startup through a rough patch. This may be worth considering and in the long-term interest of the university's startup track, especially when the stakes are high and a breakthrough or joint venture is just around the corner. Many well-known businesses were at some point on the brink of bankruptcy. An executive change often helped declutter their business model and bring them back onto the path to profitability. When things get hairy, that is where entrepreneurial experience comes in. You cannot learn this by reading a book—only from living entrepreneurship firsthand for years, through its ups and downs.

Throughout this book, you have repeatedly read my recommendation to tap into the experience of an established entrepreneur to assist university startup teams. This can be an alumnus of the university who has achieved great business success. Instead of hiring an alum to make a keynote speech, the university could ask him or her to work with their startups as an advisor. This can also be a person in a related field whom the team has identified as someone they would like to have on their board to offer ideas and criticism. The university cannot reasonably expect a startup team made up of students or researchers to learn the ropes of entrepreneurship overnight. Of course, they should know some management basics when they run their own company, but navigating real problems successfully is a rare skill.

Access to an outsider's opinion for a few hours, focused on a specific challenge that a startup is struggling with, can make all the difference. I have seen this firsthand several times. The startup team was at their wit's end and ready to give up, but a few tweaks in their product and business model brought them back to their intended trajectory. The input that an established entrepreneur may give can seem trite in retrospect; it is often not sweeping changes but sticking to the basics that provides a startup with an extra boost. Subtracting something is frequently more powerful than adding more to the mix. When

Chapter 7 | Troubleshooting

the journey gets rough, the founding team is often too close to the problem to see what they should do. Together with an outsider, they can shed light on a challenge from a new angle and solve it in an unexpected way.

Whenever you experience headwinds with your startup, use the checklist in Figure 7-1 to help you navigate.

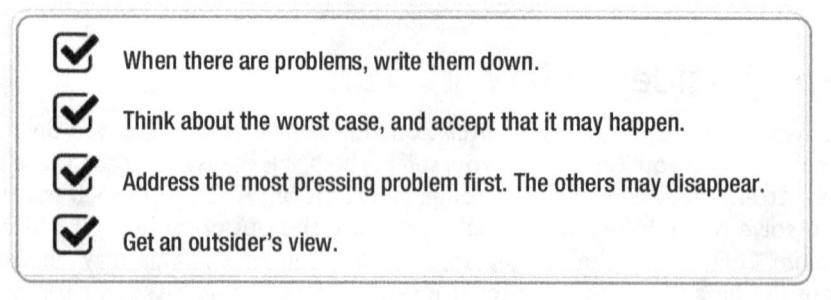

- ☑ When there are problems, write them down.
- ☑ Think about the worst case, and accept that it may happen.
- ☑ Address the most pressing problem first. The others may disappear.
- ☑ Get an outsider's view.

Figure 7-1. Checklist for troubleshooting

CHAPTER 8

The Financial Model

Although researchers are generally comfortable talking about their technology and its features at length, they are often much less well-versed in the business and financial aspects of their undertaking. Entrepreneurs need to be in a position to answer a few key financial questions about their venture. What are we producing that has a value in the market? Will the market pay us enough to be profitable? How exactly are we transferring money from customers into our bank account? The business-model canvas answers the first question, but the other ones require a financial model made with spreadsheet software.

When you sit across the table from venture capitalists, they will grill you about your financial model. You should know the size of your potential market, your expected market share, how long you believe it will take you to sell a product in this market, and how you plan to turn your market share into profit for your company. If you cannot answer a few basic financial questions, no one will take you seriously as a startup entrepreneur.

That being said, there is one thing investors know with certainty about your financial model: the model will be wrong. Investors are well aware of that, so they want to see the assumptions that underlie your forecast, much more than the forecast itself. Putting together your financial model will give you an impression of the time it will take for your startup to achieve some level of profitability. You will also have worked out your own overhead and capital needs, often called the *burn rate*. All this is what investors look at, not the hockey-stick revenue-growth chart that all other startups have in their models as well. *How* you put together your financial model is more informative than the individual numbers.

Chapter 8 | The Financial Model

Financial models and projections can be simple, but there are some pitfalls to avoid. I once made the mistake of proudly announcing that "If we sell widget X to 1% of the people in China for $1 each year, we will make $10 million in revenue." The venture capitalist had of course heard this lame pitch many times before, and responded, "You expect just 1% market share? What kind of small-minded company is this? I only invest in companies with 80% market share." With that, the discussion was over. A $10 million market seemed big for me at the time, but less so for anyone who has been in the business longer. A good market starts at about $100 million per year in sales revenue.

Basics of Financial Business Modeling

If you are already familiar with accounting and building financial models for startups, feel free to skip this chapter. If not, then here is a quick primer on the most important terms in a financial model. This is my personal approach, and I realize there are many different opinions about how to do it right. The procedure I explain in this chapter is one that I find workable without knowing much about corporate finance. It helps jumpstart the discussion about a startup's finances without much spreadsheet programming. If you prefer another modeling technique, that's fine. As long as you can explain what you are doing and why you are doing it, all roads lead to Rome.

The important terms in your financial model are revenue, cost, profit, and profit margin. Their formulas are as follows:

$$\text{Revenue} = \text{number of units sold} \times \text{price charged per unit}$$

$$\text{Cost} = \text{fixed cost} + \text{variable cost}$$

$$= \text{fixed cost} + (\text{number of units sold} \times \text{cost per unit})$$

$$\text{Profit} = \text{revenue} - \text{cost}$$

$$\text{Profit margin} = \frac{\text{profit}}{\text{revenue}}$$

Let's look at each of these in a little more detail:

- *Revenue* means the total proceeds from sales. It is the money brought into the company by its business activities. You calculate this amount by multiplying the number of units sold by the price per unit. The term *revenue* is sometimes used interchangeably with *sales*, and the two mean the same thing. Many people confuse the *revenue* with *profit*. Even though your company may have $100 million in revenue per year, its profit may still be zero or negative.

- *Profit* is the money left in your account after you pay all costs incurred by the company. When calculating profit in your spreadsheet, also make a clear distinction between *pre-tax profit* and *after-tax profit*. Because taxes are a percentage of profit, you simply multiply the corporate tax rate by the pre-tax profit. Startup entrepreneurs often forget to make this distinction, but it can make a big difference, especially if your tax rate is high.

- The percentage of revenue that you keep as profit is called the *profit margin*. This number shows how profitable your company is. Because it is a ratio, you can use it to compare the profitability of different companies.

- *Costs* consist of fixed costs and variable costs. *Fixed costs* are the overhead of the company that stays the same regardless of the number of units sold. Rent paid for offices, support services, all salaries, and so on, are fixed costs. *Variable costs* change with the number of units sold. For example, if you are producing a car, then these include the metal, plastics, engine, tires, and so on. If you pay licensing fees for patents per car sold, then these fees are also part of the variable costs.

These are the most important terms. There are of course many more formulas in financial accounting, but these should be enough for a simple financial model for a startup. If you think accounting is exciting, then feel free to pick up any book on the subject to learn more.

It often takes entrepreneurs by surprise to hear that the most vital parts of their model are the *costs* and the *assumptions* that underlie the revenue projection. Revenue and profit projections in themselves are less important, because you cannot predict them accurately. Regardless, you should set up your business model so that your startup can achieve high revenues. If a company has high revenue, it can improve its profit by reducing fixed and variable costs, courtesy of economies of scale. Building 1 item results in a higher cost per item compared to producing 100 items. A bigger factory can often turn out a product at a lower cost than a small one.

When you begin building the financial model, first fill in the parts that you know already. These may be the fixed cost and variable cost per unit sold. You may have a validated assumption about the price charged per unit. With this, you already have half the model. The tricky part is the speculation about how many units you can sell each year. I discuss some guidelines for this later in this chapter.

How Investing in Startups Works

When investors give you money, they obviously expect something in return. Where does this return come from? Not from revenue, but from the profit your company makes in the future. With their money, investors buy a certain number of shares in your company. This number of shares, as a percentage of the total shares in the company, controls the percentage of profit each investor is entitled to receive.

Let's say you can make the case that your company will turn a profit of $10 million in year 3, $11 million in year 4, and $12 million in year 5, as shown in Table 8-1. Before year 3, profit was negative. This projection enables you to make a ballpark assumption about the value of your company today. There are many ways to arrive at such a value, and to explain them all here would be outside the scope of this book. A straightforward procedure to arrive at a speculative number for the value of your company is to discount the projected future cash flows by their probability and sum them up, as follows:

Company value = 1×(-$100,000)+1×(-$200,000)

+ 0.5×$10,000,000+0.4×$11,000,000+0.3×$12,000,000

= $12,700,000

Table 8-1. Projected Future Cash Flows

	Revenue ($)	Cost ($)	Profit ($)	Probability
Year 1	0	100,000	-100,000	100%
Year 2	0	200,000	-200,000	100%
Year 3	11,000,000	1,000,000	10,000,000	50%
Year 4	13,000,000	2,000,000	11,000,000	40%
Year 5	15,000,000	3,000,000	12,000,000	30%

This is an example to illustrate how the numbers in your financial model work in context. Of course, it is an extreme simplification, and specialists in finance will cringe when they see me advocate this technique. Venture capitalists will look at your underlying assumptions and come up with a valuation of their own. As a quick hack, the probability method is workable without going back to school and learning about corporate finance. Most important, this number will put into perspective investment offers you may be receiving.

Let's say you have arrived at the projections just outlined. The big jump in revenue in year 3 results from talks you had with a potential joint venture partner. He wrote you a letter of intent saying that if you can develop your technology to a certain point, he will be willing to form a joint venture with you. Because this partner is a leading multinational, you can expect better distribution channels, instant economies of scale, and larger projects. Your own costs will increase, but because your profit margin is high, you can reasonably expect high profits. Now a venture capitalist visits your startup and offers you $250,000 for 10% of the company. Does this sound like a good deal? Let's see: if 10% of your company cost $250,000, then 100% are worth $2,500,000. The numbers you calculated paint a different picture: your company value at the current time is $12,700,000, so 10% equals $1,270,000. Based on your own numbers, you should expect a much better offer from the venture capitalist. According to your calculation, she should get roughly 2% equity in your company, not 10%, for her $250,000 investment.

With the assumptions gained in putting together your financial model, you can begin a negotiation without flying blind. The number you calculate as the present value for your company is either too high or too low. You need to check and update it often and get feedback from others about it. But now you see how your startup's numbers work. They are not rocket science, but they also are not immediately obvious. An entrepreneur who has no clue about the value of his company will be taken advantage of by shrewd investors. Most of all, they will doubt he is genuine in his efforts if he comes across as financially illiterate. As soon as you can lead a qualified discussion about your financial model, investors will take you more seriously.

It is unnecessary to hire an MBA or a financial advisor to program the financial model for you. Much more important is that you understand the drivers and underlying assumptions of the model and what they mean for your business. You should be able to modify the model yourself.

A joint venture partner will often value your company differently than a venture capitalist—for example, in terms of costs the partner can save by buying your R&D, or in terms of the IP advantage gained over a competitor. Nevertheless, it is useful to have your own model at hand. Most likely you will need it only when you speak with investors or potential partners.

Identify Your Market

Previously I skipped the discussion of how to arrive at the number of units sold in your startup. Before I address this, you first need to understand the different kinds of markets. Author Steve Blank summarizes them in the following manner:[1]

- *Existing market:* A new entrant is stealing a slice of a market. Users abandon competitor products when they start using yours. Instead of increasing the pie, you just take a slice.

---

[1] Steven G. Blank, *The Four Steps to the Epiphany: Successful Strategies for Products That Win* (K&S Ranch, 2007).

- *Re-segmented market:* You increase the pie by selling to customers who otherwise would not buy at all—for example, by introducing a less-expensive product that adds price-conscious customers to the market.

- *New market:* Your technology is new, and by definition you own 100% of the market. You must explain to the market what the product is and how to use it. Customers will still use other products when they start using yours.

The most important thing to show in your financial model is what Steve Blank calls *Product/Market Fit*.[2] Netscape founder Marc Andreessen describes this as "being in a good market with a product that can satisfy that market."[3] Most companies are re-segmenting markets in one way or another. A rule of thumb for achieving Product/Market Fit is that at least 40% of users should say they would be "very disappointed" without your product.[4]

What does this mean for your financial model? Most important, you need to demonstrate that you can sell to at least 40% of the market. If yours is an existing market, then you can find out its size relatively easily courtesy of Google. Perhaps there is even a market study available. Or an academic paper or trade journal in your library. Or a footnote in the quarterly report of the industry leader.

Re-segmented markets are more complicated to assess, because you have to make some assumptions about the size of the slice you are adding. Calculate several scenarios, starting from 10% up to 50%. In either case, your projected annual revenue should land somewhere around $100 million and upward. As I said before, investors know that this number is mostly fiction, but it should be achievable with your startup if everything goes well.

Let's forget about new markets for now, because they are rare and the most speculative to assess.

The number-one thing not to do is to conjure up hockey-stick growth, where in the first years you have no sales, and then, magically, in year 3 the business takes off like a rocket, doubling or tripling its income year after year. If you have real commitments, like the joint venture discussed in the example of company value, then your financial projections are much stronger, and you can explain the underlying assumptions for hockey-stick growth. But if you cannot, then the hockey stick will look silly. Future revenue projections are not all

---

[2] Steven G. Blank and Bob Dorf, *The Startup Owner's Manual: The Step-By-Step Guide for Building a Great Company* (K&S Ranch, 2012).
[3] Marc Andreessen, "Product/Market Fit," Stanford University, June 25, 2007, www.stanford.edu/class/ee204/ProductMarketFit.html.
[4] Brant Cooper and Patrick Vlaskovits, *The Entrepreneur's Guide to Customer Development: Cheat Sheet to The Four Steps to the Epiphany* (Newport Beach, CA: Cooper-Vlaskovits, 2010).

that important. What counts is a strong business model that harvests demand today and in the next few years from existing markets. At the end of the day, everything else is fiction. Unless you have a classic business model, such as a real-estate investment with a large sunk cost of several hundred million and rental revenue over the next 20 years, projections into the future make little sense. For a tech or hardware startup in the early stages, they are little more than wishful thinking. Just show the size of the market, the share you aim to achieve eventually, and how your pricing strategy fits into that equation.

When you know the market size and your market share, then you have to fit that around your pricing model for your product or service. Many eye openers along the way will show you either that you need to charge an enormous sum for your product or that your market is simply too small to allow you explosive growth. When that is the case, you can use this new insight in your future MVP testing. Look for other products and services, and other markets, and test those. Your costs may also be too high to let your startup achieve profitability, in which case you need to reduce them. The lean canvas and the financial model are like sparring partners that can help you do so.

The Story Matters More Than the Numbers

Every serious investor knows that financial projections for a startup are rarely going to come true, so you must prepare to answer questions about the underlying assumptions that led to your projections. Don't get me wrong: you still need the financial model; it is an essential tool to help you form useful assumptions about your market, your business model, and your strategy. But it is key to be clear about the story that explains how the financial model came about. How did you discover the market your product is serving? How did you come up with the market share your company is aiming to achieve? Can you make a credible case about exactly how your company will turn a profit? How did you arrive at the timeline? All this information is more helpful for investors than an upward-sloping revenue curve. They will form their own opinion of you as an entrepreneur and combine that with their assumptions about the product and the market. If they see that you are smart and have come up with a good idea to commercialize a certain technology with profit, they will be more likely to invest in you. The financial model will be the platform on which this discussion takes place.

Make sure the output of the model fits on one page, where you also explain all the underlying assumptions. With this and the lean canvas, you will have condensed your entire business proposition onto a few sheets of paper. When you meet with investors or potential partners, present your business with both the business-model canvas and the financial model. See what they gravitate toward and what they remark. Then incorporate those new findings into the next version of your documents.

Chapter 8 | The Financial Model

These are the basics you should be familiar with when building financial models. If you have heard enough about finance and economics, feel free to skip the rest of this chapter. Otherwise, read on to see how economic theory is not all that useful in startup entrepreneurship.

A Word about Economic Theory

As you already learned, becoming an expert in economics or corporate finance is unnecessary to create your financial model. More often than not, it may even be a disadvantage. It is good to know some basics of economics, because they are helpful for explaining things in hindsight. But when you are putting together your financial model, it is better to be blissfully ignorant. Let's find out why.

The discipline of modern economics is a strange conglomeration of sociology, psychology, and philosophy. On the basic level, it splits into two main sections: microeconomics and macroeconomics. The former concerns itself with the theory of individual firms and addresses supply and demand for products, price theory, market structures, and so on. Macroeconomics applies itself to the workings of all companies together in an economy as a whole, and the interrelationships with other economies. How the size of a company affects its production costs is a matter of microeconomics, whereas the amount of money in circulation and the effect on a country's GDP is part of macroeconomics. When talking about individual companies, we are operating in the domain of microeconomics. The most basic model in this discipline is the so-called supply-and-demand model, which you may be familiar with from Economics 101 (see Figure 8-1).

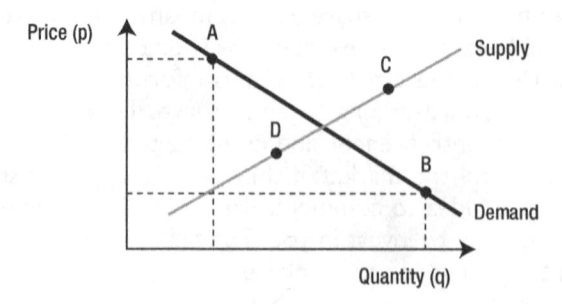

Figure 8-1. Classical supply and demand model

What does this model express? Look at the demand curve first. This shows how much of a product people buy in relationship to its price. When the price of a product is high, such as at point A, the quantity demanded is low. Fewer people are able to afford the high price, or people may be unwilling to pay more than a certain amount for a certain product. At point B, the price is low, and the quantity of products demanded is higher. This is assumed to be the case because people can buy more of the good with $100 when the price is low than when the price is high.

The supply curve works in a similar way. This curve shows the relationship of price and quantity supplied from the manufacturer's point of view. How much of a certain product does the company produce and make available in the market in relationship to the price it can charge? Assume the price is high, such as at point C. The supplier has an incentive to flood the market with product, because the company has the potential to make much more profit when it sells the product at a high price. But when the price is low, as at point D, the supplier is not interested in producing much, because overall profit is lower in a low-price environment. At the point where the supply curve and the demand curve intersect, the market is in equilibrium.

This is the story of the supply-and-demand model. Does it make sense to you? Most likely it does. But let's look at an example that flies in the face of this neat model and relegates it straight to the garbage bin.

In the last decade, there was a huge boom in real-estate prices. Many investors doubled their investment with real-estate speculation in the United States, China, and other parts of the world. When prices were low, real estate was not that attractive, because most people could not imagine that a sizable return would ever come to pass. But when things picked up and prices soared, more and more people became interested in real estate and began speculating. Demand increased as soon as prices increased. Is this what the supply-and-demand model would predict? No—quite the opposite. Figure 8-2 shows how the real-estate boom looks in the supply-and-demand model.

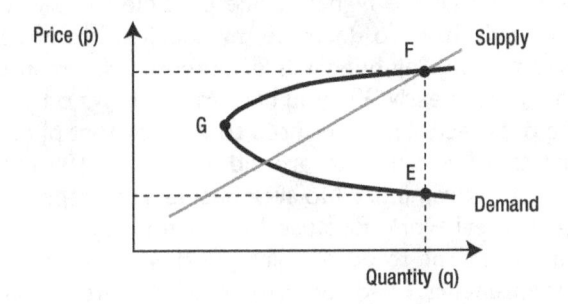

Figure 8-2. Supply-and-demand model in a real-estate boom

Chapter 8 | The Financial Model

There are now two possible prices for each quantity. One is in the low-price environment, where those with little money can purchase a house (E). When prices go up, fewer of those people can afford a house, and demand declines. Then comes an inflection point (G), where rising prices spur a real-estate boom and speculative buying. This designates the beginning of the high-price environment. Everybody who can piles into real estate, and demand increases. More and more speculators are attracted to the market. They buy second and third homes. Demand goes up, and prices go up in tandem (F). In such a market, do high prices lead to fewer or more units sold? It depends. There may be fewer units sold in a low-price environment, but more units sold in a high-price environment. You will not find this supply-and-demand model in an introductory economics book, but you may have witnessed the dynamics of a real-estate boom firsthand. Would you say the classical supply-and-demand model is useful to analyze such a boom, or other transactions in the real economy? In this light, probably not. It would lead you to the wrong assumptions and might cost you a lot of money. Uncertainty and complexity have no place is most economic models.

This goes to show that economists hardly have all the answers, even though they like to think they do. If you hire an MBA or economist to work out your financial model, the danger is that they will tell you with much authority how this *has* to be done. More often than not, their knowledge is firmly rooted in theory, which has proven to be precisely wrong more than once in history. Much better than basing your financial model on economic theory is to look at the real numbers and comparable firms already active in the market. Pair this information with your own assumptions about the future, and make your own scenarios.

When I started my first company, I had no idea about economic theory. It felt intuitively right to charge the highest price possible for my services. And it was clear that I would have to decrease my overhead to increase my profit. I knew that I had to cold-call hundreds of potential clients in order to get a foot in the door. In your early 20s, you have many things on your mind other than cold-calling prospects. How I wanted to destroy that phone at times. Yet it was clear that there was no way around it, and the 189 remaining names on the list were a stark reminder. No slick business strategy could have saved me from doing the real work. Because I knew nobody who would bankroll my startup, hiring someone to do the dirty work was out of the picture. Like many other entrepreneurs, I had to make do with limited means. Knowledge of economic theory would have been nothing more than a distraction. It was unnecessary at the time.

Years later, when I actually studied economics at the London School of Economics, many "aha!" moments occurred. It was satisfying to know the theory to explain in hindsight why some of my businesses had worked and others had not. But I still find economic theory and business school knowledge to be of little use for startup entrepreneurs. This is true not only for the simplest of all models, the supply-and-demand model we just looked at. Porter's *Five Forces* to formulate competitive strategy,[5] Christensen's *Innovator's Dilemma*,[6] and many other theoretical concepts are nice to know but by no means necessary for startup success. A business consultant for a multinational company may benefit from being familiar with some of these concepts, but startup entrepreneurs should focus on the tasks at hand with "build, measure, learn" and many other practical strategies explained in this book. If you are seriously interested in learning more about economics later down the road, then it may be worth looking into in more detail. But avoid distracting yourself in your first startup. Make all your brain power available for things that really matter.

Never Rely on Specialists

Some entrepreneurs are deeply averse to anything that has to do with finance or business modeling. They feel they should focus on the core of their technology and prefer that someone else handle the rest. Students and researchers are not immune to this. Somebody may suggest including an MBA student on the founding team to bring in expertise about running a company and leading interactions with the world outside the university. I think this is the wrong approach. It is like hiring somebody else to go on a holiday for you and report back to you in detail about their adventures while you sit on the couch at home. Startup entrepreneurship is a learning experience that encompasses disciplines outside of your domain. It is a mindset, not a job. With that mindset, you should embrace the opportunity to integrate new skills into your life. You may discover a talent that you never knew you had.

Luckily, the financial part of a startup is relatively small, so all you have to learn are the basic functions of Excel to put together your financial model. More than that is not necessary. Nobody expects you to know about depreciation schedules and the Double Irish with a Dutch Sandwich. Your tax accounting should be outsourced to an accountant. They can file your taxes for a few hundred dollars. But the financial model cannot be outsourced. It is one of the core building blocks of your company that the founders must understand. Each time new findings emerge, you should be able to adjust the financial model yourself. Handing this off will be a disadvantage for your startup. Figure 8-3 provides a recap for using financial models effectively.

---

[5]Michael E. Porter, *Competitive Strategy: Techniques for Analyzing Industries and Competitors* (New York: Free Press, 1980).
[6]Clayton M. Christensen, *The Innovator's Dilemma: When New Technologies Cause Great Firms to Fail* (Boston: Harvard Business School Press, 1997).

Chapter 8 | The Financial Model

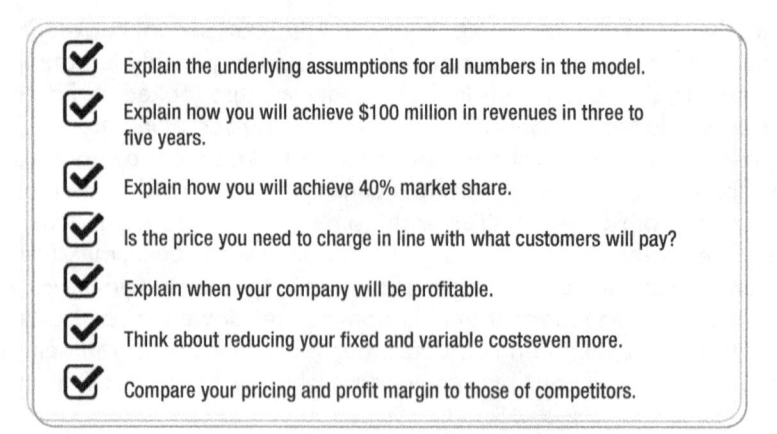

> - ☑ Explain the underlying assumptions for all numbers in the model.
> - ☑ Explain how you will achieve $100 million in revenues in three to five years.
> - ☑ Explain how you will achieve 40% market share.
> - ☑ Is the price you need to charge in line with what customers will pay?
> - ☑ Explain when your company will be profitable.
> - ☑ Think about reducing your fixed and variable costs even more.
> - ☑ Compare your pricing and profit margin to those of competitors.

Figure 8-3. Checklist for financial models

Sales and marketing are a similar story. Learning how to interact with others professionally will be a huge asset to you as an entrepreneur. Engaging third parties with a proposition that is in their own best interest applies to more than sales and marketing. Giving them actionable next steps to obtain the benefits of your product or service will be at the heart of your startup's success. Forget the cliché of the vacuum salesman who shuffles from door to door trying to sell a gadget that nobody needs. Getting others to buy something is mostly a communication skill. It has little to do with spending millions of marketing dollars to push your product in front of clients. If they see no obvious benefit, they will not buy—it's as simple as that.

Just as basic finance skills, communication skills need to be native to the startup's original founders; they should not be purchased from an external source. As the saying goes, business has only two functions: marketing and innovation. Spend a few weeks learning the ropes yourself. Learn to lead engaging discussions with others, and you will lay the centerpiece for your startup success. Turning the discussion away from features to the benefits of a technology is the first step, and this is a skill best acquired by doing. An MBA (or any other degree) has very little to do with sales and marketing success, or business success in general. Make yourself a smart and likable person, and sales and marketing will become a natural communication process for you.

CHAPTER

9

The Legal Setup of Your Startup

Startups are distinct from research projects. They are businesses, not projects. For example, different minimum viable products are projects of your startup: each may have a budget and a deadline. Thinking of your venture this way helps put things into perspective and approach it more professionally.

When you engage people outside the university, they need to perceive your startup as a business. Part of this is having the proper legal setup and financial structure. However, most university startups are never properly incorporated; they put this off until an investor or venture capitalist knocks on the door with an investment proposal. This is a classic catch-22. Startups wait to set up their business structure until they have interest from an investor; but to attract this interest, a professional business structure has to be in place. As long as entrepreneurs see their venture as a project they can abandon anytime, how can they expect serious investors to jump in?

To get out of this feedback loop, the startup's structure should enter the founders' minds as soon as they decide to launch their company. Until there is a business entity, the startup does not exist. It is just a research project and an idea.

So far, this book has focused more on the practical aspects of entrepreneurship than the organizational ones. The main goal of the book is to give you an outline of how to move your venture forward and engage others who can help you develop it in the best way possible. Legal proceedings of company foundation, such as agreements between founders and licensing contracts, are discussed at length in the business literature. One thing you cannot ignore, though, is how you set up your startup as a legal entity. You should make the move from a research project to a company as soon as possible after you decide to become an entrepreneur.

This is particularly important if you plan to scale quickly and want to attract joint venture investment or venture capital. If you do not have a proper corporate structure and a corporate bank account, how can a venture capitalist invest in your startup? It will be impossible. Change the way your startup is perceived by yourself and others by professionally incorporating it. Doing so will move you in a new direction when you establish contact with other businesses and investors.

When I speak about the legal setup of your startup, this does not necessarily mean registering a company in your country of residence. Some jurisdictions put up high barriers for new businesses, especially those with high taxes or a shaky court system. There are many ways to gain legal status with an entity incorporated abroad. No investor wants to see their capital eroded by taxes and other fees, so be aware that there may be offshore options to consider. Explaining them here goes beyond the scope of this book. If you feel you need a more complex solution, you should consult a trusted advisor. I only cover basic questions of incorporation in this chapter.

In America, several legal entities to conduct business exist. These occur in similar forms all around the world. I chose the American jurisdiction because it is straightforward to lead the discussion about startup incorporation. The terms for legal entities may be different in your particular country, but at heart, they will be similar. Let's now look at the most common structures for small and medium enterprises.

Sole Proprietorship

This is the simplest legal form a company can take. It is basically a one-person business with a self-employed founder. You may conduct business under your own name, or you can file a DBA (doing business as), which allows you to legally use a fictitious company name. Examples are a web designer, a painter, a tax consultant, and an ice cream stand. There is no distinction between the entrepreneur and the business, so as a sole proprietor you are fully liable for all your actions. If you cause damage through the business, you have to pay from your personal bank account.

Registration and administrative costs are minimal. Outside investment is not straightforward, because a sole proprietorship has no shares to sell. Investments are personal loans to the sole proprietor.

Partnership

A legal partnership is a sole proprietorship including more than one person. Small ventures are often partnerships. An example would be a group of friends buying a house and fixing it up for resale. Again, there is no distinction between the owners and the business, so they are fully liable with their personal assets.

Registration and administrative costs are minimal. Outsiders cannot readily invest in partnerships. Just as a sole proprietorship, investments are personal loans to the partners. Likewise, a partnership does not sell shares.

Limited Liability Company (LLC)

The LLC is a common form of business in America. It can have one or several owners and can issue shares. In contrast to the sole proprietorship and the partnership, the LLC is considered a separate entity from the owners. There is therefore a firewall between the company's assets and the owners' assets. This is great because you as the founder cannot be held responsible for any damages your business or your employees may cause. If the startup incurs any cost that it cannot pay back, then creditors will be unable to sue you personally and repossess your TV and your bicycle.

Registration costs range from a few hundred to a thousand dollars, depending on the state in which you incorporate. The LLC also comes with some administrative costs, but these are small. Investment by outsiders is straightforward: they simply buy shares in the company from the founders. Loans are also possible. All in all, this is the legal setup recommended for startups.

Corporation

There are several kinds of corporations: S corporation, C corporation, and so on. I will not go into detailed descriptions here. The corporation is one step up from the LLC: you could float this company in the stock market and sell shares to the public in an IPO. Registration is expensive, and so is administration. You also need a unique form of accounting for a corporation, which can be costly. Investing in a corporation is clear-cut and simply involves buying shares from the shareholders. The legal structure of the corporation makes sense for bigger companies. For example, Microsoft and Apple are corporations.

Which Legal Form Should You Choose?

The best form for a startup is often the LLC or a local variation of it. Two things are crucial: ease of investment and clarity about ownership. Because the distribution of shares in the LLC reflects ownership, one glance at the capitalization table explains the whole story.

Chapter 9 | The Legal Setup of Your Startup

This discussion about incorporation is nowhere near exhaustive. Find out if the university can hire an attorney who will explain the different legal entities to you in detail and help you select the right one for your purpose. Have an attorney write the incorporation agreements for you. If the university covers this cost, then accept it as a generous gift. If not, then pay the bill yourself. Incorporation is standard legal practice and will seldom cost more than a few hundred dollars. Taking this step makes you a real business. The sooner you address this with your team and the university, the better.

Avoid Ambiguity About Ownership

More than once, I have met with startup entrepreneurs who were months into product development and asked them about their legal structure. A puzzled look appeared on their faces. They believed I was asking about their informal agreements with the university regarding ownership of the product, so they answered something like, "All the founders together own 70% of the invention, university X owns 20%, and professor Y owns 10%." Did they put this in writing? Of course not. What happens if one founder quits? No idea. What if a venture capitalist wishes to invest? Silence.

Once the discussion about setting up an LLC has begun, confusion about ownership and investment becomes a thing of the past. There can be vesting agreements about shares, so if founders leave before a certain time, their ownership will be reduced, often to zero. If outsiders wish to invest in the company, which involves nothing more than buying shares from the existing shareholders, they can complete the transaction in an afternoon without a headache. Entrepreneurs need to have clarity about possible issues related to their company before they arise. Ownership of the startup and its assets are problem zones that proper legal setup helps clear up.

Make Your Startup Investible as Early as Possible

Here's another philosophy: money is like water. When you make space for it, that's where it will flow and accumulate. Put another way, if you make no space for it, money cannot flow to you. You think that is absurd? Bear with me for a minute, and let's look at an example.

Assume you are currently working on a research project at your university. In your PhD, you study a certain application of Li-ion battery technology. You publish some of your findings and eventually submit your thesis. Would venture capitalists invest in this PhD project? Most likely not, because there is no way for them to do so. Investing in something means buying shares in it or making a loan with interest. The research project has no corporate structure as an independent entity. It is just a line item in your university's annual budget. Unless your startup is a proper legal entity, it is a research project.

On the other hand, assume you are working on the same PhD, and you have decided to set up a startup based on some of your findings. Your startup exists in form of an LLC, where ownership and share distributions are clear. Now venture capitalists can invest easily. They know what percentage of revenue they will receive, according to the number of shares they buy in your company with their investment. Does this mean a venture capitalist will invest? No, of course not. But the potential for money to flow to you is there. Without the LLC, it is not and never will be.

Never Spend Money to Make Money

You know why rich people have money? Because they keep it and don't spend it. Duh, you may say. That was my reaction when I heard this piece of timeless wisdom from a neighbor at the age of eight. But three decades later, his words still ring in my ears. What will you do if you find a hundred dollars in the street? Buy fireworks, or lottery tickets for everyone? Or will you save it in the bank at 0.01% interest because you are afraid to be robbed? Whatever your answer, your attitude toward money will largely determine your wealth and the success of your startup.

Most people complain about money and their lack of it. A tennis partner of mine had a film production company. When I asked him how business was, he made a sour face and started off on his usual rant. The shrinking margins in the business. The new kids on the block who lured away his clients. And the new technology that turned everybody and their cousin into filmmakers. Without a miracle, he said, he may have to close shop soon. After our tennis match, we took out our calendars to set up the next one. This would have to wait a few weeks, my friend announced. He would be on another continent, on a golf holiday with his wife. When we walked to the parking garage, I couldn't help but notice his brand-new Range Rover. Nice toy, eh? Yes, he always wanted the new model XYZ, and because he could trade in his Jaguar, it was a steal. His reasoning for driving luxury cars was that he needed to project an aura of success to his clients—spending money to make money. What attitude toward money does this man have? Not one that is helpful to launch a startup or stay in business when times are rough.

A misconception about launching your own company is that it is expensive. You need to pay your suppliers, buy computers, rent an office, hire staff, pay for expensive advertising and marketing, and so on. Nevertheless, if you are launching your startup straight out of university, none of these costs applies to you. Even if you cannot fall back on an existing infrastructure, you do not need to break the bank. Work out of your house or apartment, attract another founder with skills that complement yours, and launch the company as a team. Test your product in the market before you have it mass-produced. And, of course, lower your own bills as much as possible.

Even though you may not plan to go on a golf holiday or buy a new luxury car, there are still many ways to rein in your monthly bills. Do you really need that data plan that sets you back $50 per month? How about HBO and DirecTV for another $100 per month? Is the old iPhone really not good enough anymore? And do you need to take a taxi to the university for $20 each day when the train only costs $2? With a few simple adjustments, you may be able to save several thousand dollars each year. This can make or break your startup in the early phases. As a startup entrepreneur, get used to bootstrapping with little or nothing as early as possible. Forget about spending money to make money. Even if you have funding, make it a point to use as little as possible and spend only when necessary. Use all the synergies and free infrastructure you can, as long as possible.

The checklist in figure 9-1 sums up what you need to know about moving your startup up a notch.

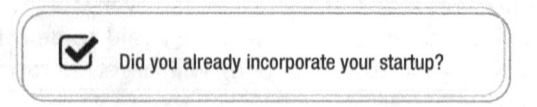

☑ Did you already incorporate your startup?

Figure 9-1. Checklist for a startup's legal structure

CHAPTER 10

Communication Skills and Meetings

Talking about their project with outsiders is an important skill that entrepreneurs often overlook. How difficult can it be to present something to a visitor? Presentation skills are often taken for granted, but in reality, good communication is the lifeblood of entrepreneurship. Because startups rarely take off in isolation, it is worth spending some time mastering communication skills. Students and researchers may find tactics related to communication too salesy or otherwise unfit for academics. Overcoming that hurdle is one of the points of this book: leave the ivory tower, and get feedback from the real market. The sooner university entrepreneurs warm up to this concept, the better.

PowerPoint

Researchers are used to presenting their findings to other academics, so they naturally assume that they already know how to give talks to third parties. What they fail to consider is that non-academics are used to a different presentation style and format than academics. A startup entrepreneur should avoid addressing potential partners and investors as if they were faculty. I have sat through hour-long presentations of 200 mostly unreadable PowerPoint slides, most of which the presenter skipped with the remark "I don't have enough time to show this here." Many of the slides were brimming with justified 12-point type, intricate diagrams, and tables of even smaller type. In addition to being utterly boring, such feature-laden demonstrations lack any actionable steps to engage the audience. Presenters simply beam data down to the listener, and when the time or the information runs out, they stop. This may be OK when you are presenting to a specialist who has an interest in such detail, or anyone unfamiliar with a better presentation style. However, when pitching a potential joint venture partner or investor, such a practice may reflect badly on you. It shows that you are going through the motions with little understanding of how the business and investing world works.

To be fair, it is not only individuals from universities who lack presentation skills. Most presentations given by startups and multinational corporations are rather dismal. There is a lot room for improvement in all domains. Effective communication is never a one-way street. It is not just a question of *telling* but also of *listening*. Entrepreneurs are hardly the only people who must learn this.

So how can a startup make its presentations more palatable? Let's establish a few ground rules and technical parameters that make it much easier to tailor your presentations to diverse audiences and applications.

The 10/20/30 Rule

A framework often used in Silicon Valley is the 10/20/30 rule put forward by author Guy Kawasaki: 10 slides, 20 minutes, minimum font size of 30 points.[1] This technique is daunting for most people on first sight. However, it works. You must fit all the essential information on ten slides, excluding the title slide. What information, you ask? Most third parties want to see the following points:

1. Problem
2. Your solution
3. Sales and business model
4. Technology
5. Marketing and sales
6. Competition
7. Team
8. Projections and milestones
9. Status and timeline
10. Short summary and call to action (next steps)

---

[1] Guy Kawasaki, *The Art of the Start: The Time-Tested, Battle-Hardened Guide for Anyone Starting Anything* (New York: Portfolio, 2004).

When you pitch to a joint venture partner, you may adjust some of the slides. Instead of a sales and business model, at point 3, you may put the partnership model that you imagine. You may omit point 5, marketing and sales, and replace it with distribution channels. 10/20/30 is open and malleable, as long as you follow the iron rule of a maximum of 10 slides with a minimum font size of 30.

The most important slide is number 10: the call to action. Only with this last step will you engage your audience. Never leave your audience with the task of coming up with the next steps to take. If lunchtime is five minutes away, they will rarely spend much effort on this. As an entrepreneur, you need to do the thinking for other people and tell them what you want them to do for you. This is also where your one-page proposal fits, as an extension of this final slide.

The large font size is paramount for several reasons. First, when you present with a projector, the contrast in the room may be weak, and small fonts will be unreadable. You could darken the room, but then people will fall asleep. It is best to avoid this problem by using at least a 30-point font size. Second, when you print a presentation and show it on paper, the people you are presenting to may have bad eyesight. Most of them will skip unreadable tiny print and will politely nod, so you will never know that most of the information went over their head. And finally, because a large font acutely limits the space available per slide, it forces you to condense. Cut out anything that is unnecessary. Producing a lot of text is easy; the magic lies in making your presentation concise. People have gotten used to reading 140-character Twitter messages that include a lot of information, so you will be at an advantage if you master the skill of keeping it short. (By the way: the same goes for e-mails and any other written documents. The shorter, the better.) You can still make a long version and include links to your in-depth publications, should anyone ask for them. Most people have little time and just want to find out the overall gist of your project.

What about tables, which need to use a much smaller font size to fit on the slide? What does not fit has to go. Simply omit anything that is incompatible with the 10/20/30 framework. You can always convey the same information with fewer words. Figure 10-1 is an example from an actual project I was working on: this is the original slide with some names obscured. It contains information about the benefits of a certain platform for patent-licensing offices. The 15-point font is difficult to read, especially from a distance. The colored table format provided by PowerPoint looks good in print, but the contrast is too weak for an overhead presentation. The audience starts reading at top left, makes their way down to the second line, and then gives up. You may be talking or explaining what you mean to say with this table, but the slide and your words will be incongruent. As you may have guessed, this slide is unpresentable.

Beneficiaries' perspective

Participants	Examples	Need	Give	Get	Alloc.
University IP licensing office		Licensees for patents, 3rd party funds	Access to patent database	Licensees, more effective brokering of licensing deals	5%
Large research projects		3rd party funds, pilot projects	Educate talent, global awareness, Secure Res. Funds	Funding, jobs for post-doc students, link to the market, assistance for start-up track, network	5%
University spin-offs/start-ups		Funds for regional expansion, network	Equity share, board seat	Funding, assistance, guidance, synergies, network	15%
SMEs		Network, leverage, POC Studies	Equity share, board seat	Funding, assistance, guidance, synergies, network	25%
R&D team of MNC or Joint Ventures			Equity share, board seat, test bedding, project outline	Debt/equity funding, synergies, network	25%
Reg. expansion of tenders from gov't		Support to win government tender (>5 Mio)	Share of won tender	Debt/equity funding, assistance, synergies, network	25%
Underwriter		Products with fee income	2 mn seed, access to support team	80% of fee income and revenue	n/a

Figure 10-1. PowerPoint slide before applying 10/20/30

Figure 10-2 shows how to improve this slide. Even though it contains more or less the same information, this version looks clean and makes sense at a glance. There is no fancy formatting: just clear information. On the left you see the beneficiaries, and on the right, the benefits. The columns for the motivation and contribution of each party are unnecessary to drive home the point that the platform has value, so you eliminate them.

Omit all information that confuses the story or makes it difficult to understand. If anyone has specific questions, they can ask after your presentation, which only lasts 20 minutes. This leaves the audience with enough energy to follow up if something is important. If the missing details are key for the overall story, you can print the table and make it available to those who wish to know more.

Assume you are in a day-long workshop to hammer out the terms of a potential project. Each speaker has one hour to make a presentation. Instead of fretting about how to fit your 200 slides into 60 minutes, stick to the 10/20/30 rule. Speak for 20 minutes, and then get feedback from the other attendees. What exactly is their problem? How have they addressed it in the past? Has this worked for them? Why or why not? What happens if they keep doing what they have been doing? How could your solution better solve their problem? Use the SPIN technique described in Chapter 5 to link the benefits you

University Startups and Spin-Offs

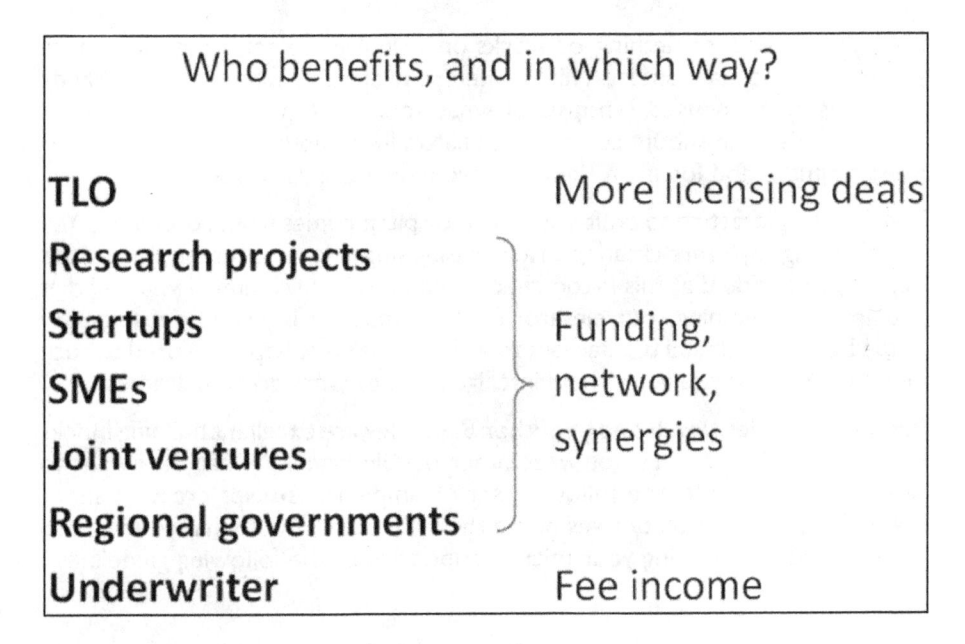

Who benefits, and in which way?	
TLO	More licensing deals
Research projects	
Startups	Funding,
SMEs	network,
Joint ventures	synergies
Regional governments	
Underwriter	Fee income

Figure 10-2. PowerPoint slide after applying 10/20/30

can bring to the table to the needs of the other parties. Your presentation becomes a platform for discussion, and you engage others in your project.

Communication about your startup goes far beyond PowerPoint. It is a skill and a mindset that applies to all your interactions with others. Once you have internalized a few ground rules, you can apply them to various situations.

Have a Backup Plan Ready

It goes without saying that if you need to hook your computer to a projector, you should do this before the presentation to make sure everything works. If the projector fails to link up with your laptop, have the presentation available on a USB stick and use another machine. As a last resort, bring a printout of the presentation that you can photocopy if all else fails. When the presentation begins, you should have checked that everything works and should have taken all possible steps to make it work. Blaming the technology or the technician and shrugging your shoulders will only reflect badly on you, so do not go there. It is your full responsibility to make your presentation work.

Elevator Pitch and Micro-Scripts

It can always happen that you meet someone in the proverbial elevator, and they ask you what you are currently working on. As a startup entrepreneur, be ready to pitch your project at all times. Who knows? Perhaps the other person can help you with something, or works on a similar project, or can introduce you to an influential contact. This is when your elevator pitch comes in handy. It is a highly condensed synopsis of what your startup is about and why it matters. This pitch should come across naturally without sounding rehearsed. Keep it simple, and focus on the most prominent points of your venture.

The following practice to craft your elevator pitch comes from advertising. Yes, you heard right: you are creating an advertising slogan for your university startup. Before you decide that this is too cheesy and un-scientific, remind yourself that you are not publishing your elevator pitch in *Nature*. It is just a brief summary of the benefits your startup delivers to a client. Businesspeople are used to such pitches, and when you apply them intelligently, they work great in academia.

Micro-script rules, developed by author Bill Schley, are excellent building blocks for elevator pitches.[2] "It's not what other people hear, it's what they want to repeat," as he puts it. The following set of simple rules helps create a short, memorable message that drives home the main point about what you want to communicate. In creating your micro-script, stick to the following guidelines:

1. One attribute.
2. The narrower your focus, the wider the message goes.
3. Simple always wins. The average length of successful scripts is less than six words.
4. Be specific.

There are further rules, but these are the ones I find most workable.

Now you have a recipe to cook up your elevator pitch. Let's see how this works with an example. For this, we go back to the battery startup from Chapter 2. What is their product's one quality? Potential candidates are "rechargeable in ten minutes" and "biodegradable." Because "rechargeable" did not make the cut in MVP testing, this is easy: we focus on "biodegradable." The narrow focus means the startup's first product is a *car* battery, as they found out in MVP testing. Specificity means the battery is not just "good for the environment": it is so many times better, or it saves so many lives or so much soil or water from contamination. For illustration purposes, some possible micro-scripts for the battery startup are as follows:

"The biodegradable car battery that reduces water pollution from heavy metals by 50%."

"Each car battery helps protect one acre of farmland from heavy metal pollution."

"The car battery that dissolves to compost."

---

[2]Bill Schley, *The Micro-Script Rules* (New York: N. W. Widener, 2010).

It is helpful to avoid touting the features of your technology, but rather the benefits. A feature would be the chemical composition of the battery acid. It's better to speak about the benefit of biodegradability, which listeners can then repeat to other people after they hear the micro-script.

This is just an example to show that you need to be creative with your micro-scripts. Write down several of them, and test which ones work best. These short sentences can be the building blocks of your elevator pitch.

So how do you use your elevator pitch? Let's find out with a fictitious example. Assume the following situation: Ben and Christine from the battery startup are waiting at a taxi stand. In line right behind them, Ben notices the CEO of Big Battery Corporation (BBC) waiting for a cab. Ben recognizes the CEO from a news article he saved—he wanted to write a letter to BBC about a potential joint venture. The taxi line is barely moving, and Ben figures he has three minutes to speak with the CEO. He seizes the opportunity and introduces himself.

Ben: "Hi, Mr. CEO. I recognized you from the article in *The Business Post* last month. My name is Ben, and this is Christine. We just founded a battery company. Here is my card."

CEO: "OK ..."

Ben: "We are working on a biodegradable car battery that can reduce water pollution from heavy metals by 50%. We're testing the battery now in the market with very good results."

CEO: "Hm."

Ben: "Yes. I planned to write to your R&D department and introduce our company. We are currently looking for a joint venture partner to raise some funding. We are actually raising $250,000 right now, which should be enough for the next six months to refine the technology, and I would like to ask your company if ..."

CEO: (Interrupting Ben) "Listen, it's 10 p.m., and I had a busy day. We already work on similar technology and have no headroom for another joint venture."

Ben: "Oh, really!?" (Long pause.) "Uhm, OK. Well, good luck with the technology you are working on ..."

Did this go well? Not at all. But that happens when you forget to rehearse your elevator pitch and are unclear about what you want from the other party as the actionable next step. Even though Ben started out fine with his micro-script, the rest of his elevator pitch was much too straightforward. Begging others for money is the last thing that should come across in your elevator pitch. Instead, focus on what you can do for the other party. Move the conversation just one step forward by breaking down your goals into smaller steps. If you move ahead steadily in interactions with others, you will reach the goal faster than if you try for a home run every time. Let's rewind and see how the situation could have played out better:

Ben: "Hi, Mr. CEO. I recognized you from the article in the *The Business Post* last month. My name is Ben, and this is Christine. We just founded a battery company. Here is my card."

CEO: "OK ..."

Ben: "We are working on a biodegradable car battery that can reduce water pollution from heavy metals by 50%. We're testing the battery now in the market with very good results."

CEO: "Hm."

Ben: "Yes. I planned to write to your R&D department and introduce our technology. It could be in line with your new sustainable product line Z. Would it be possible for us to make a presentation?"

CEO: "Listen, it's 10 p.m., and I had a busy day. Why don't you call the office and set something up with R&D?"

Ben: "Great, I will do that. Oh, here's a cab. Why don't you go ahead of us? Have a safe drive home, and we'll be in touch tomorrow."

Was this interaction successful? I think so. Even though the CEO was still grumpy, Ben got to the next base. He of course still has a long way to go to secure funding and a joint venture, but he is one step closer to a potential partner. The CEO has no reason to reject him. Ben can contact BBC tomorrow and refer to the CEO's recommendation to call the office. He may even send a greeting card to the CEO and thank him for his time and his suggestion to call. Thereby he has set up a link to a potential partner that may be of much value to both of them down the road.

Prepare and Rehearse Your Pitch

Your message has to be clear and refined, and this never comes overnight. Most important, whenever you give your elevator pitch to someone, do not ramble. This is a sure deal-breaker. Keep it simple and short, and use memorable phrases like your micro-scripts. Make sure you give the other person enough space to breathe, and take breaks between your sentences. To deliver your messages with perfection, make sure you have rehearsed them properly. It is more difficult than you think to bring across your information confidently and still make it sound unrehearsed. This needs practice. But it is well worth doing and will go a long way.

Get your team together, and start pitching to each other. See which microscripts work well by testing them frequently in casual conversations. Practice does not always have to be in front of the mirror. Get in the habit of obtaining feedback about your ideas everywhere you go. Over time, this prepares you to get it right and make it sound natural at the same time.

Unless you practice your elevator pitch, the right words will elude you under stress. As the example of Ben and the CEO shows, always think in terms of next steps. If you can advance the dialogue, it is successful. Interactions that linger in indecision are unsuccessful and a huge time waster. If you fail to pay attention, you may not notice this is the case, with actionable steps postponed from one meeting to the next. When you are setting up a meeting, clearly think about what you want from it.

What Is the Actionable Next Step?

Being too straightforward right away is a turnoff. The first contact should just be about getting to next base, in this case a formal meeting to present your technology. It could also be MVP testing with a company already active in the marketplace. Or general feedback about your approach and your assumed target market. When you meet a person in the elevator, refrain from pushing your entire PowerPoint pitch deck on them. The actionable next step is to organize a meeting where you and your team present the entire pitch. Whatever it is you want, be clear to approach it in small steps.

With the SPIN questions (situation, problem, implication, need-payoff), it is much easier to frame the discussion around the benefits of your products instead of their features. Going into the meeting to "just get to know" the other party is not enough and will rarely move the interaction forward. With this, you are depriving yourself and the other party of potential value that could come out of a potential collaboration down the road.

Note how all the techniques and the work done on your startup so far build on each other. With MVP testing and the business model canvas, you found your unique value propositions, which you highlight in your elevator pitch. With your financial model, you can lead an informed discussion about pricing and your needs when it comes to forming a joint venture or raising investment. And the right communication skills tie it all together. Without them, nothing else would matter because you would be unable to bring it across when you meet a decision maker. The strategies outlined in this book are straightforward and may even seem simplistic at times. However, putting them all together, you will end up with a workable approach to entrepreneurship that has been successful for many startups. Only when you have a clear picture of your startup can you express the exact next steps you want others to take on your behalf.

Take Control of Unexpected Situations

Have you ever given an interview to the news media? They are usually very short, sometimes just 30 seconds. The interviewer asks a generic question, and you answer the best you can until the next question rolls around or the interview is over. Most people are in a reactive mode during an interview, and this is *not* how an entrepreneur should use this opportunity. Instead of nicely answering the interviewer's questions, have your pitch ready, and be prepared with the story that you want the world to know.

Let's see how this works with another fictitious example. Assume there was a volcanic eruption in Indonesia yesterday, and a news team is now filming an interview at your university. As the team lead on the volcanic-eruption module, you are slated for the interview. Let's see how this unfolds:

Interviewer: "As a leading expert in volcanic-eruption modeling, what is your prediction for future volcanic activity in Indonesia?"

If you are like most people, you will respond the best you can to the question about volcanic activity in Indonesia. After all, that's what the interviewer wanted to know, right? Perhaps you say that no models could predict what happened and that we do not know when the next eruption will be. Or perhaps you speak about the history of eruptions and note that this one was actually long overdue. You play nice with the interviewer and tell her what she needs for her news bite. She will politely thank you and move on to the next news item. This is how most such interviews progress.

Assume, however, that in addition to being a leading expert on volcanic activity in Indonesia, you are also a startup entrepreneur. The startup you incorporated two days ago, let's call it *Seismic Software*, already has a tentative joint venture pact with a multinational sensor company, *SensorX*. You have worked on a model that has in lab tests outperformed other models. You feel it has a wide variety of applications not only in eruption modeling but also for earthquakes, tsunamis, terrestrial explosions, and so on. By chance, you find yourself standing in front of a camera for the national news media, and a reporter asks you about the volcano in Indonesia. What do you do? You can play along with the interviewer and give the generic answer that 99% of all other researchers would give because they are excited to be on TV. Or you can hijack this opportunity and take matters into your own hands:

Interviewer: "As a leading expert in volcanic-eruption modeling, what is your prediction for future volcanic activity in Indonesia?"

You: "Thanks for asking me this question. This latest activity in Indonesia has been largely a surprise, which is mainly because most models date back ten years. My team and I at Seismic Software are working on an advanced model that holds much promise. We predict not only eruptions like the one we have just seen, but also earthquakes and tsunamis up to ten minutes earlier than current systems in use. We're currently testing our model in Japan with SensorX, our joint venture partner. The first tests are promising, and it will be exciting to see how we can improve prediction in the future. In fact, this short simulation video shows how we predict future eruptions with our software." (Shows 20-second video clip on a laptop.) "You see here how we get a clear signal of seismic activity about ten minutes before the felt impact on land. This is mainly thanks to the way our software communicates with the SensorX sensors. In this video, you see our team from Seismic Software at a test site in Indonesia." (Shows other 20-second video clip.) And so on, and so forth.

What just happened? The interview is now about your company and your product and not about Indonesia. If the interviewer has time for another question, she will most likely follow up on your model, your tests, or your company. Or she may want to show your videos with the credit of your company in the news bit. Do not worry about talking too long—the news team can always edit your interview. The elevator pitch should be short, that's true. But that applies when you pitch under time constraints. When you have the chance to tell your story to the world on the news, you should have a lot of interesting material to talk about. In the example, you made a powerful pitch that put your own company and also your joint venture partner in the spotlight on the national news. Make sure to exchange business cards with the film crew and anyone else on the set. You could double up and invite the news crew to your lab to film a special report about prediction software.

You never know what these encounters may lead to. The most important thing to remember is that entrepreneurs first and foremost have the benefit of their own company in mind. When there is a chance to get a platform, make the platform your own. You could not possibly buy the visibility you get from these opportunities.

A Word about NDAs and Confidentiality

Attorneys advise you to have third parties sign a non-disclosure agreement (NDA) when you show those parties confidential information about a technology and want to discourage them from copying or stealing your invention. If you have a patent (pending), then your invention is somewhat protected from plagiarism, but you still have to enforce against potential infringement. This can be time-consuming and expensive. An NDA should, in theory, protect you from intellectual property theft. The reality is that NDAs are impractical. Better than relying on NDAs and patent protection is keeping the crucial parts of your invention under wraps. My experience has shown that an NDA often frames a discussion in a negative light, because it presupposes the other party will naturally steal your intellectual property. Many venture capitalists will tell you straight out that they never sign NDAs. If you insist, the meeting is over.

A better strategy than an NDA is incremental disclosure. First, by focusing mostly on the benefits of your technology and not the features, you avoid revealing the secrets behind your invention. In the example of the battery startup, they should avoid disclosing their product's chemical composition in the first meeting. But they should highlight all the benefits it brings: biodegradable up to X%, contains no heavy metals, protects water and soil, and so forth. When the potential joint venture partner asks sensitive questions, you sidestep with the answer that you can discuss those in a later meeting. If your invention is obvious—for example, if one glimpse at the battery immediately tells the other party about the technology behind it—then leave it in your top secret lab. Bring a mock-up or a diagram with the sensitive parts obscured. The more the relationship progresses, the more you show. When you have signed a joint venture agreement, then all the intellectual property is shared, and there are no more secrets. Only when you think in terms of features, not benefits, will you be afraid of intellectual property theft.

What Should You Bring to a Meeting?

Let's say you have a first presentation with a potential joint venture partner. How do you approach it? Let's revisit the collateral you have produced so far and see how they are put to good use. This is what you should bring to a meeting:

1. Short summary for the meeting, with points to discuss
2. PowerPoint presentation on a laptop or printed
3. Business model canvas
4. Financial model
5. One-page proposal, if you have something to propose
6. Additional materials

Let's look at each item in more detail.

Points to Discuss

When you go to a meeting, make sure you are coming from a position of preparedness and strength, not from a stance of begging for sponsorship or capital. The grant track focuses startups exclusively on securing funding from day one, but capital is hardly the most important asset others can provide. When you approach others, their experience and the synergies they bring are the most valuable assets for your startup.

Make it a point to lead the meeting with confidence. As an entrepreneur, you want to come across as goal-oriented and determined. When you communicate this way and the other party reacts strangely or withdraws, then you may have found out that they are not up to speed to work with you. Be glad you recognized this early. Use the meeting to show your worth and to test the other party regarding their ability and commitment.

Business Model Canvas or Lean Canvas

Whichever canvas you choose (I recommend the lean canvas), you should tailor it to the other party in each presentation. Parts of the canvas will flow into your PowerPoint presentation: for example, the slides where you explain the problem, solution, business model, and so forth. You may bring several canvases to address specific situations, such as your joint venture partner's market and also the global market. Because you open the meeting with the PowerPoint presentation, the canvases are just backups in case the discussion progresses beyond the most obvious points.

Financial Model

Even though a joint venture partner will value your company on their own terms, the financial model is important to show the assumptions under which you operate. Do you project $1 million in sales or $100 million? Does your product cost one dollar or one cent? What is the potential profit margin, and what are the effects of scale economies?

The underlying logic of your startup and the market are more important than the numbers in the model. They show others how you think and operate. Make sure you explain your assumptions concisely as well. Bring the financial model with the output printed on one page for easy discussion.

One-Page Proposal

This document condenses onto a single page the entire discussion about your proposal for a joint venture or other proposition: your status quo, what you can do for the other party, and what you want them to do for you. Of course, never break out a joint venture proposal at the first meeting, before you even know the other party and have an understanding about how you could work together. This proposal makes sense when you have met the other party several times and are ready to extend or receive an offer. You can also prepare several different proposals.

In any event, before you go into a meeting, know what you want out of it. In a first meeting, you should ask for a follow-up meeting to discuss other parts of the technology, or get feedback on an MVP, or look at the joint venture partner's processes to learn something new.

Technical Drawings, Sketches, Photographs

You should bring anything to the meeting that makes the point of your product being valuable to the other party, unless it gives away your intellectual property. If you have photographs of people using the technology, or drawings, or certain statistics that make a point, then bring those printed on separate pages. You will rarely need to show everything; just have more material ready as a backup.

What Should You Leave After the Meeting?

Print out the ten-page PowerPoint presentation and leave it there, unless it contains confidential information. Do not leave the lean canvas, the financial model, or any of your technical drawings. If you have presented a one-page proposal, leave that also, because you want a reply in the next few days regarding the next steps. Other than that, avoid flooding the other party with paper. You should make a sharp impression with your presentation and leave them wanting more.

Business Cards

Do you need your own business cards? Well, of course. When you are out and about as an entrepreneur, avoid giving people the card from your university. Print your own business cards at a professional copy center. They should include the following information:

- Your name and degree: for example, Dr. X, MBA.
- Your title at the company: for example, CEO.
- The name of the company.
- The address of the university lab where your startup is hopefully based in the beginning.
- Your personal mobile phone number.
- Your personal e-mail address. Get your own dot-com domain for your startup at a web-hosting company like Godaddy.com. This costs about $15 per year and comes with free e-mail accounts. Setting up your page and e-mail address takes ten minutes. This looks infinitely better than a faculty e-mail or Gmail address.

Your title is important. First-time entrepreneurs are often unsure about their role in the company. Are they the founder, the chief executive officer (CEO), the chief scientist, or all of the above? Avoid using the title Founder.

If you are the boss of your team, then use the title CEO, or Managing Director, or President. If you are working more in the background on technical issues, put CTO (chief technical officer) or CIO (chief information officer). Read about these abbreviations on Wikipedia, and choose the one that best fits what you are doing. Use only one title, even if you have several roles.

The Business Lunch

A business lunch is distinctly different from getting together with your friends and family at a restaurant. The focus is on *business*, not on lunch. Eating together and sharing food is a gesture of goodwill among humans today just as it was in ancient times. It is more informal and cordial to meet over pizza than in a conference room. The topics discussed during the lunch are also different from those in a meeting, but they are still based on the premise of benefits over features, asking instead of telling, and actionable next steps.

I discuss the business lunch in a little more detail than the other skills in this chapter. This is because it is easy to spot a beginner during a business lunch. A great number of entrepreneurs blunder their way through lunches and lose much previously gained respect as a result of their amateurish behavior. I have no intention to micromanage your business lunches; this discussion simply shows you the moving parts that come together in this meeting ritual that looks so simple on the surface.

Let's assume you had a brief meeting at a science summit with the CEO of a company that you may want to partner with later. You exchange cards, and he suggests that you get together for lunch sometime. You set up a meeting next week at a restaurant close to the CEO's office. How do you make the most of this meeting (see Figure 10-3)?

Chapter 10 | Communication Skills and Meetings

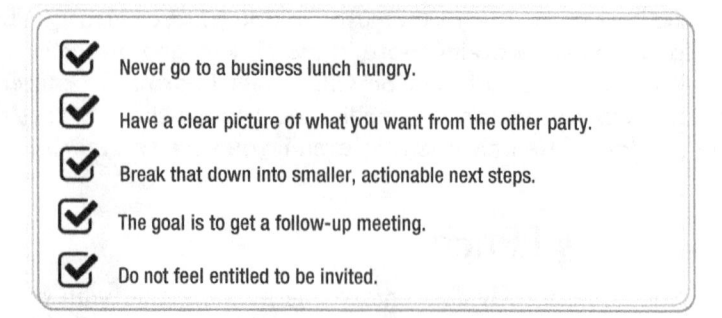

- ☑ Never go to a business lunch hungry.
- ☑ Have a clear picture of what you want from the other party.
- ☑ Break that down into smaller, actionable next steps.
- ☑ The goal is to get a follow-up meeting.
- ☑ Do not feel entitled to be invited.

Figure 10-3. Checklist for a business lunch

First, be sure you are early. Familiarize yourself with the place, and then wait for the other party to arrive. Do not arrive at the restaurant starving. Make sure you ate a good breakfast and perhaps a little snack just before lunch to avoid arriving at the restaurant undernourished, only thinking about food. Wolfing down your lunch seldom makes a good impression. In general, let the other party order first, and then order something similar. If it turns out the other person is a vegetarian, then refrain from ordering a bloody steak; order a small soup dish or salad. Always order a small plate so you have more time to address the issues you would like to discuss. Definitely avoid messy food, such as crab legs or anything similar, unless the other party orders the same and insists that you join them.

It is a good practice to stay away from alcohol at lunch, even if the other person orders a beer or glass of wine. You are not drinking buddies just yet. If it happens that the two of you become friends, then it is of course OK to go out drinking, but the first lunch meeting is hardly the time to drink together. Apply common sense. Make sure your lunch does not interfere with the business part of the meeting.

When it comes to paying the bill, the CEO will most likely invite you, but have enough cash on hand to cover your part. Offer to split the check. Be as persistent as you must, depending on your local customs. When you are invited, thank the other party for the lunch. However, never assume because somebody is richer or older than you that they must pay your bill. A sense of entitlement can be a deal breaker.

You need to have your business agenda planned in your head when you go to the lunch. Do not bring any paper, such as bound prints of PowerPoint presentations, unless the other person expressly asked you to bring them. Remember, you want to move each interaction to the next one. If the CEO wants to see more, then set up the next meeting where you will show your full presentation. Most first-time entrepreneurs make the mistake of wanting to hit a home run right out of the gate. That is hardly how relationship building works. Move step by step. The business lunch is a good opportunity to suss out the other party informally, get to know their opinion, and then present actionable next steps. What those are should be clear to you before you go to the lunch.

Let's assume you want to ask the CEO if he can sponsor your product development with hardware. In a first meeting, such a commitment might be a stretch. What would the CEO get out of it: perhaps access to your other testing data, or insight you gained in developing prototypes? Present something of value before you ask for anything. Try to find out whether the CEO already has the data you collected. See if it would be helpful if you shared your findings. Ask him how his team approached a certain problem that you are struggling with. Offer the insight you gained from solving a similar problem. As the actionable next step, offer to show him some of your results directly at his company's R&D lab. In that next meeting, you can begin inquiring about the possibility of potentially working together, perhaps by using their lab or some of their hardware.

Every meeting exists to lay the groundwork for the next one. Look at your meetings this way, and you will see them in a whole new light.

You Can Always Ask

As an entrepreneur, you must let go of your fear of asking other people to do things for you. Of course, I am not suggesting you bum out your friends with silly requests to buy dinner for you or let you crash on their couch for free with no end in sight. Those kinds of favors only go so far and end up alienating everyone around you. I mean well-researched requests that you may want to ask others to fulfill.

Let's assume you want to meet the CEO of a company with which you would eventually like to form a joint venture. You have no personal connection to this CEO yet, nor does anyone in your network. At the same time, you think it would be good to get on the radar of her firm and hear her feedback about your MVP. What do you do? You should make contact with the CEO and ask her for a meeting to get her feedback about your early-stage product. Most people are open to giving their opinion about your work. They want to help others, especially if they can identify with them in one form or another. But remember that all relationships are give and take.

How do you contact somebody you have never met? Luckily, there is the Internet, which solves many of our problems. Most CEOs have an account on LinkedIn; make sure you connect there first. But a hurdle comes up: to connect with a person on LinkedIn, you often need to know their e-mail address or show that you have some other connection with them.

Chapter 10 | Communication Skills and Meetings

You can often guess e-mail addresses from the URL of a company. Most of them use the format *first-name.last-name@company.com*. Try that and see if it works. You can also say that you are a friend of the CEO. Sometimes you can choose a LinkedIn group that you are both a member of: join the same group as the CEO, and off you go. Try a few times, and see what happens. Eventually it will be possible to connect.

Why not simply send an e-mail to the company? E-mails from strangers fall by the wayside: most decision-makers receive hundreds of them each day. It is better to use alternative channels, if they are available.

Of course, you can also call the company and ask for a meeting. I recommend this only if you are well advanced on the path of MVP testing and can make the case for providing value to the company. Only go into a meeting if you are prepared and ready with actionable next steps for the other party. Never go "just to get to know them." This will annoy the other party and make the next meeting more difficult to get when you need it.

With that in mind, you can meet anybody you desire in this world. Celebrities, billionaires, Nobel laureates—they are all just people in the end. If you appreciate their time and engage them in the right way with something they perceive to be of value, you will eventually prevail.

I once wanted to meet a famed investor to get his feedback on a project of mine in Asia. Because he ran several investment funds that had been active in Southeast Asia and China for over two decades, I was sure he would have some insight about these markets based on his experience. He often appears on CNBC and Bloomberg TV, speaks at various investment conferences, and is generally perceived as a jet setter, so chances were slim that this man would ever lend his time to me. So how did I approach this challenge?

First I sent an e-mail to his investment company in Hong Kong, not sure whether an executive assistant would screen them. For three weeks, I sent an e-mail each Tuesday morning with the request for a meeting in either of the two locations where he has homes. These e-mails went unanswered. So I switched to LinkedIn, as mentioned earlier. But there were several accounts with his name, some obviously fake. I connected with the two that looked real. To do that, I used the Classmate feature with my alma mater, for lack of a better alternative. Surprisingly, a few days later, both connection requests were approved. Once you connect on LinkedIn, you can see your new friend's full profile and send them messages. That is what I did:

Dear X,

I would like to introduce myself in person to you. Would you be available for ten minutes this or next week by phone or in person? I am happy to meet you either in Y or in Z, at your leisure.

Notice that my first message contained no flattery about that person's achievements. There was no word about admiring his work. Such statements put you in the position of a *fan*. Nobody wants to be friends with a fan. They only want to be friends with people on the same wavelength. There was also no time lost explaining who I was. That information was visible on my LinkedIn profile. Keep these introductory e-mails as short as you possibly can. Omit all fluff, and get right to the point. What did I want as the first action? I could have written that I wanted feedback about an idea, but this would have been an immediate turn-off. I just wanted to get face time. Afterward, I could bring forth my request for a follow-up meeting to present my project. You cannot force others to interact with you, but you can lead them gently with patience and persistence.

The answer I received was brief:

Sorry, I'm traveling.

At least there was a direct line now. What do you do when someone obviously has no time and no motivation to meet with you? Do you become a nuisance and pepper them with requests until they give in? They never will. You will brand yourself a spammer and will end up on their blocked list. Or do you put the ball in their court, sending your phone number and asking them to connect when they have time? You will never hear from them. Instead, be politely persistent, yet respectful of their time. You can always ask—but ask the right thing at the right time. This is a delicate skill that takes time to master.

It took two months until my first meeting with the investor came to pass. The first meeting took place in a "gentlemen's bar." I introduced myself and told the investor that I was an entrepreneur, and that some of my ventures had been in the Internet space. Before the meeting, I had prepared several suggestions for the investor's personal blog, which could have used a makeover. I had also mapped out a strategy for a mobile app and a podcast that he might consider to reach a wider audience. All this I gave away without asking anything in return. This was about providing value to the other party and establishing the notion that this was not to be a one-sided interaction. I noticed that he relaxed slightly. He had probably expected an investment proposal, or a request for advice. Instead, most of this discussion circled around digital strategy and how he could use it to his advantage. This meeting was engaging and lasted several hours.

After that first meeting, it took another two months to set up the next. This time I asked for the investor's opinion about an idea I had been working on. About five one-sentence e-mails later, mostly stating that he had no time or was abroad, the get-together was finally organized. Printed PowerPoint presentation in hand, I arrived at that same bar. Two hours later, all the bar girls had introduced themselves to me, but the investor had not shown himself.

It dawned on me that this would most likely not happen today. When I returned to the hotel, I wrote a short e-mail asking whether everything was OK and whether a meeting in the next few days might be more convenient. The temptation to give up is strong in such a situation, and so is the danger of choosing the wrong words. Never write an e-mail when you're angry or disappointed. Keeping it simple and to the point is the way to go.

Long story short, I eventually got what I wanted. The investor gave valuable feedback about the idea and even introduced a contact of his to help develop it further. This interaction was two-sided, and that is why it was productive. Few startup entrepreneurs I meet are thinking about first providing value to others. You can of course only provide value to others if you have something to say that cannot be read in a book. This is another reason to develop skills beyond your area of expertise: you never know when you or something else can use them.

Figure 10-4 sums up the most important points about meetings and communication skills.

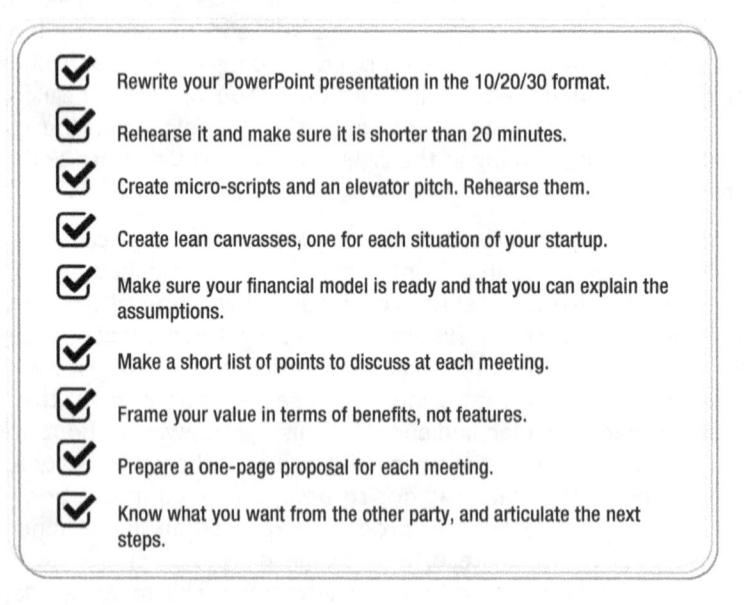

- ☑ Rewrite your PowerPoint presentation in the 10/20/30 format.
- ☑ Rehearse it and make sure it is shorter than 20 minutes.
- ☑ Create micro-scripts and an elevator pitch. Rehearse them.
- ☑ Create lean canvasses, one for each situation of your startup.
- ☑ Make sure your financial model is ready and that you can explain the assumptions.
- ☑ Make a short list of points to discuss at each meeting.
- ☑ Frame your value in terms of benefits, not features.
- ☑ Prepare a one-page proposal for each meeting.
- ☑ Know what you want from the other party, and articulate the next steps.

Figure 10-4. Checklist for communication skills

CHAPTER

11

Startup Grants: Can Government Programs Stimulate Entrepreneurship?

A discussion about startup entrepreneurship out of universities would be incomplete without touching on the subject of grant funding. Many first-time entrepreneurs believe the initial order of business is to get a grant. Obviously, entrepreneurs need to pay bills and have to eat, and product development requires capital. All this makes it necessary to spend some time writing a good proposal, then submit it, and hopefully impress a panel of experts enough to receive some money. This tides over the startup team for the early months while they labor in their lab on a better mousetrap. This is the mainstream view under which most people operate, because most have never started a business and see this adventure through the lens of the employee. Nobody would show up at their job if they were not paid, so why should the entrepreneur? A result of this thinking is that first-time entrepreneurs are often more concerned about paying for their health insurance than market-testing their product.

Chapter 11 | Startup Grants: Can Government Programs Stimulate Entrepreneurship?

This, unfortunately, is exactly the wrong approach to entrepreneurship. A fundamental misunderstand about funding and its usefulness lies at the heart of it. Startups need funding only when they have a validated product, ready to launch in the market. This is possible only when they have proof that enough people need this product and are ready and willing to pay for it—after they have repeatedly tested their ideas directly in the market, confirmed their approach and business model, and have done much soul-searching about whether they have the willpower to see their startup through. When a startup stands ready to launch a validated product, that's when raising funds makes sense. The investment is necessary to scale up the startup and help produce its final product. Any money collected before then dilutes the focus of the startup and sets it off on the wrong trajectory.

Launching a startup has little to do with asking for permission from a panel or with sitting quietly at a desk, writing proposals and business plans. True game changers often go against the grain of what the mainstream accepts as normal and useful. How often have you read the story of a first-time author who sent a new book to 100 publishers who all thought it was not worth the paper it was printed on? The 101st publisher relented and accidentally ended up making a fortune when the book turned out to be an international bestseller. Similar stories abound, and it is the same with disruptive startups. They will never receive grant funding, and the public will rarely deem them worthwhile until they have launched and proven that their product or service is something that nobody is willing to live without.

Early Funding Can Be an Early Grave

In my opinion, early funding can be an early grave for a startup. It avoids all the inconvenient questions that build a foundation for success down the road. Startup founders should not ask themselves, "Where can I get $50,000?" but "Do I really *need* $50,000?" When the government makes startup grants available, this question is bypassed and drowned in months of concentrated grant-proposal and business-plan writing. This happens at universities that funnel their startups into the grant pipeline. Theoretical planning and scrambling for funding replace firsthand experience in the market. The startup must have an entrepreneurial fire that puts everything else in second place. If this is absent, then it will be very difficult to compete with those who have that fire burning in them, despite any amount of funding.

Grants make sense much later, after the entrepreneurs have undergone some soul-searching and idea testing and have launched a prototype of their product or service. Additional capital may even be unnecessary at that point, if the venture is already profitable or has found a joint venture partner.

During the initial unfunded startup stage, some founders learn that they lack what it takes to be a startup entrepreneur—they fail to launch a valuable product or stop much earlier than that. A grant would have just delayed the inevitable and would have wasted taxpayer money.

Network Effects and Other Government Programs

There are obviously ways in which a government can assist startups, other than grant funding. Undoubtedly, entrepreneurship benefits from network effects: if there are 20 other startups nearby, a new one benefits form existing infrastructure; support services such as lawyers and patent specialists; inexpensive co-work spaces; and other positive externalities. Such a setup depends on the entrepreneurial climate and the ease of conducting business in a country.

Government policy can help lower the boundary to entry for new startups by making incorporation simple and straightforward. The less bureaucracy and the fewer roadblocks exist, the better. The environment may even attract entrepreneurs from abroad. At this point, an entrepreneurial ecosystem may be in the making, from which additional network effects originate. The first step of introducing or removing a certain government policy may seem insignificant, but when it starts to take effect, change can occur rapidly.

Unfortunately, governments hardly have the best reputation for helping startups succeed. Author Josh Lerner lists the following examples of government policies that were meant to boost entrepreneurship but that went wrong[1]:

- When hurriedly rolling out the Small Business Investment Company program in the early 1960s, the U.S. Small Business Administration poured capital into hundreds of funds whose managers were incompetent or corrupt.

- The incubators in Australia's 1999 Building on Information Technology Strengths (BITS) program captured the principal share of the subsidies aimed toward entrepreneurs by forcing startups to buy their overpriced services.

- Malaysia opened a vast BioValley complex in 2005 with little consideration about whether there would be demand for the premises. BioValley became known as the "Valley of the Bio-Ghosts."

---

[1]Joshua Lerner, *Boulevard of Broken Dreams: Why Public Efforts to Boost Entrepreneurship and Venture Capital Have Failed, and What to Do About It* (Princeton: Princeton University Press, 2009).

- Britain's Labor and Conservative governments heavily subsidized and gave exclusive rights in the 1980s to the biotechnology firm Celltech, whose management team turned out to be inept at exploiting those resources.

- Norway wasted much of its oil wealth in the 1970s and 80s by propping up failing companies and funding new businesses that were badly planned by relatives of parliamentarians and bureaucrats.

Money Cannot Buy Entrepreneurship

Grant funding is a great idea in theory, and it made some sense when it was much more expensive to start a company. With today's advances in IT and rapid prototyping, entrepreneurs can test their assumptions much more quickly without spending $50,000, $10,000, or even $5,000. This applies not just to Internet startups, but to any other project as well. Once they have proof that the market is ready to pay money for the technology, the startup is already up and running. If the market has no interest in a product, then there is no business, and the entrepreneurs have to decide whether they want to go back to the drawing board or abandon their venture. Money will hardly help entrepreneurs come up with fantastic new ideas, but internal drive will. Taking months to write business plans and grant proposals is time spent unwisely. It will chip away at the internal drive of otherwise motivated entrepreneurs.

When entrepreneurs are pushed down the grant track, they get the wrong impression of what startup entrepreneurship entails. As in a feudal society, this approach makes it seem as though entrepreneurship is an exercise in sending a proposal to an all-knowing entity who gives it the thumbs-up or -down. If the gatekeepers like what they see, startups may proceed. Otherwise, their ideas need further research. This is more akin to school than the reality of launching a company.

Furthermore, the silliest-sounding ideas are often the best ones. Those ideas are like the book that fell through 100 times before it became a bestseller. They have the power to become blockbusters, not the ones that everyone agrees on. Entrepreneurship is about taking matters into your own hands and staking a claim, regardless of what a bureaucrat or professor thinks.

Grants Crowd Out Investors and Advisors

At the 21st Singapore Economic Roundtable, organized by the Institute of Policy Studies and *The Business Times* in 2014, an angel investor raised the issue that grant funding made it harder for angel investors to invest in startups. He also argued that early support from the government enabled less-innovative companies to survive.[2] This investor brought up an issue that many others were aware of but hesitated to mention in the open. And its relevance is not limited to Singapore. The revolving door from incubator to incubator has created a situation where startups rely on the government to cover their overhead without coming up with innovative products.

Authors Paul Miller and Kirsten Bound make a comparable point: they suggest that startup accelerators may be more attractive for B-grade companies. In their opinion, if a business finds an accelerator or incubator attractive, it probably will be less successful than a company that does not need support.[3]

When startup entrepreneurs land early government grant funding, all their problems seem to have come to an end. They often stop seeking advice and keep working on their challenges with the logic they have always applied. Working with investors with extensive startup experience is the better choice. Their support goes beyond money and includes advice from seasoned experts in the field. This is useful, especially when things are not going smoothly; as the saying goes, "It's too late to make friends when you need them." Startups can benefit greatly from having experienced investors or entrepreneurs on their side, but they get crowded out by easily accessible grants.

But Startups Need Funding, Right?

How can we fund all these university startups, if not through grants? As already mentioned, funding makes sense only when a startup is ready to hit the market with a validated product. If the bar was higher for startups to collect grant money, much less of it would be necessary. Talented students and researchers would launch products and attract joint venture partners, and those with weak motivation to get their ventures off the ground would give up before they qualified for grants. Still, many startups collect grants as the first order of business, because such funding is often extremely easy to get.

Let's look at exactly what is being funded with all this government grant money. Is it groundbreaking technology that needs a large investment to get off the ground? Is it a drug with the potential to save millions of lives that requires expensive trials to get to market? Or a special device aimed at improving living conditions in developing countries that can only be produced inexpensively in huge amounts? None of the above. The lion's share of grant money goes toward the high salaries of startup entrepreneurs and the bills of external advisors and specialists. Conversely, high salaries and reliance on external specialists are outrages for private investors. When a startup raises seed-round

---

[2]Kelly Tay, "Government Grants Seen Crowding Out Angel Investors," *Business Times* (June 9, 2014).
[3]Paul Miller and Kirsten Bound, *The Startup Factories: The Rise of Accelerator Programmes to Support New Technology Ventures* (London: Nesta, 2011).

Chapter 11 | Startup Grants: Can Government Programs Stimulate Entrepreneurship?

funding in Silicon Valley, the salaries for the entrepreneurs should be zero or low; and they must be able to do the core work in-house, because they are the brains behind the operation. If entrepreneurs cannot do with little money, how can they reign in the finances of their startup?

I know an entrepreneur who received a grant of about $200,000 for his software startup. As they always do, the grant came with strings attached: for example, how much of the grant could be paid in salary to the founders. The entrepreneur's first and foremost concern was how to double his salary allotment through subterfuge. The next step was finding a foreign contractor who would do all the work for the remaining amount of the capital. Did taxpayers fund innovation with this grant? It all went toward someone's salary and a foreign programming firm. The product was derivative and untested in the marketplace, and it has not yet seen the light of day.

Sadly, early grant funding props up businesses that have not undergone a single test in the market. In most cases, considerable money and time are spent building a better mousetrap, only to find out that the market is largely oblivious to the expensive prototype. Taxpayers should see their money put to better use.

The issue is that researchers often approach startup entrepreneurship as an afterthought. This may be because they are unaware that a startup is an available choice early in their career. Or it may be that when their research project ends, they scramble for a way to stay on board and stumble on the possibility of a startup, which then becomes their lifesaver to stay at the university a little longer. Whatever the case, the motivation to become an entrepreneur should never be entitlement or complacency, but an unquenchable drive and desire to make an impact in the world with your ideas. If this is the case, then you will find a way to begin the startup process in your free time while still being on salary with the university, so no further capital is necessary. You can also leverage your research work and infrastructure directly into the startup, removing overhead costs for offices, a workshop, and materials. If your technology is patentable, then take advantage of the university's invention-disclosure process to pay for the patent. If you need a certain person's expertise, try to get them on your startup team as a co-founder. Before you know it, your startup costs will be close to zero. This is the true power of a university as a launch pad, not the availability of easy government grants. Make do with less. Recycle and leverage, instead of turning on the faucet and trying to fill a bucket that is full of holes.

CHAPTER 12

Venture Capital and Angel Investors

Students and researchers often misunderstand the function of investors, even if they have a business or finance background; they see them as a source of capital only. Entrepreneurs should consider investors in broader terms than that. Expertise, network, and influence are much more important than paying the next round of salaries. This chapter explains the most common sources of early-stage capital: venture capital firms and angel investors. It describes which other benefits these investors may have for startups and at what stage of development entrepreneurs should approach them (hint: much later than most people think).

Venture Capital

Venture capital is funding invested in startups and small companies with the goal of long-term capital appreciation. It bears high risk, but the promise of large returns in the future compensates for the possibility of total loss. When a venture capital firm invests in a startup, this often entails more than just money. Because venture capitalists (VCs) often have an entrepreneurial background themselves, they can provide worthwhile advice to startups—for example, about how to negotiate partnerships or how to scale the business when it achieves certain milestones. Strong networks with well-connected law firms and investment bankers add to the lure of venture capital.

Chapter 12 | Venture Capital and Angel Investors

This model of investment is nothing new. In fact, it has been around since the end of the World War II. In 1946, the first two venture capital firms were founded in America.[1] Yet it was not until the first dot.com boom in the 1990s that VCs made a foray into mainstream consciousness. Venture capital sounds very good in theory. But when I speak to startups with venture funding, a slightly different picture emerges. I often get the impression that there are two kinds of startups: those that desperately want venture capital, and those that want to get out of the deal they have with a venture capitalist. Let's discuss this in a little more detail.

Venture capital firms often visit universities to look for technology and early-stage startups to invest in. More often than not, they leave without writing a check. This is largely because VCs look for low-hanging fruit: investible start-ups with capable management teams and promise in attractive markets, in which they can buy equity relatively inexpensively. Most university startups are too early stage for VCs. They lack business models and financial models, and often they are still unsure themselves what exactly they will do and whether they even want to do it. Venture capital firms look for a relatively painless 10X return. Unless your company can make a credible case that high returns are on the horizon, VC funding will go elsewhere.

Students and researchers should understand what venture capitalists are looking for. Then they will be less disappointed when the next one turns up and leaves without investing. Startups can save a lot of time if they learn to first develop their businesses ideas without any outside funding. Then all the VC visits could take place later, when their contribution makes sense.

Venture capital is a fantastic tool when a startup company already has a proven business model and a product the market wants. Capital then serves as an accelerator to expand the business and help it grow rapidly. The goal of this expansion is achieving higher revenue in the market, which results in a higher value of the company and a higher payoff for the invested capital. The Holy Grail is an initial public offering (IPO), where VCs can sell their shares to the public with a high multiple. This is the ideal scenario. But unfortunately, things seldom turn out this way in the real world. When the business underperforms or the founders have no desire to go down the path the venture capitalist suggests, problems begin. The once-friendly VC turns into a micromanaging control freak. More often than not, the original founders lose control of their own company, and the venture capital firm installs a new CEO at the helm.

Contrary to public opinion, venture capitalists rarely invest their own money. Just like any other investment fund, they raise capital from private high-net-worth individuals (HNWIs) and institutional investors. A venture capitalist

---

[1]Spencer Ante, *Creative Capital: Georges Doriot and the Birth of Venture Capital* (Boston: Harvard Business School Press, 2008).

with a sound track record can raise several hundred million dollars this way, which the VC then divides over several portfolio investments. The few blockbusters in the portfolio more than compensate for the failed investments, or so the story goes. In the tech boom running up to 2000, venture activity increased at a pace that was unsustainable. Institutional and individual investors—attracted by the returns enjoyed by venture funds—poured money into the industry at unprecedented rates. Many venture capitalist firms staggered under the weight of capital. As always happens in boom times, groups that should have not raised capital garnered considerable funds.[2] We all know how it ended. After the boom came doom and many paper millionaires ended up with nothing.

The media only reports about the big winners in the venture game—the Googles, Facebooks, and Tesla Motors. This has imbued startup founders with the Hollywood version of venture capital. In reality, many small and medium funds implode and result in a total loss of investment. Successful portfolio companies usually go public with huge returns, so calculating a meaningful average return on investment (ROI) in venture capital funds is biased toward these rare blockbusters.

Looking at the actual numbers, venture capital returns have been less than stellar in the last decade. With selection-bias correction, the mean log return of venture capital during the first dot.com boom has been found to be about 7% with a -2% intercept and a standard deviation of close to 100%.[3] This and the fact that some entrepreneurs have expressed frustration with the management style of their venture capital firms have earned them the unflattering nickname "vulture capitalists."

Angel Investors

Angel investors have the reputation of being the better VCs: less greedy; less complicated when it comes to due diligence, deal terms, and checking on progress; and altogether more willing to open their wallets. In contrast to venture capitalists, they invest their own money in startups: usually smaller sums, around $50,000 for a seed investment. Some successful entrepreneurs become angels after they sold their first company. Celebrities may become angels. Wealthy local business people may become angels. They often do this to remain connected with young entrepreneurs for image or networking

---

[2] Joshua Lerner, *Boulevard of Broken Dreams: Why Public Efforts to Boost Entrepreneurship and Venture Capital Have Failed, and What to Do About It*, (Princeton: Princeton University Press, 2009), 41.
[3] John H. Cochrane, *The Risk and Return of Venture Capital* (Cambridge, MA: National Bureau of Economic Research, 2001). http://www.nber.org/papers/w8066?

Chapter 12 | Venture Capital and Angel Investors

purposes. Some also invest purely for the fun of it so they get to coach startups and help them avoid rookie mistakes. Angels would love to see a profit on their investment, but a large part of angel investing is giving back to society. Conversely, venture capital investing always aims at a financial payoff.

The link between angel networks and universities is weak. This may have something to do with the fact that university startups usually operate behind closed doors. Often they only enter the public light after they have collected grant funding. Because government grants are competing with seed investments, angels are being crowded out of the university startup game.[4] This is not the situation with independent startups, and angel investing thrives in innovation hubs all around the world. Angels are often very engaged with the startups they invest in. If they have relevant experience, they can be valuable, trusted advisors in the early and later stages of a company.

Most recipients of angel capital are first-time entrepreneurs with no proven track record. They have exhausted the FFF round (capital from friends, family, and fools), but the project is still too small to be interesting to venture capitalists. Tech hubs in the United States, such as San Francisco and Austin, have large angel networks that entrepreneurs can tap into to get a small amount of cash to start. Smaller angel networks are sprouting up all around the globe. This is an alternative to grant funding: less bureaucratic and with less time between the first meeting and the investment.

However, just as grant funding gives a false impression of what entrepreneurship is all about, so does early angel and venture capital. When you have raised your first investment round, it will look to the outside world as if you have already made it. This is a cool feeling, no doubt. But reality will catch up with you, because the funding removes constraints from your startup. Constraints on both time and capital (human and financial) are the lifeblood of innovation. They focus entrepreneurs on profitability early on and cut out all the fluff that is contributing little to the creation of a sustainable business. If you cannot achieve some level of profitability on your own without external funding, you may have to shut down the business and move on to the next idea. It's often as simple as that.

In a nutshell, entrepreneurs have to reach "Ramen profitability" before starting to fret about raising any outside capital. It is more comfortable to have funding than to work in a garage on a shoestring. But much more time will be available for the founders to work on their idea if they forget about raising capital. Dealing with a micromanaging investor can be a nightmare. Many profitable businesses you never heard of have been built without any funding.

---

[4] Kelly Tay, "Government Grants Seen Crowding Out Angel Investors," *Business Times* (June 9, 2014).

When you are just starting out on your entrepreneurial journey, stop thinking about venture and angel capital. Begin building a prototype today, and you will be in good company.

The Fallacy of Failing Fast

"Failing fast" is a paradigm loosely associated with the Lean Startup method.[5] I mention this here with venture capital and angel investment because you should have some reservations before wholeheartedly embracing the notion of failing fast. They are related to the fact that a failed startup is completely at odds with the expectations of investors.

The idea that entrepreneurs learn just as much from failures as from successes is nothing new. Failing fast stipulates that the sooner entrepreneurs get business failures under their belt, the better. This will lead to faster learning and better entrepreneurship in the future, so the reasoning goes. I can second this, because my failures have always yielded bigger lessons than my successes. Still, there exists a fundamental misunderstanding regarding failing fast. Embraced by a prominent Stanford professor in her creativity class, failing fast has become a means to justify when a startup has gone belly-up after its fleeting life. "Celebrate your failures, and move on to the next idea," is the way she puts it.[6]

The mindset of welcoming failure into your life is problematic. Suddenly, first-time entrepreneurs are urged to fail, as a means for them to graduate on their journey. If things in a startup become difficult, the first reaction is to fold the venture and celebrate, writing it off as a learning experience. However, here's something that I find to be an even better learning experience: pulling a startup from the brink and getting it back on track to turn a profit. This process may often be far from elegant, but investors prefer it any time. Folding a startup at the first sight of stormy weather may be fine in an *in vitro* school experiment, but the real world works differently.

For every investor in their right mind, failure is *not* an option. To frame the total loss of capital as collateral damage on the startup founder's learning path is not OK. If entrepreneurs like to celebrate their failing experiences on their own dime, that's fine. Unfortunately, all too often, investors or the tax payer end up paying the bill for the entrepreneur's education. Personally, I am wondering how failing fast can help create a sustainable track record of success and execution at universities. What looks like a failure at the beginning

---

[5]Eric Ries, *The Lean Startup: How Today's Entrepreneurs Use Continuous Innovation to Create Radically Successful Businesses* (New York: Crown Business, 2011).
[6]Tina L. Selig, *What I Wish I Knew When I Was 20: A Crash Course on Making Your Place in the World* (New York: HarperCollins, 2009).

occasionally ends up being a massive success, if the entrepreneur can weather the storm. But if failing fast is an available choice, entrepreneurs will never dig deep enough to eventually strike gold.

About half of my own projects went under, some of them with a bang. In one case, external capital suffered; but in most cases I hurt the most of all the participants involved. Pivoting the business model can sometimes help avert a calamity, but still, every time a project fails, I feel miserable.

When a failure occurs, you need to analyze it thoroughly. Once you understand what happened, you can step up a notch to take measures and be sure it will not happen again. Lifelong learning to succeed is the goal, not looking for experiences to fail fast.

Investors and angels should screen diligently for the fail-fast mindset. As a founder, better avoid writing it on your flag that you are looking for opportunities to fail fast, just because you picked up the term in a startup book. When you become an entrepreneur, it is time to grow up. You need to use your creativity to pivot business and revenue models until they work, and never give up before you have tried everything to avert disaster. If you play with other people's money, failure is not an option you can embrace under any circumstances—even if a professor from Stanford University tells you it's OK to do so.

CHAPTER 13

Incubators and Accelerators

Both incubators and accelerators provide startup aid in the form of advice and services. In comparison to venture capital firms, which focus on investment capital, incubators and accelerators house startups at their offices and are in daily contact with them about challenges at hand.

Both may have what they call an *intake*, which marks the term of a new batch of startups admitted to enter a program. These programs begin at certain times during the year, similar to university semesters. When a program has run its course, the startups are often shopped to first-round investors on a demo day.

Most people use the terms *incubator* and *accelerator* interchangeably, but there are some small distinctions between them. This chapter explores these modern forms of startup support and their usefulness for university entrepreneurs.

Incubators

In contrast to research and technology parks, which provide business infrastructure for established companies and government agencies, incubators firmly concentrate on companies in the startup stage. Many research and technology parks house incubation programs, but they are not incubators themselves. Incubators provide offices and other real estate, along with various business support services, to fledgling companies in a wide variety of fields. Resources provided include help with business basics; networking activities; help with accounting and financial management; access to bank loans, loan funds, and guarantee programs; links to strategic partners; access to angel investors or venture capital; advisory boards and mentors; intellectual property management; and more.

As author Linda Knoop mentions, about one-third of business incubation programs are sponsored by economic development organizations. Government entities (such as cities or counties) account for 21% of program sponsors. Another 20% are sponsored by academic institutions, including two- and four-year colleges, universities, and technical colleges. In the United States, most incubation programs are sponsored privately. About 25% of all incubation programs take equity in the companies they hatch. The others provide a service as nonprofits that they hope will create jobs, improve the community's entrepreneurial climate, or kick-start community revitalization.[1]

Unlike with many freely available business support programs, entrepreneurs who wish to enter a business incubation program must apply for admission. Acceptance criteria vary from program to program, but in general only those with feasible business ideas and a workable business plan may join.

Accelerators

Accelerators (also called *seed accelerators*) are comparable to incubators. A clear distinction between the two is seldom made, but you could say that accelerators are for-profit versions of incubators. They are also more common in the technology and software space. Authors Paul Miller and Kristen Bound identify the following criteria that distinguish accelerators from business incubators: the application process is open to all and competitive, they give a pre-seed investment in exchange for equity, the focus is on small teams rather than individual founders, support is time-limited (around 90 days), and cohorts or classes of startups exist rather than individual companies.[2] The business model of accelerators consists of producing venture-capital-style returns. The first seed accelerator was Y Combinator. Started in Cambridge, Massachusetts, it moved to Silicon Valley in 2005. In short succession, Techstars, located in Boulder, Colorado, followed in 2007. Seedcamp, calling London its home, opened its doors in 2008. There are now many incubators in startup hubs around the world, some of them with billions of dollars of funding on the backend. New startup hubs are seeing an increasing number of privately funded accelerators pop up. The accelerator model seems to work not only for the accelerators themselves, but also for startup entrepreneurs.

---

[1] Linda Knoop, *2006 State of the Business Incubation Industry* (National Business Incubation Agency [NBIA], 2008).
[2] Paul Miller and Kirsten Bound, *The Startup Factories: The Rise of Accelerator Programmes to Support New Technology Ventures* (London: Nesta, 2011).

One of the most established seed accelerators, Y Combinator, had an acceptance rate of around 2% in 2012.[3] The primary value for the entrepreneur consists of world-class mentoring, connections, and the recognition of being part of the accelerator. Gaining access to a high-powered network of entrepreneurs consisting of Y Combinator alumni and the who's who of the Silicon Valley billionaire club is clearly a huge advantage for startups. Famous examples out of Y Combinator include Dropbox and Airbnb.[4] The accelerator likes to describe itself as a "new college for entrepreneurs."[5] Such seed accelerators can be a pre-filtering mechanism for later-stage funding.

There may be an incubator or accelerator in your city. Someone from an accelerator may even have reached out to you and wants to find out whether you would consider joining them. Should you? Here are some things to consider.

Shortcomings of Accelerators

It is important to remember that accelerator programs are not free government programs, but for-profit operations that need to produce a return with the startups they seed. Prominent venture capital firms often fund them with massive backing. They are mostly focused on software and technology startups, and technology firms may support these programs because they see additional business for the startups using their technology. Facebook, for example, ran its own accelerator for a while to encourage startups to use its platform.

Because startup costs for software companies have shrunk in the past decade, with prices for server space and computing power rapidly racing to the bottom, software startups can be lifted off the ground with small investments. This is where accelerators shine. However, programs geared toward hardware startups—for example, in the field of robotics, material science, or transport technology—are relatively rare. If you are a tech startup, great; accelerators cater to your needs. But if you are a hardware startup, an accelerator may not work for you.

---

[3] Ryan Lawler, "With a 50% Increase in Applications, the Next Y Combinator Class Will Be 80 Strong," TechCrunch, May 22, 2012, http://techcrunch.com/2012/05/22/ycombinator-80-strong/.
[4] Y Combinator company list, www.yclist.com.
[5] Tomio Geron, "Top Startup Incubators and Accelerators: Y Combinator Tops with $7.8 Billion in Value," *Forbes*, April 30, 2012, www.forbes.com/sites/tomiogeron/2012/04/30/top-tech-incubators-as-ranked-by-forbes-y-combinator-tops-with-7-billion-in-value.

There are a few criticisms of accelerators, as Miller and Bound point out, both for the startups they seed and the investors who fund the programs[6]:

- They focus on smaller companies. It is highly unlikely that an accelerator could help build a Facebook or a Google. They concentrate on companies that already have a business model and that a bigger fish can buy soon after launch. Only then will the 10X or 100X gain the accelerator is looking for become reality.

- Useful companies may fail after accelerator programs. Because the program's support is brief, companies still have much to learn about how the actual market works. The hype around the accelerator program may dull their senses and lead to complacency about how hard it is to establish a successful business.

- Startup founders may feel exploited. Some startup entrepreneurs have publicly expressed anger about "rich guys starting a startup accelerator so they can rip off founders."[7] Some of the seed capital to startups exists in the form of loans that startups have to pay back—yet accelerators still demand an equity stake of around 7% in the company. This may be marginally acceptable when the value of the alumni network is significant and the accelerator's support is large. But if an inexperienced group has started an accelerator as a profit center, then the practice of demanding a high equity share for a small loan is questionable.

- Accelerators have a reputation for being more attractive for B-grade companies. This point is up for debate, but it can be argued that if a business finds an accelerator or incubator attractive, it probably will be less profitable than a company that needs no support.

- Accelerators are creating bubbles. Although many small companies are bought each year, the market for acquisitions is still only in the hundreds. If many more accelerators pop up and begin turning out new companies in the thousands, then a crisis of confidence in the sector may develop, because most of the new companies will go under. Accelerators subscribe to a "spray and pray" approach to

---

[6]Miller and Bound.
[7]"Let's Mug a Startup Founder," Treehouse Blog, May 10, 2011, http://blog.teamtreehouse.com/lets-mug-a-startup-founder.

investing, where they make many small investments in the hopes that the tide will lift all boats. Some investors have the opinion that targeted investments would be a better and more sustainable use of investors' money.

- Accelerators are just startup schools. Some see accelerators simply as a reaction to the defects of the university system in creating sustainable businesses out of their research. They doubt the benefit to the investors whose money is invested in the startups, because many founders see the accelerator track as an experience worth mentioning in their CV more than a serious try at building a business. This may undermine the ecosystem of accelerators in the long run, when sustainable success stories dry up.

Here is another damper for you: 93% of companies backed by Y Combinator fail, despite the best efforts of the accelerator and the entrepreneurs themselves.[8] The venture capital model focuses mainly on quick-turnaround equity funding. Scalability with the potential to monetize 100 million users relatively soon is also one of the cornerstones of tech accelerators. It is unclear whether this model makes sense for smaller-scale startups that need longer-term development, or for startups in non-tech fields.

Long story short: the incubator and accelerator model is promising. For tech startups, it is an alternative to going it alone. The alumni and founder networks of some accelerators are excellent and can help build synergies for founders early on. However, not all accelerators are created equal. The superstars may be valuable to their portfolio companies, but there are many second- and third-tier accelerators. These may have limited benefits for entrepreneurs past the usual advice and a little funding, in exchange for a large chunk of equity.

Can Universities Benefit from Accelerators?

Unless accelerators have a proven track record of success with strong networks that can provide real value, they may add little to what the university as a platform already has to offer its startups. Universities have many synergies available, most of which currently evaporate, unused. It is a matter of reactivating them and directing them toward adding value to the university's startups. I address approaches to achieve this in the second part of this book.

---

[8]Henry Blodget, "Dear Entrepreneurs: Here's How Bad Your Odds of Success Really Are," Business Insider, May 28, 2013, www.businessinsider.com/startup-odds-of-success-2013-5.

Chapter 13 | Incubators and Accelerators

As soon as accelerators have expanded their focus to sectors outside of tech, they may become interesting platforms for startup founders from university research labs. In either case, startup entrepreneurs should never rely on someone else to carry out their work. First and foremost, they need drive and an open mind. They need the right presentation and communication skills with which they can actively seek out synergies and potential industry partners to give them feedback about their processes and minimum viable products. As soon as they know how to develop their value propositions, engage third parties, and move interactions forward with goal-oriented next steps, they can begin building their own networks on the platform of the university. With the right mindset, a strong startup environment can add a lot of value. Without it, even the perfect ecosystem will only make a small difference.

CHAPTER 14

Moving Past the Startup Stage

The prospect of having to micromanage their company's taxes, accounting, payroll, and sales calls and handle all the other unpleasant byproducts of entrepreneurship is often a turnoff for students and researchers. Whether they are good multitaskers is another question. A world-class entrepreneur should not waste time filling out a tax return that an accountant could complete for $100. But to reach the point that you can delegate all the support tasks, you need to understand what it takes. The first stages of entrepreneurship are yours and yours alone. Doing everything in the beginning does not mean things will always be that way. It is important to realize that your venture will graduate from bootstrapping and MVP testing mode at some point. In order to be a business, it must eventually launch a final product and take off.

I have discussed the most important three analytical tools in your startup toolkit: the lean canvas, the financial model, and the one-page proposal. You have learned many approaches that can help you leave the building and get real feedback about your product. You know how to incrementally develop products the market wants, using "build, measure, learn." And you have become acquainted with several techniques to engage others with next steps and improve communications so they see a benefit in what you offer. Your startup may be in MVP testing mode or may have launched products. You may be bootstrapping, or you may have made sales. In any case, you have taken the first steps and are now an entrepreneur. That's the most important thing, and

I applaud you for following through. You cannot skip the first stages of startup entrepreneurship discussed in this book so far. They lay the foundation for everything that follows.

After being a startup entrepreneur for a while, you understand what it takes. There will be a time when you are ready to pull the trigger and move past the startup stage. Then you can decide if you want to continue running the business yourself. Perhaps you have found your entrepreneurial stride and are fully comfortable managing your company from here forward. This is an exciting endeavor, and when your startup has taken off, the hardest part is often behind you.

Alternatively, you may begin to look for synergies from the outside. Once you have tested various MVPs and confirmed your value and your growth hypotheses, you have armed yourself with enough knowledge to engage a joint venture partner or raise capital from a venture capital firm. If you do, you will no longer be responsible for everything and will integrate an established company in your operations. This is a viable option that could help you tap into a larger network and scale your operations.

The legalities of entering a joint venture deal or signing a term sheet with a venture capital firm are complex, and other sources discuss them at length. This chapter gives you an overview of what to expect when going down either path.

Seeking a Joint Venture

Small and medium enterprises (SMEs) and multinational companies may approach universities for collaborations with research projects. These collaborations are often limited, with a knowledge transfer in favor of the company. Because most universities are far from being startup hubs, companies cannot be blamed for that. Startups that currently launch out of universities have little traction in the market and little conviction about their business models and future direction. Naturally, they cannot make many demands on industrial partners. As a result, they frame discussions with established companies not as being about real joint ventures between startups and industry, but rather as being about sponsored research partnerships.

R&D can be costly for companies, but by sponsoring research teams and tapping the knowledge of a university, they can save millions of dollars. With more and more university startups on the horizon, the focus of such partnerships is beginning to shift. Students and researchers have more strategies available to develop products that satisfy a genuine need in the market. When market testing shows that enough people are willing to pay for their products, university startups are standing on stronger footing. They are viable companies, often with existing revenue and a sizable present value. This opens the gateway to an entirely new value proposition: instead of a collaboration between a company and a university research team, a joint venture is a collaboration between two companies. The expectation is a two-way knowledge exchange where the startup entrepreneurs learn as much about doing business as the joint venture partner learns about technology—a win-win situation for both parties. University startups should begin to lead the discussion in this different light.

Unless someone on your team is a natural born manager, I recommend you look for a joint venture partner around the time when you are ready to launch your final product. There is of course no surefire way to land the joint venture of your dreams. The only certain thing is that the collaboration should benefit both parties. After you have validated your value and growth hypotheses, you will be in a good position to approach potential joint venture partners. You may already be in contact with companies that service the same market as you. Investigate whether they can bring synergies to your venture: scale, better distribution, or access to better manufacturing technology. At the same time, the feedback from your MVP tests, along with your financial model, should make the case that your company is a decent business worth considering as an investment. You may still have no revenue, but if your final product and outlook are a match for them, joint venture partners may want to collaborate with you.

You will rarely convince a joint venture partner with numbers and logic alone. Chemistry and mutual trust are often more important than anything else. Unless your company already makes millions of dollars a year, you should look for a joint venture partner who likes and appreciates your team, your history, and your effort. If you have developed a product with MVP testing and have validated your hypotheses, this entrepreneurial achievement may be the deciding factor that causes a company to partner with your startup instead of another one that is still deliberating how to get started.

SMEs can be very good joint venture partners. The founders of these companies are often still at the helm as CEO, so they may sympathize with young entrepreneurs who have made something out of nothing. Conversely, in a multinational, daily business is dictated by shareholder demands. In such top-down bureaucracies, the human factor is less prevalent; thus it may be more difficult to start a discussion with a partner who is a giant in a market.

Let's say you identify a few potential joint venture partners. How do you approach them and open the discussion? As you may have guessed, you apply the same communication tools you used to get your startup off the ground. The world has not changed much in the meantime. Third parties still want to see the benefits of your product; they want to know how those benefits relate to solving their current challenges, and you must engage them with actionable next steps.

Show them the test results from your MVP testing and your incremental product development. Introduce the final product that you determined is desired by the market. Your lean canvas should summarize how this relates to the potential joint venture partner. The assumptions behind your financial model will open the discussion about pricing and cost structure. Then move the discussion along with one-page proposals. This involves several steps, with the ultimate goal of selling shares of your startup to the joint venture partner and becoming part of their network.

A joint venture is simply an offer to another businessperson that they see as valuable. You should already have learned how to do that several times over in this book. The exact structure and terms of your joint venture is outside the scope of what we are discussing here. When you reach the point that negotiations and legal agreements enter the picture, I recommend you work with your lawyer.

Raising Venture Capital

I have previously talked about venture capitalists and how they can help your startup with capital and expertise. Although I said that early venture funding may be a disadvantage for a first-time entrepreneur, it can make sense when a company has developed far enough to launch a final product. This product should have solid, confirmed market demand. Revenues are therefore on the horizon. With this value proposition, your startup becomes interesting for a venture capital firm as an investment.

Before you sign the investment agreement with a VC, you should have a clear idea of what raising venture capital entails. Other books sufficiently explore the legal side of this. I will simply present an overview of the process of entering into business with an investment firm in case your startup chooses to go down that road. Note that this is a different proposition than passively meeting venture capitalists who approach your university. You will see later in this chapter that your active participation is paramount to identify the right venture capital firm.

Before reaching out to investors, develop a clear idea of what your company needs; only then can you scan the venture capital landscape and pick a firm that matches your vision. Do your own due diligence on these firms. There is a great variety out there, each with a distinct focus and track record. Study all the information you can find, and think about whether this firm can bring you value other than money alone. Firms that randomly approach your university most likely will not make that shortlist.

University Startups and Spin-Offs

Venture capitalists Brad Feld and Jason Mendelson give a good outline of the process of raising venture capital from the perspective of startup entrepreneurs.[1] Their recommendations include some the points explained in the rest of this chapter.

Determine the Amount of Capital You Need

The amount of capital you need tells you which venture capital firms to approach. VCs specialize in terms of the stage they fund. A firm focused on later-stage funding will hardly consider a startup that incorporated yesterday, just as an early-stage fund will not invest in a company that aims to raise funds pre-IPO. A smaller firm or angel investor may seed amounts up to $500,000. If your startup is raising $10 million, then a larger VC firm will be a better partner.

Have a clear idea of the number you are aiming for. Never offer a range of, say, $4 million to $6 million. You must know whether you need $4 million or $6 million. Instead of letting the other party figure out what is best for you, work it out for yourself, and then confidently ask for it.

Have Your Fundraising Materials Ready

The materials you need include the following:

- Executive summary, compiled with the saying "less is more" in mind. Fit as much information as you possibly can on one page. Avoid any fluff. Fancy design is unnecessary.
- PowerPoint presentation in 10/20/30 format.
- Elevator pitch with your micro-scripts.
- Lean canvas. You may have several, according to different scenarios.
- Financial model. As I said before, more important than impressive numbers are the underlying assumptions of your financial model. Be able to explain how you arrived at the numbers in your model.

---

[1] Brad Feld and Jason Mendelson, *Venture Deals: Be Smarter Than Your lawyer and Venture Capitalist* (Hoboken, NJ: John Wiley & Sons, 2011).

Chapter 14 | Moving Past the Startup Stage

- Demo or prototype. This may be more important than all the other documents together. Even if it is still in early development, a demo shows the VC what you are working on. If you already have your final product, then bring that. If it is too big, bring a video, or invite the VC to your lab. Having a prototype available shows that you are serious with your startup and ready to move to the next stage.

- Due-diligence materials. When a venture capital firm is ready to sign a term sheet with you, it will ask for capitalization tables (how the shares of your company are distributed), contracts and material agreements, employment agreements, licensing agreements, board meeting minutes, and so on. You do not need them in the first meeting with a VC. Regardless, make it a point to assemble these materials early so you can easily access them when needed. You should never hide anything unpleasant, such as a current dispute or similar issues. It is better to bring those up right away and be clear in the future.

Despite what anyone else may advise, forget about writing a business plan. Most VCs have not read one in years. The same goes for what is called a *private placement memorandum* (PPC). This is necessary only when your negotiations have progressed significantly. Bringing one with you to the first meeting is overkill and will only raise red flags. A venture capitalist will most likely ask you to e-mail something first, so make sure your documents are light enough to be attachments.

Finding the Right VC

Hopefully by now you have a sizable network of fellow entrepreneurs in your city and beyond. Ask them about their experiences with VCs and which ones they recommend. It is much more powerful to be introduced by another entrepreneur who already knows the venture capital firm than to cold-call them. A good VC firm receives thousands of submissions per year. You need to cut through the clutter any way you can, and personal introductions go a long way.

Research the different firms on the Internet. Carefully study which other companies they have invested in. Examine their track record. Google whether there are any lawsuits against this venture capital firm or any of its partners. Just as VCs investigate your startup, you have the right to know what they are doing. Ask for a list of entrepreneurs the VC has worked with and startups it has funded. Call some of those startups and ask what their relationship with the venture firm was like. The best VCs will give you this list. If not, feel free to ask. If a firm balks at providing references, then ask yourself whether you want to work with an nontransparent partner.

As mentioned before, most VC firms will not sign an NDA with you. This is less alarming than it may seem. Reputable venture capitalists are busy and have no time to steal your ideas. You should have weeded out untrustworthy firms long ago with your own due diligence.

Of course, a meeting with a venture capital firm is no guarantee that it will invest in you. Even after prolonged due diligence, the firm may pass on the deal. This can happen directly or indirectly, when the VC simply stops returning your e-mails. If a firm turns you down, you should try to find out what happened and why it chose not to invest. This information is important for your path ahead. Persistently probe until you find out.

If everything goes well and both the VC and you feel that working together is in your mutual interest, a deal will come to pass. This stage is often split into two separate activities. Part one is signing the so-called *term sheet*, a document that outlines the final deal structure. As Feld and Mendelson explain, the most important aspects of the term sheet are *economics* and *control*. Economics relates to how the venture capital firm will share in profits, through either a sale of the company or an initial public offering (IPO). Control refers to how the VC can influence the direction of the company either directly or by vetoing certain decisions of the CEO.

Without going into more detail about joint ventures or raising venture capital, your startup is well on its way when you have reached this stage. Serious contact with established companies or investors will seldom take place early in the life of your startup. As you have seen, you must have validated assumptions about your product and your market before you can move on. You should have a clear picture of your business model and what your startup can provide to others. And, most important, you must have explored whether entrepreneurship is for you. As much as you may want to, these steps cannot be skipped. They are necessary to build a strong foundation for your startup.

PART

II

Strategies for Universities

Congratulations—you made it through the first part of this book. Maybe you are an entrepreneur, or perhaps you think about how your university could enable more startup success. Either way, you have seen by now what it means to launch a company out of a university. It may have surprised you that little theory is necessary for that purpose. That a startup has more to do with tinkering and incremental product development than careful grant-proposal writing may also have been news to you. With a fresh approach to communicate ideas, startups engage third parties with actionable next steps to build on synergies for their success. The most important part of the process is to begin and to collect individual experiences and feedback as soon as possible.

Just as launching a startup has a great deal to do with experimentation, so does setting up a startup track at a university. Think about the process of building the entrepreneurship program at your university as a startup in itself. You will need the very same skills to make it work.

Universities are magnets for smart people. Traditionally, they have educated students in specialized domains and critical thinking. However, graduates and researchers often struggle to apply their knowledge in their first job in the real world. All the way up to the doctorate level, they have acquired deep theoretical knowledge that makes them stand out. Entrepreneurial experience in their own startups can greatly improve their skill sets. In light of stricter requirements in the job market today, universities may want to think about extending their role. They can prepare graduates with the full spectrum of skills that help them become more successful, both in the workforce and in their own companies. Establishing a stronger foundation for entrepreneurship is an effective way to do so. The most important building blocks exist already; they are just waiting to be assembled.

Universities enjoy a privileged position. Governments, businesses, and other organizations love to collaborate with them, either on research projects or via in-house R&D. Academia provides a walled garden for acquiring knowledge and going about your affairs undisturbed. This safe-haven function should extend to launching startups as well. Building a bridge to the market and people outside of academia will expand the reach of university research. The motivation for launching a startup out of a university should be the desire to make a measurable impact on peoples' lives. Through the mechanism of the market, this is possible. It will allow promising technology to influence the lives of people where it matters most. Giving you a better understanding of what it takes to access this mechanism is the goal of this book.

To quote Peter Drucker, this means "if you want something new, you have to stop doing something old." There will be setbacks along the way. Experts inside and outside of your university will tell you with considerable authority how you should set up your startup program. Some people may fear for their jobs. Others may feel threatened by the new wind that is suddenly blowing through the institution. Much confusion will ensue, and staying the course will require strong conviction. With persistence, you will eventually uncover an individual setup that works for your university. Set out on the path to find what works best for you with the mindset of an entrepreneur.

In the long run, universities need to integrate entrepreneurship one way or another. It will no longer suffice to *try* to launch startups. Success must be measurable. When that time comes, it will be too late for some institutions, and they will miss the boat. If this is not the fate you have in mind for your university, then please read on. The suggestions in this part of the book may stimulate your thinking along the path of introducing entrepreneurship at both the degree level and the research level. Some of the things I suggest may already be in place at your university. Others may seem too simplistic, too cumbersome, impractical, unrealistic, or not feasible. Remember, this part of the book is a collection of thoughts to keep the dialogue going about university entrepreneurship. There is no definitive answer of how to do it. One thing is certain, though: doing nothing will never enable more startup success.

Many universities already have some startups and talk about the numerous spin-offs that have launched out of their institution in the past. They may have an entrepreneurship class and refer to grant X and startup program Y, which is supported by the government. But how is the success of these initiatives measured? By the number of students attending a specific program? By the number of startups collecting grant funding? Or by the number of startups registered as companies? Unfortunately, most of these metrics are *vanity metrics*. They may result in good-looking statistics, but the real impact disappoints. After all, does grant funding guarantee startup success? Of course not. Just *wanting* to be an entrepreneur hardly means you will have entrepreneurial success.

Despite their best efforts, most startups fail. Focusing on good-looking numbers may deliver satisfaction in the short run, but when attention shifts to the bottom line, things will get uncomfortable. How many customers have your startups reached? How much revenue have they earned in their first, second, and third year? I am not saying that universities and governments deliberately close their eyes to the real numbers behind their current startup support; but when it becomes common practice to show measurable impact, they will be forced to catch up fast.

Your university may have to achieve certain key performance indicators (KPIs), which is why you are reading this book. Or more researchers and students may be asking for advice for their startup ideas. Or it may interest you personally to make this complex property called *entrepreneurship* work. Just as in part 1, where we looked at strategies for startup entrepreneurs, part 2 collects approaches that have worked for other organizations when creating a favorable startup environment. These are not only universities, but also private organizations and corporations. When it comes to commercializing innovation, the private sector has a leg up on universities. We'll take a look at their playbook and see what we can borrow to power up university entrepreneurship.

As you may have guessed, the task of setting up a startup track and measuring its success hardly happens over night. If a change agent comes up with ideas that "break all the rules," the people responsible for things running smoothly may put up a defense. To avoid such a fate, it is often best to avoid proclaiming that you have all the answers. Prescribing sweeping reforms is the wrong way. Don't be the bull in the china shop. An entrepreneurship program needs to grow incrementally, just like a startup. With this in mind, the Lean Startup method can be used to set up the program in phases. Think in terms of minimum viable products: carry out a small change, test it, review it, and adapt it. Do this repeatedly, and you will achieve more than going for a home run right from the start.

Some of the ideas in the following chapters come from the world of venture capital, and some from corporate R&D. Universities use some of them today, whereas others are new to academia. Wherever you are on the path of integrating more entrepreneurship in your institution, I encourage you to keep an open mind.

Should Universities Care About Startup Success?

Historically, most universities had little motivation to compete in the market, and by their own admission, they still are not all that interested in the commercial success of their research. There is no urgency to change, at least in universities with access to ample state funding. Framing the startup debate purely in terms of money ignores the fact that more than profit encourages founders to launch companies. Real-world impact beyond academia is equally important for many entrepreneurs. If a technology can make a difference, it should be available as a product or service. If it has the potential to save lives, then even more so.

Academic research often addresses pressing issues of developing countries that are in desperate need of innovative solutions. However, when a PhD or postdoc program ends, research teams disband and their intellectual property evaporates. In the best case, the university has patented their technology and makes it available for licensing through the technology licensing office (TLO). Universities' passive approach toward commercialization leaves it up to the private sector to find the proverbial needle in a haystack, so most academic research has a small impact and therefore no relevance to most people outside universities. Framing the discussion about startups purely in commercial terms therefore misses the point.

When stepping off the well-trodden path, universities often fear that startup initiatives may pose a risk to the institutions' good reputation if they fail. Will universities become the subject of ridicule if it turns out they promised too much with their entrepreneurship initiatives? Will their reputation suffer if they launch a startup program that fails to bring forth the next Mark Zuckerberg? To make matters worse, unexpected success brings its own problems, because high market returns can cannibalize a university's government funding. The budget should show a deficit at the end of the year to justify an increase the next year. Massive startup success is therefore disruptive to those with an interest in preserving the status quo. At the same time, university KPIs are beginning to demand a certain number of startups to justify research funds spent, which puts universities in a bind. They must find a compromise between incorporating more entrepreneurship and keeping their funding from the public sector as high as possible. In any event, universities have a lot of catching up to do with their startup initiatives. They are becoming more open to advice on how to set up startup programs and incorporate more entrepreneurship into their operations.

The amount of money sunk into research at universities is staggering, with some annual university budgets in the billions of dollars. In Europe, universities have traditionally relied on state funding almost exclusively and have had a tendency to look down on commercial ideas and efforts to commercialize their technology themselves. But their American counterparts have a long history of seeking links to the private sector and their own successful alumni and are therefore more entrepreneurial, with a track record as startup hubs. Modern Asian campuses are also more open to commercializing their research and seeking a return on investment, but they often lack the flat, democratic structure and independent critical thinking that help startups achieve momentum.

In addition, they are often more bureaucratic and risk-averse than other universities, despite their stated goals of aiming for high-impact commercialization and aggressive monetization of research. But again, their KPIs demand a certain number of startups or spin-off companies per year, so they need to satisfy their statistics one way or another.

It is important to reiterate that it is not the intention of this book to reform universities and the way they work now. I respect the current system and see its many benefits. Nevertheless, when presenting commercialization ideas to universities, I have heard statements like, "I think these are good ideas, but the board will never approve." And, "The university is not a hedge fund." As much as I understand these concerns, thinking about how university startups could launch in a better way is important. If more successful startups came out of universities, everyone would benefit. Their research can make a measurable impact on people's lives, and the university can gain new network effects in addition to those it already enjoys. It is in the best interest of universities to care about their startups and take the necessary steps to improve their chances at success.

CHAPTER 15

How Do Universities Measure the Impact of Their Research?

University startups have existed for a while, but it has become easier in recent years for students and researchers to launch a company. Startup grants, entrepreneurship programs, a drastic decrease in the cost of IT technology, and rapid prototyping beckon researchers to take the plunge into startup life. Students and researchers are beginning to take advantage of lean methods. I applaud this trend and think it paves the way for a promising future. At present, however, the startup initiatives of most universities still amount to little measurable impact in the market. How much relevance does university research have outside academia? How many university startups launch products and achieve profitability in the real world? Universities rarely collect impact-driven metrics, and it is still the revenue from patent licensing that validates a technology as a commercial success.

This overlooks a whole new breed of lean startups composed of fluid teams who never even think of patenting their ideas. Facebook launched out of a university dorm room but bypassed all existing infrastructure aimed at startup support. It licensed no technology, applied for no grant, and sought no permission. The environment of the university enabled the founders to test their ideas in the walled garden of Harvard University. Yet Facebook is hardly a poster child for the success story of a Harvard startup.

Author Melba Kurman recommends that universities update their performance metrics and include the following measures (among others)[1]:

- Ability to turn research into public benefit
- Impact on industry—that is, ability to add value to the industry
- Commercialization impact

Such upgraded metrics should paint a more realistic picture of how exactly research translates into public goods. Lord Kelvin sums up the entire debate: "When you can measure what you are speaking about, and express it in numbers, you know something about it; but when you cannot express it in numbers, your knowledge is of a meagre and unsatisfactory kind."[2]

Most research projects never have an effect on the taxpayers who funded them. They never attempt to solve the challenges they study in the developing countries where they could make a difference. This is a serious matter, and the managing directors of some university research centers have taken notice that the status quo of commercialization lacks measurable impact. The first step is to upgrade their metrics and get a clearer picture about where research projects stand on the impact scale. This will simplify the discussion in moving toward a more entrepreneurial ecosystem at universities.

Patents and Tech Transfer

Without talking about patents and technology transfer, a discussion of the impact of research would be incomplete. Traditionally, universities have thought in terms of patents to commercialize their research. After all, research is expensive, and there should be a means to recoup at least part of the cost. If a technology is patentable, the university hires an attorney to file for patent protection. The in-house technology transfer office (TTO) or technology licensing office (TLO)—both names are used interchangeably—licenses pending and granted

---

[1]Melba Kurman, *Tech Transfer 2.0* (Ithica, NY: Triple Helix Press, 2013), 103.
[2]Sir William Thompson (1st Baron Kelvin), *Popular Lectures and Addresses Vol. 1: Lecture on Electrical Units of Measurement* (London: Macmillan and Co., 1889), p. 73.

University Startups and Spin-Offs

patents to those who are interested. Protected intellectual property is accessible to industrial companies that can license the technology and integrate it in their product lines.

Alternatively, the research team that invented a patented technology gets a license from the university for its own use and ventures into business by itself. This model works for university entrepreneurs if they have the wherewithal to transform the technology into a real business. Because most academic spin-offs of the past centered on patents, the TLOs of many universities became the overseers of startup and entrepreneurship programs. And that is where the problems begin. Licensing is seldom the main issue with startups; rather, the issues are time to market and approaching the venture from a solid business standpoint. When the TLO is in charge of startups, entrepreneurial advice is often limited to workshops or theoretical support by the TLO staff or the business faculty. As a result, commercialization efforts fall short of expectations. Lack of mission of the TLO is the core problem. It is unclear what it means to achieve "effective university technology transfer."[3] As long as the TLO can make the point that they are within historical benchmarks, then any extra effort introduces risk into their daily business. The bar is set low at 1% of all patents ever finding a licensee, in the best case.[4] Leaving startup programs to those in charge of patents can be counterproductive. Filing a patent has little to do with innovation, let alone entrepreneurship.

Despite the fact that they cost money and perform poorly, universities are proud of their patent portfolios. The number of patents filed sometimes even stands in as a synonym for innovation. This appears to be a trend especially in Asia. For example, with the goal to declare Singapore the IP Hub of Asia,[5] the government of the city state pointed to the many patent filings by domestic universities. This seems to make the point for Singapore as hotbed for intellectual property, as long as nobody is asking about the amount of licensing revenue or the quality of the patents. The liberal approach taken by the intellectual property office in Singapore has led to rapid growth in the number of granted patents over the last ten years, including patents with little or no real merit.[6] Certain key performance indicators (KPIs) for universities and the government may check out, but it is doubtful that such portfolios will ever attract the interest of potential licensees. The patent revenue could be exactly zero—nobody knows for sure. Realizing the flaw of mistaking the number of

---

[3]*Ibid.*, 34.
[4]*Ibid.*, 46.
[5]IP Steering Committee, *Intellectual Property (IP) Hub Master Plan* (Intellectual Property Office of Singapore [IPOS], 2013).
[6]Lau Kok Keng, "S'pore's New IP Regime a Boost for Businesses," *The Business Times*, June 20, 2014, www.businesstimes.com.sg/premium/editorial-opinion/opinion/spores-new-ip-regime-boost-businesses-20140620.

patent filings for innovation, Singapore vowed to improve patent quality with a "positive grant" system at the beginning of 2014 that requires a positive, substantive examination report before a patent is granted.[7]

Singapore is no outlier when it comes to patents with low commercial value. Research shows that university patent portfolios are performing poorly. A report from the Brookings Institution makes recommendations for increasing support for startup formation but implies that most university TTOs are not self-supporting through patent-licensing income. As Brookings shows, universities spend most their licensing revenues rewarding inventors or funding new research, not supporting technology transfer.[8] An older study came to similar conclusions, arguing that most American research universities lose money on patenting and licensing technologies.[9] Almost 75% of universities in America and Canada with TTOs have difficulties to cover the costs of filing patents and their own operations with licensing revenue. About 15% barely break even, recouping less than 4% of university research spending, and an estimated 99% of patents never make any money.[10]

To boost their performance, TTOs often ask for additional funds. If only they had more funding, they could hire new staff who would undergo entrepreneurial training to coach students and researchers about launching a startup. I doubt this approach will solve the problem, because a larger bureaucracy will hardly spawn more entrepreneurial success. Only a mind shift can get the debate about university research's lack of impact out of its rut.

Open IP

Open IP promises to replace the drive to patent by making technology freely accessible. Under this notion, researchers immediately publish their findings and thereby release any intellectual property into the public domain. This so-called *bazaar approach*, a term borrowed from open source software development, should spawn more collaborations between industry and research teams and therefore hopefully improve market impact.[11] In the software world, open source has become a huge success. Some open source projects like Linux are competing head to head with industry giants.

---

[7]Ibid.
[8]Walter D. Valdivia, *University Start-Ups: Critical for Improving Technology Transfer* (Washington DC: Center for Technology Innovation at Brookings, 2013). http://www.brookings.edu/~/media/research/files/papers/2013/11/start-ups-tech-transfer-valdivia/valdivia_tech-transfer_v29_no-embargo.pdf
[9]Dianne Rahm, "Academic Perceptions of University-Firm Technology-Transfer," *Policy Studies Journal* 22, no. 2 (1994).
[10]Kurman, 46.
[11]Eric S. Raymond, *The Cathedral and the Bazaar: Musings on Linux and Open Source by an Accidental Revolutionary* (Cambridge, MA: O'Reilly, 1999).

University Startups and Spin-Offs

Whether open source has resulted in a larger impact by university research is up for debate. When universities talk about open IP, the term comes with strings attached. Ownership of projects is often unclear, with several research parties claiming that a certain technology was invented by their faculty.

If open IP were on the rise, then the number of patent filings per year should be decreasing. But the opposite is happening, both in industry and at universities. According to a report by the World Intellectual Property Organization (WIPO), international patent applications filed through the Patent Cooperation Treaty (PCT) have rebounded strongly since the global economic crisis. Growth in the number of filings has picked up by 5.7% in 2010, 11% in 2011, and 7.1% in 2012. The total number of filings made via the PCT system amounted to 195,308 in 2012, which is more than double the figure recorded in 2000.[12] Data from the U.S. National Research Foundation (NSF) shows the same trend. U.S. universities filed 18,163 patent applications in 2009, with a positive annual growth rate between 0.10% and 12.25% between 1999 and 2009 (see Figure 15-1).[13] This is hadly proof of fewer patents, nor is it a case for open IP taking off on a large scale. There is no evidence that this trend will reverse in the coming years.

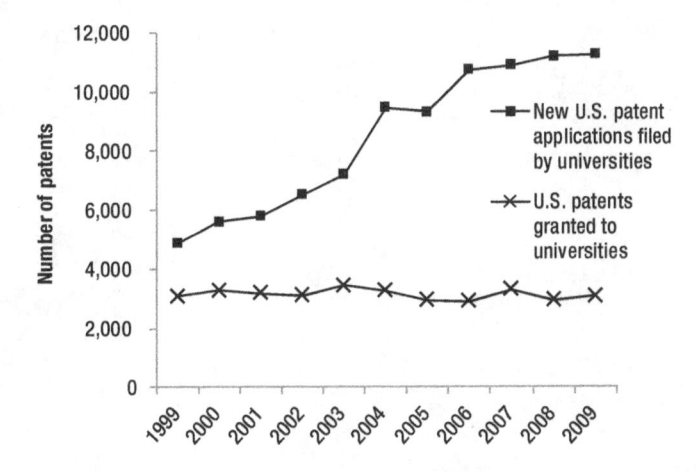

Figure 15-1. Number of university patents filed (data source: U.S. National Research Foundation)

Open IP is a noble idea in theory, but many universities are less open with their intellectual property than they could be.

---

[12]World Intellectual Property Organization (WIPO), *World Intellectual Property Indicators – 2013 Edition* (Geneva, Switzerland: WIPO, 2013), www.wipo.int/ipstats/en/wipi/.
[13]National Science Board, *Science and Engineering Indicators 2012: Patent-Related Activities and Income* (Arlington, VA: National Science Foundation, 2012), www.nsf.gov/statistics/seind12/c5/c5s4.htm#s5.

CHAPTER

16

Why Are University Startups Not Taking Off?

This chapter looks at the gaps that exist in the entrepreneurial ecosystem, which we encountered in part 1 of this book. To overcome those gaps and improve the startup launch pad, both entrepreneurs and universities need to make a concerted effort. Dabbling in entrepreneurship will not work—you either do it or you don't. Dabbling always results in mediocrity, not only in entrepreneurship, but in everything you do in life.

A university may have startup initiatives in place. Grants and workshops about entrepreneurship may exist. The library may carry copies of *The Four Steps to the Epiphany*[1] and *The Lean Startup*.[2] business-plan competition and exchanges with the university's MBA program may be carried out to stimulate the entrepreneurial drive of students and researchers. Although these are all good

---

[1] Steven G. Blank, *The Four Steps to the Epiphany: Successful Strategies for Products That Win* (K&S Ranch, 2007).
[2] Eric Ries, *The Lean Startup* (Ne. York: Crown Publishing Group, 2011).

intentions, they do too little to actually make a startup successful. More firepower is required to get startups off the ground. With this I mean more than massive funding. Despite large government grants, most universities are still uncertain about how to build an ecosystem for entrepreneurship.

Thinking About Startups in Terms of Opportunity Cost

A good approach to think about startups is in terms of opportunity cost. What if technology keeps lingering in patent portfolios without ever making an impact. What will happen if universities fail to build the bridge to the business world? Cost is measured in terms of more than money. The loss of a much-needed public good or social change may be as painful as losing millions of dollars.

Because startups are beginning to make inroads in universities' key performance indicators, it is only a matter of time until someone looks at the impact of these startups. It will no longer be sufficient to have startups on paper that never gain any real traction. University research can be extremely valuable, but only if it is available as a product or service in the real world. Roadblocks to startup success result in great losses for humanity. Forgoing the opportunity to make an impact with its research and to foster a success story costs the university prestige and future funding.

Jumpstarting Knowledge Exchange

Most universities have only weak ties to established companies and multinational corporations. Hold on, you say. There is plenty of interaction between the business community and university research. Yes, companies do sponsor research modules and work directly with research scientists. This is a convenient practice for corporations to outsource their R&D and save money and human resources by hiring researchers inexpensively to do work for them. This results in maximum knowledge transfer to the corporation and zero knowledge transfer to the university about how business and entrepreneurship work. Hardly a prestigious arrangement for the university, if you look at it in this light.

Universities and their startups often set the bar too low regarding what they expect from corporate joint venture partners. They are often delighted that a multinational even talks with them. They ask for a small allowance to buy materials, a few months of overhead, and free use of certain machinery. Nonetheless, the multinational will save millions in R&D that it would otherwise have to spend. Universities overlook this part of the bargain. Such practices have created a strange dynamic between corporate partners and research teams—one that is unsustainable for startups in the long run. I believe it would be much more helpful for universities to engage with industry earlier and with the more targeted goal of forming genuine joint ventures with researchers. Not only would this create more of an entrepreneurial dynamic for the university's startup track, but it would also transfer valuable business skills from corporations to the startups. This two-way knowledge transfer is currently lacking. It may exist in short workshops, but rarely in true business interactions.

In a nutshell, the current environment in most universities fails to foster startup success. Ingredients that could make a real difference are missing. As a consequence, universities' current commercialization efforts fall short of expectations and promises. Entrepreneurship initiatives are well-intentioned, but they are far removed from the reality of how startups thrive. Startup entrepreneurs often have the wrong impression of what it is like to run their own company. They also have minimal incentives to make their startups work, because they can go back to the safe haven of the university and take on a paid position. Contemporary relationships with the business community are one-sided and tilted toward the benefit of corporations that let taxpayer-funded research teams do their R&D. As a consequence, close to zero university startups ever make an impact in the market. This is quite a dire summary, but there is hope on the horizon.

University research is very valuable. Countless inventions used today in the market originated from university research. But research institutions need to catch up with the new model of startups and entrepreneurship. In the last decade, there have been tectonic shifts in the practice of launching and running businesses. Advances in IT technology, automation, rapid prototyping, and digitization have made it easier to commercialize research right out of the university lab. Entrepreneurship is a skill that is becoming increasingly important. Students and researchers should learn this skill to compete on a global scale.

Universities are still on the vanguard of relevant research. They have noticed that they should include more entrepreneurial thinking in their structure, but they still need to find the right approach. Startups and universities should get used to the fact that they need to go all the way to make a measurable impact. A Ferrari without gas in the tank will not get you anywhere. Holding one more brainstorming session or inviting an expert for a morning workshop will barely move the needle. To have true success stories that can compete on a global scale, both startup entrepreneurs and universities must take extra steps beyond the obvious and beyond their current efforts. To bring about change, they must leave their comfort zones.

Stronger Entrepreneurship Networks

A peculiar trait of university entrepreneurs is that few of them know anyone who has launched a profitable startup. The same is true for universities, which are rarely in contact with experienced businesspeople or startup veterans. Yes, there are many business-plan competitions, but few of them ever result in profitable businesses that last beyond the semester. University startups therefore often have zero firsthand insight into what it means to start a company. They have nobody to turn to for hands-on advice.

Being in contact with experienced entrepreneurs would be most helpful to students and researchers. If they can tackle challenges together and actively work on their own startup process with a startup veteran, they can benefit greatly. The impact of such direct knowledge goes far beyond weekend workshops in business-plan writing. An entrepreneur-in-residence program (EIR), described in chapter 20, can be a step in this direction. Such a program requires planning and administration by the university and will not come to pass overnight. Until stronger networks and connections to entrepreneurs exist, students and researchers should know that they cannot rely on the university or the government to build connections for them. Once more, they have to learn how to do this themselves.

Hands-Off Approach

Noncompetitive thinking plagues not only universities but most large organizations. For employees who are going through the motions until 5:00 p.m. rolls around, entrepreneurship and learning have no mindshare. Most large organizations focus not on innovation but on continuing operation and efficiency.[3] They are on the declining end of the industry life cycle. A strategy to escape their certain downfall is to buy new companies with fresh ideas, who then help the aging giants reinvent their business model. Entrepreneurship and innovation rarely originate in these large institutions: they develop elsewhere and find their way into the existing framework through takeovers or joint ventures.[4]

Even though there may be voices in a university who speak for more entrepreneurship at all levels, initiatives that yield measurable impacts are far and few between. When the rubber hits the road, startups cannot launch passively with a hands-off approach. This applies to students, researchers, and university staff alike. In the startup game, competition has to enter the minds of those

---

[3]Vijay Govindarajan and Chris Trimble, *The Other Side of Innovation: Solving the Execution Challenge* (Boston: Harvard Business Press, 2010).
[4]Kathryn Rudie Harrigan and Michael E. Porter, "End-Game Strategies for Declining Industries," *Harvard Business Review* (July 1983).

who want to play. This is at odds with the present-day model of universities. They prefer to do the research, publish a paper, and then let someone else commercialize. This surrender is unfortunate and wastes the natural synergies that are waiting to empower university startups. With a more competitive approach to entrepreneurship, universities could learn to take advantage of all the energy that is right in front of them.

Limited Startup Expertise at Universities

Few people at a university or tech-transfer office have ever launched a company, so they cannot be blamed for not being startup experts. Yet they are the ones coaching and guiding entrepreneurs, firmly anchored in theory without applied experience. At the end of the year, the university may have achieved its key performance indicators of X startups or spin-off companies, but the impact in the real world still hovers around zero. All this reinforces the notion that entrepreneurship requires great effort and a huge body of knowledge to get right. The conclusion is often that somebody else should deal with it.

Roughly speaking, there are two schools of thought about entrepreneurship: that an MBA degree and advanced business skills are required to have a real shot, and that entrepreneurship is simple and requires little more than a 10-step program (or 20-step, depending on which book you read). Depending on which ideology your university subscribes to, it will either focus on theoretical knowledge and procedures that need to be followed, or it will take a laissez-faire approach. As you may expect, the reality lies somewhere in between. Startups require certain business skills that are not native to academic life. They should also be free of rules, processes, and theory, with enough room to experiment and explore which approach works best for them. Just like students and researchers, startup advisors at universities and the government should understand that entrepreneurship is first and foremost a mindset. A startup can succeed with no theory but the right attitude. If a team lacks motivation and an open mind, the best advice and coaching will fall on infertile ground.

Most researchers I work with are passionate about their plans but lack the entrepreneurial mindset and the tools that only first-hand experience can bring. Because they were researchers their whole life up to this point, they often lack the know-how to take their ideas from the lab to the market. To make matters worse, university startups are often given the run-around by a system designed by bureaucrats who are more concerned with statistics than startup success. Unnecessary politics and requirements for lengthy proposals to apply for this or that grant can break the creative flow of startups and sap their energy. This leaves them resorting to the path of least resistance: complying with the rules, one eye already on taking a teaching position when the venture inevitably tanks. Hardly a good place to start.

Instead of theory about entrepreneurship, passionate students and researchers interested in launching a startup need to learn first what it means to run a company, warts and all. Most workshops at universities focus a particular strategy, with too much focus on a single piece of the equation. Somebody may recount their own startup success story, using a specific approach. In this light, a startup seems like a fun ride that students and researchers are anxious to try right after the workshop. But the entire picture is often missing. Inevitably, they get stuck because they lack the know-how to proceed after the initial enthusiasm has worn off.

Startups Defy Standardization

There is no all-purpose approach to launch successful startups. Just as their technology, products, and business models are all unique, the personalities and tempers of their founding teams are diverse. And that is good: otherwise, entrepreneurship would no longer be innovative. Trying to press all startups into the same cookie-cutter schema may homogenize them and make them easier to manage, but it will do little for their success. Unfortunately, the best entrepreneurs are put off by the bureaucracy of a standardized system and may give up if it is the only way to launch a startup at their university. Entrepreneurship is an individual affair. It goes against the grain of any standardized process that a university or government puts in place for startups. More important than fixed procedures is the freedom to experiment. There must be room for this freedom in one form or another, to let entrepreneurs find their stride.

Many universities *say* they want to advance their startups, create a more entrepreneurial culture, and enable their students and researchers with the know-how to start a spin-off company from their research assignments. Putting these words into practice is often another story, and doing so is much more complex than the university imagined when it made the commitment. Entrepreneurship is not a neat thing that can be put in a box, which results in confusion and frustration for many students and researchers who give it a shot. When the startup team has had enough of their lack of success, they throw in the towel, return to their research positions, and chalk up the experience as an interesting experiment. At least they *tried*, they rationalize. Grand Maste. Yoda once more has the perfect answer: "Do. Or do not. There is no try."[5] However, *what* exactly to do is the question, and there are no standard answers.

What worked for this startup may not work for that startup. What was gospel yesterday may find itself in the garbage bin today, only to reemerge tomorrow. The one thing that stays consistent is that entrepreneurs need the

---

[5] *Star Wars Episode V: The Empire Strikes Back*, directed by Irvin Kershner (1980).

right attitude to achieve success. Setbacks are unavoidable, and entrepreneurs need to be able to face them effectively. A simple set of techniques that help develop a marketable idea quickly and incrementally is the starting point. From there on, startups have a real chance to get feedback in the market and engage with others. By writing their own manual, they find out how to bridge the gap between being a student or researcher and a startup entrepreneur. Then can they decide whether this journey is something they wish to embark on.

Entrepreneurship as a Job

The tenure track is less appealing than it used to be for many researchers. Lifetime positions at universities have become rarer, and the lure of excitement at a startup has caused many PhDs and postdocs to think about the road to entrepreneurship.

If your research finds a solution to a pressing problem that enough people struggle with, the university is the ideal springboard for a startup. It is far harder to launch on your own. Imagine if you had to reproduce all the infrastructure made available by your university: an air-conditioned office, a working high-speed Internet connection, a print room, IT, tech support, expensive machines and tools, workshops, and so forth. On your own, the cost of this infrastructure would quickly amount to thousands, if not tens of thousands, of dollars per month. But most important, universities provide other benefits for startups. They are platforms on which different parties come together, including governments, intergovernmental organizations, NGOs, the business community, and the financial sector. All this can help startups succeed, given the right approach. None of it is available to startups outside of universities. You should seize this huge advantage if you can.

However, there is a flip side to the wealth of resources readily available for startups at universities. Researchers sometimes see a startup as a convenient way to extend their university assignment, without having a genuine interest in making their company work. They take the lottery approach to entrepreneurship: writing a business plan, applying for a government grant, and hoping they win. When they do, they breathe a sigh of relief because their salary and overhead at the university are secure for a few more months. They dabble in entrepreneurship, in effect doing the same work they were already doing on their research assignment. Despite their lack of a sellable product, they hope to hit the jackpot when a venture capitalist or joint venture partner comes along and invests millions of dollars in them.

This approach has little to do with the reality of successful entrepreneurship. At the root of it, once more, is a false notion of what a startup is and how it comes about. As long as this thinking prevails, university startups will struggle to achieve results in the real world. Because universities are comfortable environments, they indirectly encourage researchers to take the lottery approach to entrepreneurship. If they hit the jackpot, great. If they don't, nothing changes. Most of these startups inevitably fail. Unfortunately, the verdict is often that these failures are the result of insufficient funding for startups. In reality, the opposite is true: *too much* funding exists, providing life support for students and researchers who lack the motivation to make their startups succeed.

Launching a startup and a job at a university are two different animals. Entrepreneurs and employees have completely different motivations, expectations, and schedules. Students and researchers should understand this as early as possible. Otherwise, they might confuse a startup with a paid position at a university.

CHAPTER 17

How Universities Can Support Their Startups Today

Many universities are adventurous when it comes to research and new technology in a lab setting. But when the conversation turns to commercializing this research, academics often remain on the sidelines. There is still a chasm between academia, the business community, and the financial world. However, many decision-makers at universities I had the pleasure working welcome new ideas for entrepreneurship and commercialization. They have shown great interest and support, and I wish to thank them for their openness.

Clearly, no institution of higher learning can or should reform overnight and become a business school or an investment bank. Suggesting sweeping changes will therefore fall on dumb ears and will be more counterproductive than anything else. It's better to focus first on a few simple guidelines that can make it easier for new startups to embark on the entrepreneurial path. I discuss some of these in this second part of the book. All of them require active participation by the startups. If a team lacks genuine interest in learning about practical entrepreneurship, then it will be very difficult to help them succeed. Let's therefore assume that all entrepreneurs are keen to learn and are hell-bent on making their startup work.

Give Guidelines, but Don't Micromanage

Universities should stop treating their startups with a one-size-fits-all approach. As this book explored earlier, universities should refrain from forcing entrepreneurs down the grant track as the first order of business. Writing lengthy documentation, proposals, or, even worse, business plans make little sense for startup entrepreneurs. Universities should let them experiment without doing much planning. Just as the grant track paints a false picture in young entrepreneurs' minds of what it means to launch a startup, so do micromanagement and over protectiveness. All parents must at some point let their children make mistakes on their own. This process may be hard for advisors and professors who have been working closely with students and researchers, but it is essential for a startup to collect personal experiences in the real world. Without the opportunity to fail from time to time, startups will never learn to fly.

Universities can clear roadblocks and make resources available. This can enable students to develop their startups without hassles and help them to take the first steps towards entrepreneurship. They will have the best chance to succeed if non-entrepreneurial duties burden them as little as possible. Testing minimum viable products, putting together business models and financial plans, and engaging non-academics with potential partnerships are quite different tasks from the daily business of other academics. Make sure startups can do their work uninterrupted, at least part of the time. Research team members may still have other important roles to perform at the university, such as finishing their PhD or postdoc, and the team may be pursuing entrepreneurship on their own schedule. In this case, see that they fulfill their duties, and then let them run.

A startup mentor may also help set up certain guidelines to help the university understand what startup entrepreneurship entails over the first few months. Most faculty will be just as confused as the founders.

Mentors vs. Workshops

At a university I worked with, several students and researchers had the opportunity to attend workshops on Lean Startup and business modeling, one of which was conducted by author Alex Osterwalder, who invented the Business Model Canvas.[1] That weekend workshop was exciting; but the results for the individual startups were mixed, as I learned in one of my follow-up consulting sessions. The participants' PowerPoint presentations were less academic and

---

[1]Alexander Osterwalder and Yves Pigneur, *Business Model Generation: A Handbook for Visionaries, Game Changers, and Challengers* (Hoboken, NJ: Wiley, 2010).

had been tuned up with more business speak. Nonetheless, fundamental insecurities about the journey ahead still prevailed. Teams were now aware that there was a thing called the "business model canvas," but few had completed one for their startup. Those who did were staring at a piece of paper that made certain statements about their company and their market, with no idea what to do next.

When learning about the Lean Startup method, several of its concepts are far from intuitive at first sight. The main issues have to do with the business model canvas and the minimum viable product (MVP). If you are unsure what these are, then look them up in Chapter 2, where they were introduced. But let's first go back to that workshop. Over the weekend, the startups learned about the need to collect feedback from the market about their product as soon as possible. In a consulting session the week after the workshop, I asked one of the teams, a software startup, about their next steps. They did not know how to respond. Using the business model canvas, they had completed several questions about their product, their potential market, and how to serve that market. However, the most important part was missing: the startup team was unaware that they should be making a test version of their software. How could they get any feedback from the market if they had nothing to test? A software startup without software is like a restaurant without food.

The team had always assumed that a large software firm would come along, start a joint venture with them, and then do the product testing and development on its own. They saw their strength in their sophisticated algorithm and therefore never bothered with a user interface for the software. But established companies are unlikely to flock to a startup with an invisible product and no feedback from potential users. Teams have to test their MVP to understand whether anyone in the market even wants what they produce. If they do, then the next question is whether consumers are ready to spend enough money so the startup can become profitable. With this first-hand intelligence, they can later approach a joint venture partner.

The software startup without software found itself stuck in a loop: they needed to get feedback from the market about their product, but to do that, they first needed a joint venture partner to help them make the product. And to attract a joint venture partner, they needed to get feedback from the market.

I am not trying to poke fun at these entrepreneurs. They are smart individuals. Analysis paralysis is common if you have been working on a project for a long time. Even though the solution may seem obvious in hindsight, a workshop rarely solves current challenges. It can therefore be advantageous to get the perspective of a mentor. This should be an entrepreneur who can offer a fresh look at things. The mentor can help the team solve challenges as they arise. If a seasoned entrepreneur is made available during a startup's initial stages, the difference can be like night and day.

Another team I worked with wanted to create language learning materials based on certain academic research. Under "key resoruces" in their business model canvas, they listed the need to raise six-digit funding to complete a line of several books and audio programs in different languages. They would then sell this material to schools and universities. They were struggling to raise the funding at the time I got involved. A few simple questions turned up major flaws in their approach. Did they ever test a lesson with potential clients? Did it make sense to roll out the entire product line at the same time? What about testing which languages would have the deepest market? Stuck with planning and brainstorming their product line, the startup had never thought about proof of concept with real market testing. They assumed they would first have to complete the entire product line to be a real company. "Build, measure, learn" is not a household concept, and it may take some time to get the hang of it. Having a qualified outsider available for advice can make all the difference between success and giving up.

When getting feedback from potential clients, you need to be creative. In my own startups, we sometimes made software mockups in Microsoft Excel, dressed up to look like a web site (more or less). Clicking a button (nothing more than a colored cell) linked to a new sheet in the workbook to simulate the next page. Mockups can be messy; they contain bugs and often have just a tiny set of the features. But putting a simple mockup of your idea in front of people should be the first order of business. Most of the time, these take less than 24 hours to produce and require zero funding. Endless deliberating about how to start leads nowhere—the most important thing is taking the first step as soon as possible.

Creating an overall atmosphere of entrepreneurship at a university is a laudable goal, but it often leaves would-be entrepreneurs without workable strategies to achieve success. Most university staff and faculty have never started their own venture and can therefore provide only limited guidance when a startup hits the ground running. Working with a mentor one-on-one on specific challenges is infinitely more helpful. This will hardly break the bank of the university, but the benefits for the startups will be more powerful than the best business model workshop.

Integrate Startups in Management Activities

University research teams and management staff exist in parallel worlds. Startups can benefit from taking part in the everyday fabric of university life. Managing a university involves many activities in which startups could share. No sweeping changes are necessary; simply thinking of entrepreneurial students and researchers when planning events and receptions. Suppose there is a conference in town where the university has a booth. How about offering some space to startup entrepreneurs to conduct further MVP testing, interview prospects, and get feedback about their business models? Startups can profit from leaving the building to see how a tradeshow works. Make it known when such events take place, and give students and researchers the opportunity to take part.

Instead of giving visitors a general tour of the facilities, propose that they drop in on one of the startup labs that is showcasing an experiment with an MVP. When the government comes by, ask startups to pitch instead of having a professor give a lecture. Many possibilities exist to integrate startups in the everyday hustle and bustle of the university management and support.

Startup entrepreneurs can volunteer to guide certain visitors around the facility, all the while getting feedback about the problems they are working on. Because startups are learning to shift the discussion from features to benefits, every chance to reach out to test subjects can be used as practice to engage them for feedback. This creates knowledge about potential partners and clients that will move the startups further along with their business models and market studies.

Enable Industry Networking

Entrepreneurs must try to leverage everything at the university for their benefit. If your university is a certain size, it may take part in a conference or technology fair. Many small and medium enterprises (SMEs) and multinationals also attend these events. They provide an ideal platform for startups to network with potential clients, future joint venture partners, investors, and competitors right on the battlefield. Teams can collect business cards and begin a list of e-mail addresses and phone numbers that they can use in their evolution down the road. Startup entrepreneurs can never have too many contacts in their networks.

Attending university networking functions gets a new meaning for startups with a solid business model and the mindset of engaging others with actionable next steps. Because they have discovered the importance of a strong network, startup entrepreneurs know better than standing around with peers they already know, or wish they had never attended in the first place. They actively pitch their startup and engage contacts with actionable next steps. Luck favors the prepared: a single conversation or new contact can change the trajectory of a startup and give it a turbo boost.

This is all great, you may say, but our university rarely participates in such events. In this case, how can startups make more frequent contact with industry? One idea is to establish your own networking events. Hold on, you say; networking events we already have. Yes, companies may contact the university and tour the premises and labs to watch demonstrations and hear lectures about certain technologies. But are several companies ever invited together?

How about an entire sector? What about a full industry group or trade organization? Interaction may exist one-on-one, but this lacks the scale to enable a vivid exchange of ideas and true networking. The university could offer a platform to make that happen. It would also be interesting for companies to network with each other. How about reaching out to industry groups or trade organizations and inviting them for an afternoon of networking, with refreshments? Instead of lecturing them on research and technology, startup teams can ask their opinion of MVPs and market assumptions. They can use the networking event to gain as much intelligence as possible without having to leave the building. Rather than startups reaching out to companies on their own, bring companies to them once in a while.

Fail Smart and Collect Data

Of course, it is never fun to admit that an undertaking *failed*. Most people feel uncomfortable with the notion of failure. As a result, they frame all of their efforts as successes. Even if a team failed to achieve certain results, they learned something in the process—at least they *tried* to do something. Unfortunately, this mindset allows failure to become an accepted, everyday event. If you frame failures as successes, startups will lose their edge. If they think that burning through $250,000 in grant money without launching a product is OK, then they are on the wrong track from day one.

In retrospect, however, even such failures can provide valuable data for the university and startups that will follow. They should review failed startup together with the team and register their findings. How did the entrepreneurs attack the endeavor? How long were they at it? When did they declare defeat and wind down the company? How many MVPs did they test? How many potential joint venture partners did they engage? What did they ask from those potential partners? Did they launch a product in the market? And so on. Myriad questions are possible.

If a university has a startup track, it can gain insight by recording all the steps its startups take. This makes it easier to spot patterns. Then startups can be tracked and gently nudged toward taking reasonable actions when they become confused or veer off course.

What you cannot measure, you cannot improve. Having more data to mine will hardly make the university a new entrepreneurship hub over night. Even when droves of data exist, not every startup will succeed. There is no fail-safe procedure that ensures hundreds of millions of dollars in revenue within a few short years. But learning what contributes to startup failure will result in a helpful tool that makes your university's startup program smarter over time. It will take a while and several startups to arrive at a workable database. If failing smart sounds interesting to you, then you should begin collecting data as soon as possible. This may even become part of a course at a related business school.

CHAPTER

18

Building a Bridge to the Market

Currently, few links exist between universities and the business community. This makes sense, because both work differently. State-funded universities largely run as not-for-profit entities, whereas businesses with shareholders are at home in the capitalist paradigm. Regardless, universities often declare that they benefit from established links to the business community. These exist mainly in research, where corporations sponsor certain projects. However, when examined more closely, such connections do little for university start-ups—as I have mentioned, they are often nothing more than a convenient strategy for corporations to let researchers do their R&D inexpensively. Such links are not particularly valuable for universities, and the knowledge exchange is lopsided. Corporations extract know-how from university research teams, but universities gain no insight about how entrepreneurship works and how they could better commercialize research in the market. This is unfortunate, and some universities have begun to realize there is room for improvement.

Most important, it would be good if universities integrated market-oriented thinking in areas beyond the research level with their PhD and postdoc programs. On the degree level, know-how about applying academic research in the market is almost entirely missing.

The rest of this chapter presents some general assumptions about why a pivot toward more entrepreneurship may be difficult for some universities. I also offer recommendations about how to address these difficulties.

Focus on Small and Medium Enterprises (SMEs), Not Large Multinationals

Universities often try to attract large multinational corporations to sponsor research projects or collaborate in other ways. The corporations shoulder the financial risk by underwriting a part of the research. In reality, the amounts they contribute to these projects are small fry compared to their overall profits. Plus, large corporations are tax optimized, often reside in Switzerland, and pass most of the tax burden to their employees. If they hit upon a goldmine with a product developed in a joint research program, the windfall will rarely benefit the university or the researchers.

On the other hand, small and medium enterprises (SMEs) are the real drivers of economies. Companies with fewer than 99 employees are comparable to large firms in their contribution to aggregate employment.[1] They are important engines of job creation and GDP growth in developed and emerging markets.

Most universities treat SMEs as an afterthought. It is of course much more prestigious to announce joint projects with multinationals than with smaller, local companies, but this practice should change. If governments want to support the economy, they should give SMEs better access to universities: for example, in the form of tax breaks, guarantees, or risk sharing. Giving SMEs more access to inexpensive research would help make a larger impact in society. This could go hand in hand with establishing practices for a more balanced knowledge exchange that would actually help universities become more entrepreneurial.

Is the Current System Up to the Task?

Startups are inherently hands-on. Little know-how about rolling up one's sleeves and turning research into marketable products currently exists in universities. This makes universities less than ideal experts on the topic of entrepreneurship and stipulates the need for knowledge transfer from sources outside of academia. The market is by definition the battlefield on which entrepreneurship takes place. Why not tap into this source to glean some insight about how to commercialize innovation? Later, this chapter investigates how universities can build stronger bridges to the market to help their startups become more entrepreneurial and compete with businesses in the real world.

---

[1]Meghana Ayyagari, Asli Demirguc-Kunt, and Vojislav Maksimovic, "Small vs. Young Firms across the World: Contribution to Employment, Job Creation, and Growth," Policy Research Working Paper, *The World Bank*, April 2011, www-wds.worldbank.org/external/default/WDSContentServer/WDSP/IB/2012/11/06/000158349_20121106091157/Rendered/PDF/WPS5631.pdf.

Can universities reinvent themselves and suddenly become startup hubs? Most of them lack the capacity to reproduce Stanford University in Silicon Valley. Laying the foundation for successful startups will take a while. A cultural shift will need to take place, and this needs time and patience. Unfortunately, a mind shift is impossible while continuing to do more of the same—more grant funding, more lectures by MBAs, and more business plan competitions. These will be of little help in the long run. If universities want to promote startup success, they need a deeper understanding of how entrepreneurship comes into being: how they can enable it from the bottom up, not try to force it into existence from the top down.

Because universities need a radical paradigm shift, their current advisors may not be up to the task. Government officials are hardly startup entrepreneurs. Neither are MBA students, professors in economics and finance, or the technology licensing office (TLO). Considerable trust is placed in those with strong incentives to stick with the status quo. A fundamental mind shift must occur to put universities on the right track. The longer universities put off change, the harder it will be to bring about a course correction later.

Learning from the Market

A pivot toward entrepreneurship can be achieved better by learning by doing than by lecturing. To learn more about this field, universities need to build a stronger bridge to the market. Just as launching a startup is an experiment, universities need to test different approaches and find the ones that yield the best measurable results for them. They should do this by integrating applied business knowledge much earlier than in the research stage of academic education. If degree students have regular contact with market practitioners who have walked the walk and can tell war stories about their trials and tribulations, those students can gain considerable insight. When they reach the research level in their PhD or postdoc, they will already understand how the market works. This will be a huge advantage over those living in the ivory tower of academia who are exposed to business for the first time at age 35.

Universities should be concerned with empowering their students and researchers with the know-how to launch businesses in the twenty-first century. If they achieve that, many more university startups can make a difference in the lives of people who benefit from the innovative products the startups bring to the market. To make an impact, startups should gather this knowledge right at the source.

Industry Links

Entrepreneurial students and researchers profit in many ways from stronger links to industry. Universities should seek and welcome connections not only with large multinationals but also with SMEs. The latter may be appreciative and loyal partners for university startups, especially when a two-way information exchange takes place.

At present, university startups often feel that they have to go the entire distance alone. The founders take management and accounting courses and think about how to sell products and distribute them in the market. It is good to understand as many aspects of business as possible in the early stages of a startup. However, when entrepreneurs are ready to launch their final product, they need to focus their energy. They need a more effective way to manage the moving parts in their operations than doing everything by themselves.

Management and sales skills seldom come overnight, and it can be worthwhile for a startup to join forces with an established company to shoulder these tasks. Nowadays, a joint venture is often an afterthought for a university startup. If it exists, as you've seen, it is often an outsourced R&D lab of an industrial partner, who perhaps sponsors some equipment and materials and in return extracts the intellectual property the researchers create. Unfortunately, this arrangement will never allow startups to make a splash. They will remain small, tethered R&D labs forever.

Instead, startups should find a way to get joint-venture partners to form companies with them. This will take industry partners out of the pattern of seeing universities as a free technology platform from which they can cherry-pick the most promising morsels at a discount. When a company is part of a university startup earlier in the process, it can help create an entrepreneurial ecosystem from which the university's other startups can profit. Management, distribution, sales, support—all these functions will be part of the startup's daily business under the tutelage of an experienced joint-venture partner. He helps with recruiting operative personnel and support services, and from this link with professional managers, entrepreneurs gain knowledge about other fields of business that they never knew existed. Successful startups will maintain a connection with the university, and having joint ventures in the network will provide major future benefits.

Entrepreneur Alumni Networks

It is common for the founders of a successful company to exit it at some point to start a new firm. This is often the case in finance, where successful teams of managers work at a large investment fund for a few years and then split off to start their own fund. Technology and Internet firms are other examples where this occurs frequently. These accomplished founding entrepreneurs are often excellent partners for future startups launched from the university. Not only can they form a joint venture with new startups, but they may buy entire units and integrate them into new enterprises, which kick-starts an active knowledge exchange between the market and university startup entrepreneurs. Fostering entrepreneurial success and maintaining a link to alumni who have achieved it will enable network effects for the university's entire startup track. Universities should be open to harnessing this source of knowledge.

With this in mind, it becomes obvious that enabling entrepreneurial success at a university is a multigeneration task. It will rely on establishing a mechanism that launches startups, keeps strong links with the founders and joint-venture partners, and engages them in the future with attractive opportunities and applied research. Some universities may need to rethink some of their programs in this new light. If there is a choice between offering a PhD program that is doing research that is easy to commercialize and one that is not, which one should the university choose? This thinking is less relevant to universities today, but it may play a bigger role when a startup track is in place.

CHAPTER

19

Platform Thinking for Startup Success

The first part of this book explored what individual startups can do to improve their chances in the market: how they can communicate more effectively with outside partners, and how they can organize their business model and financial model around easy-to-understand principles with which they can engage others and kick-start synergies. So far, support from the university only includes providing a framework for startups with its existing infrastructure and occasional assistance such as hiring a startup coach.

There are also universities that want to take a more active role in entrepreneurship. They feel the technology they develop should have a bigger impact on people's lives, or they may be falling short on their key performance indicators (KPIs). They organize startup workshops with entrepreneurs and consultants, improve interaction with government agencies for technology transfer, and support their startups when applying for grants. They may even have a dedicated startup program with a financial matching scheme, where startup teams put money into their endeavors that someone else matches. These efforts are commendable. But there remains room for improvement, and by that I mean other things than adding more of the same. We need a mind shift to foster entrepreneurship from a fundamentally different angle at universities. This chapter explores what that could look like.

The strategies outlined so far in this book are bottom-up. They originate directly with startups, and the entrepreneurs do most of the work, plugging in to the university platform only occasionally. Currently, this is the way start-ups become successful. It is rarely the ones that play by the rules and run the length of the grant track that spin off into the market as self-sustaining entities. Rather, it is the mavericks that make the real impact.

Author Josh Lerner points out the link between innovation and growth. Innovation and new firms are strongly correlated, but public intervention to boost venture capital and innovation is largely ineffective.[1] This is a thorny issue. For a startup to succeed in the current system, it has to avoid taking part in public entrepreneurship initiatives. This may sound harsh, but it is frequently true. Few of the launch strategies discussed in this book are included in current support programs for startups. This does not have to be the case: universities could adapt to the new reality of lean models and guide their startups much earlier along that course. This part of the book addresses universities that want to apply more leverage of their existing platform to boost their startup initiatives.

Building Startup Platforms

Universities are platforms. Many diverse fields and opinions come together under one roof and mingle with each other in interdisciplinary research. An active exchange of ideas takes place between students and scientists of distinct faculties. Largely supported by the public sector, universities also interact with the government and its agencies, and even with intergovernmental organizations such as the World Bank and the Asian Development Bank. Occasionally, the business community sponsors events or holds job fairs at universities. Banks may finance research projects through university foundations. Many different stakeholders exchange ideas and energy with universities daily, creating vast potential resources that are sitting there, unused.

Platform thinking is an innovative approach to maximize these resources. Author Sangeet Paul Choudary contrasts this practice with two other paradigms that he calls the *stuff approach* and the *optimization approach*.[2] The stuff approach is the current practice of trying to solve a problem by doing more of the same. In the context of supporting university startups, this means more grants, more workshops, more business-plan competitions, and more technology licensing office (TLO) staff. You may already suspect that this will create some jobs and

---

[1] Josh Lerner, *Boulevard of Broken Dreams: Why Public Efforts to Boost Entrepreneurship and Venture Capital Have Failed, and What to Do About It* (Princeton: Princeton University Press, 2010).
[2] Sangeet Paul Choudary, "A Platform-Thinking Approach to Innovation," *Wired* (Jaunary 31, 2014), www.wired.com/2014/01/platform-thinking-approach-innovation.

increase the available budgets, but fail to deliver the results for startups that you are after in this book. Slightly better is the optimization approach, which adds algorithms to the equation. After collecting all available information, you match it with the needs of specific startup entrepreneurs. This avoids pushing them into a one-size-fits-all format, but addresses them individually with the contacts and information they need at a given time. This is an improvement, but it neglects the potential synergy effects that lie dormant at universities.

Enter platform thinking. It goes one step further beyond just collecting and matching the available assets: it creates more by tapping into synergies. When you apply leverage to all the activities and interactions of which universities are a part, a startup ecosystem emerges and grows, powered by network effects. Figures 1-1 and 1-2 in Chapter 1 show what the ideal university ecosystem and the startup launch pad in look like. On a strong platform, the whole is greater than the sum of its parts. This sounds intriguing, but how can you apply platform thinking at your university? This chapter examines some ideas and examples.

The Government Visit

Instead of addressing each stakeholder independently and catering to their individual agendas, universities can turn on network effects to help their startups. When a government agency visits, what does the university usually do? It rolls out the red carpet for the officials, who visit a certain lab where a professor makes a presentation about the research of his team on technology X. There may then be a lunch or Q&A about that technology with students and researchers. Photographers take some pictures. Perhaps there is even a TV crew. There may be a public commitment to funding this or that research in the future, and another commitment to working together on a certain challenge. Then the delegation leaves. The university is delighted that the government has shown some interest, but students and researchers hardly engaged the delegation at all. The visitors had a great field trip and are already looking forward to a similar excursion to another university next week.

I suspect that universities are often insecure when the government wishes to visit. This is the proverbial rich uncle who pays the bills, so they need to be on their best behavior. They breathe a sigh of relief when the visit is over, and the last thing on their mind is engaging the government more deeply regarding their platform. This is where a mind shift has to occur.

Let's say a university has five startups. The team working on technology X is the furthest advanced, but the other four are also promising. How about having all the startups hold short presentations for the delegation? You may object that the government agency expressly wanted to see technology X. Sure, that's what they *said* they wanted, because they were unaware of the other four startups. Why not take matters into your own hands and set a new agenda for the delegation? Show them something unexpected—something out of the box. Framing the visit as a demonstration of your startup track.

Governments love startups because they create jobs. Whenever someone takes that initiative in job creation, it looks good for the government to be part of it. The delegation will seldom get all the technical details in the presentation about technology X, nor will they take much interest in them. But they will definitely understand when you say that technology X could potentially provide 100 jobs in the next 2 years. Benefits trump features. If you have 5 startups, that may be 500 jobs in the next 2 years. Don't you think it would be possible to engage the government to a greater extent with the prospect of 500 additional high-profile jobs created by your startups?

Now suppose these startups address problems in environmental sustainability. Doesn't the government have to reach certain targets, perhaps related to Millennium Development Goals (MDGs)?[3] Let's say some of your startups are already leading joint-venture discussions with large multinationals. How about asking the delegation about public tenders for which these joint ventures could put in offers?

There are many other ways to engage the government in this particular example, but I will stop here. It is about switching from a passive stance to an active role where you engage external stakeholders and ask them to assist you. Media coverage of the visit will now be different. Instead of reporting the same old story of government officials visiting a research lab, it will tell about your university potentially providing 500 new jobs with startups that address problems in environmental sustainability. That's free advertising, and it provides leverage for your startups to reach out to the private sector with a tailwind.

For this to be possible, your startups need to move up a gear or two. Teams need to be more to the point and use the 10/20/30 structure discussed in Chapter 10 for their presentations. They need to rehearse their pitches and presentations so they fit into 10 minutes. Somebody from the university must ensure that startups are up to speed and will not embarrass themselves or the university when it matters.

The logistics of such an event will be more challenging than the run-of-the-mill reception. You need to keep an eye on many more moving parts. You should provide press kits for each startup. Staff and startup founders must be sharp and presentable. As always, there is no quick fix to jump to the next level, but the effect of channeling attention away from single research projects onto your startup platform will be powerful in the long run.

---

[3]United Nations, *Millennium Development Goals and Beyond 2015*, www.un.org/millenniumgoals.

The Industry Visit

Visits from small and medium enterprises (SMEs) and multinational corporations are another great opportunity for startup initiatives. As we have seen, links to these companies may exist, but they are often rather uninspired. The knowledge transfer from the university to industry takes place through the technology transfer or licensing office (TTO or TLO), which makes patented technology available for licensees. Alternatively, a company may sponsor a research project and extract intellectual property this way. In both cases, knowledge flows out of the university into the private sector. Learning more about commercializing technology had little mindshare for universities in the past, but this should change when their goal is to build platforms for their startups.

Turning on knowledge transfer in the opposite direction can help university startups gain valuable insight and firsthand experience in how the market works. Joint ventures with industry partners are therefore desirable for startups. I mean *real* partnerships between established companies and startups, with the goal of launching products right in the market trenches. Few students and researchers are born managers, so joint ventures can provide scale to their operations in manufacturing and management.

Assume the following scenario: technology X has attracted interest from a multinational industry giant. The company would like to see the lab and the technology and may potentially sponsor further development or license the technology for the company's own manufacturing processes. The research team happily obliges and shows the industry representatives around the lab. They present their work and speak about what they have done so far and the many problems they still need to solve. They compare their technology with others already on the market and announce that theirs will be greatly superior when it is ready for commercial application in five to ten years. They also mention that they will need additional funding soon to move forward, on the order of hundreds of thousands of dollars. The team lead, Professor A, gives a presentation that spans 200 PowerPoint slides, skipping most of them with the remark that one hour is not enough time. In the Q&A session that follows, the industry reps ask again about the team's funding needs. Professor A reiterates that the number he mentioned is the minimum funding they will need, and, of course, housing costs, cost-of-living adjustments, and business class flights are not part of this budget. In addition, he will need to hire several additional PhDs and postdocs, which will take at least six months, if he can find the right candidates.

Put yourself in the shoes of the multinational company. Is this team attractive for a joint venture? Unless their technology is a blockbuster, probably not. But this is how such interactions are carried out every day. It's how universities work and think. Most large companies know this, because many already sponsor university research projects. However, if a SME visits a university lab, it can be taken by surprise when it learns how cumbersome such a collaboration turns to be. SMEs get the impression that university joint ventures are for big companies only, which can absorb inefficiency through sheer scale.

When working in partnership with industry, universities usually take a passive stance. They answer requests the best they can, by showing visitors what they asked to see. Then they overwhelm companies with information and details about internal politics, which makes them rather unattractive as equal partners. Better is a leveraged approach. If a research team has founded a startup, they should develop themselves to the point that they can use the synergies of a joint venture partner to achieve specific milestones in their product development. When startups meet with established companies, they can address those companies directly for specific feedback to improve their understanding of the market and ways to interact with it. Such a startup brings more to a joint venture than just technology. It is more attractive to partners, who see ways to engage with university startups in a different light. Of course, not every presentation will result in a joint venture. But over time, the university can step out of the position of supplier of inexpensive R&D. University startups can present themselves as equal joint venture partners and channel know-how about business and the market to the university.

Let's get back to the earlier example and see how the interaction between the startup and the company could have unfolded differently. Assume the team around technology X has decided to launch a startup with their intellectual property. They have incorporated a company and tested a few theories about the value of potential products in the marketplace. One product is promising, and they intend to launch it first. They have a lean canvas for several markets as well as a financial model, which they improve when new information surfaces. They also know what they want from different actors: feedback about their product and assumptions, sponsoring of materials to build more prototypes, distribution channels, and funding of a precise amount to scale up production. A multinational industry giant has read a journal article about technology X. The company would like to visit the lab and see the technology and may potentially sponsor further development. The company would also like to talk about licensing the technology for its own manufacturing processes.

Instead of going through the motions of the standard dog-and-pony show, the startup uses this opportunity to collect direct industry feedback about their intended first product. Not only do they turn the visit into a testing session, but they also engage the potential industry partner with actionable next steps. Team lead Professor A has stripped down his PowerPoint presentation. He presents the startup in the 10/20/30 format, leaving enough energy and time for the Q&A session, which he actively guides toward questions that benefit the startup in MVP testing. Some comments from the corporate visitors are new to the team. They ask follow-up questions and come up with additional ideas for MVPs on the spot. This resourceful method of approaching R&D

intrigues the company. The startup team also seems advanced in creating a marketable product, not just further data about technology X. The subject of money never comes up. Companies know that good things have their price; when they really need something, the cost is often unimportant.

Let's say the Q&A has ended. Fresh insights about MVPs and the market have emerged. The startup has added several items to its to-do list, which they are anxious to test. Because the industry representatives have experience in product development, Professor A asks if his team could conduct some testing at the company's lab using its expertise and specialized equipment. The company would like to discuss this internally and promises to be in touch by the end of the week to see whether this is possible. The startup has established a connection to the company from a position of strength, not from a position where the company has all the money and power and the university is begging for funds, hat in hand. If the startup can get access to the company's equipment and personnel to test the MVP in a realistic environment, they will build a stronger bridge to the market and begin to absorb pragmatic know-how right then and there.

Instead of waiting for companies to knock on their door, universities should also actively seek contact. SMEs are in many regards interesting joint venture partners, perhaps much more so than industry leaders and giant corporations. A small company can benefit hugely from university R&D. Large corporations already have multinational R&D operations, and the thrill of setting one up wore off long ago. Universities and their startup teams should seek more contact with SMEs. They should figure out where they can provide the most value and bring their intellectual property to market in partnerships.

For this to be effective, they need to streamline the operations of their startups. An entrepreneurial mindset must replace that of being a government employee with all expenses paid. Startups need to become skillful at presentations. Endlessly droning on about features must make way for concise information about tangible benefits. Presentations must include real, tested products that could launch in the market. The basic assumptions about the startup's financial structure and business model should be clear so they can lead an informed discussion, as I addressed in Chapter 8. If startups use this information, they are ready to engage companies with attractive value propositions. It is now up to universities to enable more conversations with businesses and industry, in order to build better channels for a two-way knowledge exchange.

The Investor Visit

Large banks and financial institutions visit universities occasionally. In my native Switzerland, the banking sector generously funds universities by sponsoring certain infrastructure such as new auditoriums. The American university system is dependent on endowments, into which wealthy alumni gift small fortunes.

It is natural that sponsors want to showcase their donations to clients or influential friends. To do this, they ask to set up an event at the university's facilities, which may last a few hours to a day, often comprising a speech from the managing director of the university or a visit to a state-of-the-art research lab. However, universities often have a mixed opinion about such events.

Let's see how an investor visit may unfold in the following fictitious example. A bank has funded an auditorium at a university and would like to conduct a workshop at the shiny new facility for the college-age children of their ultra-high-net-worth clients (UHNWI). The workshop includes a tour of the campus and a Q&A lunch with some students, researchers, and the university's management team. The workshop should acquaint the affluent offspring with the importance of science and research in today's society. Because this is the third such visit this year, the university reluctantly agrees but states that this is the last time it will free up the researchers. The researchers themselves have complained about having to give the same presentation repeatedly to mostly uninterested rich kids. The workshop takes place and is somewhat interesting for the visitors, but not for the university, which just goes through the motions. The UHNWI offspring go home and quickly forget about the excursion and the workshop—there are many more exciting things taking place in their lives, such as a rocket launch in the Mojave Desert, which celebrities such as Sir Richard Branson also attend. In a nutshell, the university wasted its time, and the bank feels somewhat unwelcome. Is this a shining beacon of platform leverage? You already know the answer.

Here is an alternative scenario. The university's five startups have all been involved in MVP testing and are incrementally developing their products. Some venture capitalists have visited, but none have invested, having judged the startups "not ready yet." The teams have therefore gotten used to making do with little or no funding and bootstrapping their way through the product-testing phase. When the university announces that a bank will bring by wealthy visitors, the startups see this as an opportunity to gather additional feedback and engage the audience with actionable next steps. Knowing that such opportunities are valuable, the university proposes to formulate the UHNWI workshop so it is not about research in today's society, but about startup entrepreneurship. This will seed the visitors' minds with entrepreneurial thinking rather than yet another request for trickle-down wealth redistribution. The university asks the bank to pay for a successful entrepreneur turned billionaire to speak at the event as a special guest. This is great for the bank and also for the university, which is putting on quite a show. The event will be fun for university staff, the in-house entrepreneurs, and other visitors, such as the government and selected industry representatives who are invited to the speech.

Instead of holding lengthy academic presentations, the startups stick to the 10/20/30 format. Each of the five makes a short presentation during two morning sessions. After that, the Q&A takes place, and the startups collect feedback about their products—not one by one, but all five together on a panel with the special guest. This cross-pollinates the minds of the teams, helps them understand how others see what they are doing, and gives them ideas for how to approach current challenges from a different angle. The wealthy kids, who live an unusual lifestyle, give different feedback than the test subjects the teams usually interview. Because the MVP testing is still ongoing, some of the visitors volunteer to spend more time with the teams and promise to make themselves available for testing and feedback in the future.

The event was a resounding success, the bank asks the university to organize further similar events, this time for the parents of the UHNWI children and other institutional clients. When that event takes place, the university's startups will be well on their way to launching products with joint venture partners and will need funding to scale up operations. It is a match made in heaven, because decision-makers regarding potential funding will be present at that next event. Additional synergies may evolve on the spot. But the story is not over yet.

One of the workshop attendees boards her private aircraft after the event and shuttles off to the Mojave Desert in California to attend a rocket launch. Sir Richard Branson, who is by coincidence the young woman's godfather, asks her what she has been up to in the last few days. It is then that Sir Richard learns about a biodegradable, rechargeable car battery that is currently being developed by a university startup. As it goes at events like these, just to the left of Sir Richard stands Elon Musk, founder and CEO of Tesla Motors. He overhears the conversation and wants to find out more about that battery. Do you think it could be helpful if Branson and Musk talk about your product? Pure fiction, you may say. This never happens. Yes, it does. I have been at a rocket launch in the Mojave, standing between Sir Richard and Paul Allen, cofounder of Microsoft. The net worth of the 50 or so people at that event was higher than the GDP of a small country. People discuss this and that at such events. Whatever has mindshare with a person at any particular moment has a good chance of being talked about. This may as well be your product. If it is valuable to a billionaire, he may call you then and there. When that phone call comes, startups better be prepared. They may have wondered whether they really need that business model canvas, that financial model, and that one-page proposal—well, this is when those things are needed.

Platform Building Takes Effort

Which of the scenarios discussed here do you think made a bigger impression with the bank and its clients? Which scenario do you think is more supportive for the university and its startups? The answer is clear. The two scenarios are like night and day. However, setting up events like these never happens by accident: it requires a conscious effort from the university and its startups.

It is obviously much easier and safer to go through the motions like any other university and to deliver just enough that visiting sponsors are not turned off. Of course, universities are not event agencies, and I am not proposing that they become one. The examples outlined in this chapter cost nothing more than a few good ideas and a mind that is open to turning around the existing situation. To break away from the pack, management and entrepreneurs need to look beyond the obvious recommendations. Once they have begun to leverage the existing activities taking place on a university's platform, they will uncover synergies that are right in front of their nose.

Like when you are reading a book about mathematics, it is easy to agree with a formula and the result when you see them written down for you. Coming up with both yourself is a whole different thing. It is apparent from these examples that universities can create huge advantages for their startups by taking advantage of existing stakeholders and hidden synergies. But how should universities go about raising the bar to engage in more platform thinking? Looking at a situation from a fresh angle may steer the university in the right direction. An active dialogue about platform thinking may yield ideas from the least expected sources.

In addition to these internal efforts, an outside opinion can once more make a huge impact. Many successful serial entrepreneurs are open to getting involved with universities. Several friends of mine had successful exits from their companies and are in a position where they do not have to work to pay the bills. Their focus is on making a difference in the world and helping entrepreneurs get off the ground. They draw satisfaction from the success stories of startups they have mentored. That does not mean they will work for free for the university, but their engagement will hardly break the bank. The ideas that qualified, motivated mentors can introduce are valuable. Just like startups themselves, universities should take advantage of this readily available resource if they want to have more success stories with their entrepreneurship programs.

CHAPTER

20

More Platform Projects

Leverage Cooperations and Create Network Effects

We know that universities can take advantage of their interactions with external allies for the good of their startups. They can do this with an innovative mindset about launching startups and engaging third parties through actionable next steps. This chapter describes several initiatives to reroute energy from external parties into a university's startup track. They take place on the existing university platform but require a little more time and effort to establish than the actions described in Chapter 19.

Communication between universities and external actors creates energy. The most important thing is to prevent this energy from escaping unused. To do this, universities need to think more like entrepreneurs themselves. They should approach third parties as partners for feedback and two-way knowledge exchange. With actionable next steps, universities can move potential partners toward the specific milestones the universities want to accomplish with their startups. When something falls short of producing the needed results, universities need to collect feedback and adjust their approach.

Just as an entrepreneur tries out his MVP with potential clients, a university should test its startup platform with its external stakeholders. When it does this, students and researchers gain access to an organic ecosystem of entrepreneurship. Startups can then draw on unique practical resources and knowledge to launch companies with much more momentum.

Entrepreneur-in-Residence Program

There are two definitions of an entrepreneur-in-residence (EIR) program. On the one hand, it can mean that an experienced technologist has the chance to develop a startup as a so-called *intrapreneur* within a company.[1] On the other hand, the term describes a situation where an established entrepreneur comes into an organization to help with the organization's own startup initiatives. An EIR might also provide expertise to a portfolio company of a venture capital firm.[2] The entrepreneur may later become part of the portfolio company as a full-time executive if both feel there is a good match.

Multinationals and even governments have EIR programs. The Mayor's Office of San Francisco runs its own program "to explore ways [to] use technology to make government more accountable, efficient and responsive."[3] Some business schools are starting to carry out EIR programs as well. With the goal of inviting seasoned entrepreneurs to work with their startups, universities can borrow from the playbook of corporate R&D. The main benefit consists of bringing entrepreneurial know-how directly into the university to address specific startup challenges. As you have seen repeatedly in this book, direct access to seasoned entrepreneurs can be a major asset for startups. The impact from working hand in hand with an experienced founder trumps any workshop or entrepreneurship lecture.

At a university, an EIR program could have several modules, each with a different entrepreneur (see Figure 20-1). Every founder has their own approach and experience, so a rotation brings many facets of startup entrepreneurship to light. Each module could last between four weeks and several months, depending on the university's resources.

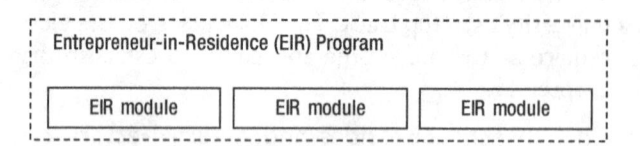

Figure 20-1. EIR program with modules

---

[1] Alexander Haislip, *Essentials of Venture Capital* (Hoboken, NJ: Wiley, 2011).
[2] Stefan Lindegaard, *The Open Innovation Revolution: Essentials, Roadblocks, and Leadership Skills* (Hoboken, NJ: Wiley, 2010).
[3] The Mayor's Office of Civic Innovation, Office of Mayor Edwin M. Lee, *San Francisco Entrepreneurship in Residence*, http://entrepreneur.sfgov.org.

Let's say there are three modules per year, and during each one a different entrepreneur comes in to work with startup teams. The EIR brainstorms with the teams, looks at their available assets, and tries new applications and combinations. The EIR works with all teams and thus serves as a connector and catalyst between diverse ideas and markets. When external parties visit the university for networking events, the EIR can lead the discussion about deeper integration of entrepreneurship to unlock synergies between the existing actions on the university platform.

An EIR program can also be the source of excellent media coverage. The university anchors its image not only as a research hub but as a center for applied, investible innovation, which may be useful when attracting partners from the business and financial community.

Universities often have an outstanding reputation as research institutes with dormant potential in entrepreneurship and startup success. When they proclaim that they would like to adopt entrepreneurship earlier in their curriculum, they can follow through by jump-starting the process with an EIR program. An initial four-week module could launch as a pilot program. This pilot serves as the guide for later modules featuring successful entrepreneurs from around the world. The risk and cost for the university are minimal. But the payoff is massive, especially considering the longer-term value of the program. Toward the end of a module, the EIR and the startups can present directly to potential joint venture partners and investors in the university's city.

Even if a module does not directly result in marketable projects or successfully funded startups, the relationships and insight gained from the EIR program will benefit the university and its students and researchers. They learn firsthand how to present projects, assess them, and launch them in the market.

Demo Days

Many ideas from Silicon Valley can be useful for startup programs at universities. Demo days are just one of them. The seed accelerator Y Combinator holds two demo days per year.[4] Each startup has seven minutes to make a short presentation. One week before the important day, there is a rehearsal day when startups can fine-tune their pitches.[5]

The demo day is a platform where startup founders can present their product and business model to venture capital firms that may wish to take them to the next step with an investment. Demo days take place at incubators and accelerators around the world. Why shouldn't universities also hold demo days with their startups?

---

[4] Y Combinator, *Demo Day*, www.ycombinator.com/demoday.
[5] Jessica Livingston, *Founders at Work: Stories of Startups' Early Days* (Berkeley, CA: Apress, 2007).

Chapter 20 | More Platform Projects

Some universities insist that they already have demo days. On closer inspection, those turn out to be little more than relatively passive showcases of non-investible ideas to a small group of government officials, industry representatives, or venture capitalists. Some university showcases I have seen consisted of a room full of tables with research props on them: here was a 3D-printed dish, there a block of cement, and so on. Some of the unmanned tables featured tablets with videos about the technology and interviews with the researchers. This may be OK for presentations of student work on the degree level, but it is a far cry from a serious startup demo day. Without professional organization, such events will disappoint. This will confirm the notion that entrepreneurship is like a lottery: very difficult and better left to others. The staff who organized the showcase will make a mental note that a university is not a venture capital firm and go back to business as usual.

As you saw in the examples of platform thinking in Chapter 19, putting startup teams in front of decision-makers and seeing what happens does hardly cut it. If startups want to succeed, they need to get their act together and engage others with attractive value propositions and actionable next steps. Just as on a demo day at Y Combinator, pitches must be short and to the point. They should follow the 10/20/30 format and should avoid beaming technology features at the audience. As the saying goes, when you need friends, it's too late to make them. A demo day that a university puts together out of thin air will never attract critical mass and will fail to interest the real decision-makers. Startups and universities must be able to draw from a strong entrepreneurial network that they should have started to build long before.

Silicon Valley accelerators hold invitation-only demo days as a first opportunity for investors to meet the startups that are part of each intake. These are full-day events that begin with a breakfast buffet at the accelerator's office. They include a series of short presentations from each of the startups, brief demonstrations of technology and products, and networking and Q&A sessions with invited industry and customers.

An incubator's motivation for putting on a demo day is to expose its teams to the market and give them an opportunity to collect feedback, network, and engage third parties with actionable next steps. If there is a commitment to invest in a project, great; but even without it, the demo day itself is a valuable field test of ideas.

Because accelerators have excellent connections with industry and investors, the demo days are brimming with energy and are usually highlights for entrepreneurs and attendees. It is less about putting a monetary value on each demo day than strengthening the foundation of the startups and the network for future events. The accelerator made powerful friends from other venture capital, industry, and finance firms before it ever needed them, and now it can hand-pick the ones it deems worthwhile to attend the demo day.

In the context of a university, such events can engage research teams with the business and financial community and serve as a fact-finding mission for business-model generation. Because demo days include all of a university's startups along with university staff not directly involved in entrepreneurship, they strengthen entrepreneurial idea exchange within the faculty. By inviting potential industrial users of technology developed at the university and potential joint venture partners, startup teams gather feedback on products, their application in the marketplace, and future partnerships. This enables students and researchers to leave the building and collect real-world data about the viability of their products. The focus is on inclusive listening to feedback and opinions, instead of beaming scientific facts at an audience. Such a practice speeds up the feedback loop to validate business models for technology developed at the university. It also teaches startup entrepreneurs what it takes to make a good impression and enables them to see how others are approaching the same problems they deal with.

To hold a successful demo day, a university needs to have something interesting to demo and relationships with influential partners to demo to. Research projects that are not actionable for partners and investors may be interesting to see but miss the purpose of a demo day. It only makes sense to invite potential joint venture partners and investors when startups have evolved along the path of MVP testing. They should have several business model canvases that give a clear idea about their direction, product, and position in the market. Their financial model should enable discussion with potential investors. And startups need to have developed a clear idea of what they want from potential partners and investors. One-page proposals should exist at least in their minds, if not on paper, so they are ready on demand.

Contacts made at demo days provide superb opportunities for startup teams to follow up. If entrepreneurs identify potential clients or joint venture partners, they can now approach them for meetings to move the startup along its trajectory.

Employing simple tools used in entrepreneurship hubs can give universities an edge with their startup initiatives. Knowing how demo days work puts a university on equal footing with top universities worldwide and improves its chances to establish long-term collaborations with industry and investors. Careful longer-term planning is necessary, as is the case for all initiatives with platform thinking. The sooner universities get started, the better.

Integrating Intergovernmental Organizations

Intergovernmental organizations (IGOs) are global organizations made up of member states. They are created by treaty or charter but are not treaties themselves. The North-American Free Trade Agreement (NAFTA) is not an organization, but the World Trade Organization (WTO) is. So are the United

Nations (UN), the International Monetary Fund (IMF), the World Bank, the Asian Development Bank (ADB), and many more.

IGOs typically have a clearly defined mission. The United Nations, for example, has the following missions: "To preserve international peace and security, to develop friendly relations among nations to achieve international co-operation in solving international problems of an economic, social, cultural, or humanitarian character, and to be a center for harmonizing the actions of nations to reach these common ends."[6] As another example, the Asian Development Bank has an important mandate: to end extreme poverty in Asia and Pacific.[7] Various publications and diligent research map out strategies for reaching that goal. One example is the ADB's *Strategy 2020*, which postulates that member countries should focus on critical strategic agendas of inclusive economic growth, environmental sustainability, and regional integration.[8]

To make a long story short, many organizations exist with massive funds that could help university startups. Some universities in Asia meet with the ADB to look into joint projects, but IGOs are still sleeping giants. That is a pity, because much university research aims at solving exactly the problems that many of these organizations have on their agendas: environmentally sustainable growth, decreasing greenhouse gas emissions, better urban planning, sustainable transport, and many more. Few students and researchers know that the ADB has a *Sustainable Transport Initiative* (STI) with an allocation of 25% of the bank's annual lending (about $10 billion in 2012).[9] The STI aims at private sector development and operations, capacity development, knowledge solutions, partnerships, and more.[10] Many other programs exist, focusing on water safety and renewable energy. What does this mean for university startups? If their products address the issues mentioned in these initiatives, they have a direct link to IGOs, which may turn out to be powerful partners for startups.

Universities usually approach IGOs with funding requests for individual research projects. A typical request for funding is around $250,000. This may seem like a lot of money, but it pales compared to the billions of dollars of an IGO's annual budget. Therefore, the economic scale and momentum they could bring to startups lie dormant. To change that, universities could try a

---

[6] The United Nations, *Charter of the United Nations*, www.un.org/en/documents/charter.
[7] Asian Development Bank, *Overview*, www.adb.org/about/overview.
[8] Asian Development Bank, *Strategy 2020: Working for an Asia and Pacific Free of Poverty* (Manila: ADB, 2008), www.adb.org/sites/default/files/Strategy2020-print.pdf.
[9] Asian Development Bank, *Financial Profile 2012* (Manila: ADB, 2012), www.adb.org/sites/default/files/adb-financial-profile-2012.pdf.
[10] Asian Development Bank, *Sustainable Transport Initiative Operational Plan* (Manila: ADB, 2010), www.adb.org/documents/sustainable-transport-initiative-operational-plan.

new strategy when approaching these organizations. Why not bundle several startups together and make them investible as a new project for an IGO? How about becoming an implementation partner (not a research partner) for an IGO and addressing issues they aim to solve with solutions built with technology from the university?

Suppose a university has five startups working on biodegradable battery technology, prediction of seismic activity, robotic manufacturing, an electric scooter, and a biodegradable glue useful for construction sites. Could they align with the ADB's *Strategy 2020* or *Sustainable Transport Initiative*? I believe so. The university would have to present this idea and find out.

Instead of approaching IGOs with a request for funding alone, startups can use them as a springboard to finalize their product, gain extra information about potential markets, and engage the organization for the next steps. IGOs work on the intersection of many different industries and finance, and they see various projects every day. They may be able to set powerful network effects in motion. What about private investors they work with? What about tenders for which startups could put in offers, perhaps together with joint venture partners?

Platform thinking goes a long way. Channeling the energy created on university platforms into startups should become a habit. Once it is part of everyday business, an entrepreneurial ecosystem will grow. As long as startups have a clear roadmap and can keep potential partners interested with good value propositions, this ecosystem will be their launch pad.

Presentations for Investors, Funds, and Banks

I have discussed building bridges to the market by engaging companies in joint ventures with startups. In the example of an investor visit, I talked about turning an event for a university sponsor into a great learning and networking experience for startups. What I address here involves actively reaching out to the financial sector. Except for business schools, universities rarely do this at the current time. Private equity funds, hedge funds, venture capital firms, investment banks, sovereign wealth funds, and all the other players in finance have a dubious connotation for many academics. Since the financial crisis of 2007/8, the popular press has done its best to slander the sector with stories about fraud, excess, and ruthless behavior. A famous example is one popular writer branding the American investment bank Goldman Sachs as "Vampire Squid."[11] This may have hit a nerve with universities, which are by nature risk-averse. Reputation risk is the last thing a university wants to burden itself with.

---

[11] Matt Taibbi, "The Vampire Squid Strikes Again: The Mega Banks' Most Devious Scam Yet," *Rolling Stone*; February 12, 2014, www.rollingstone.com/politics/news/the-vampire-squid-strikes-again-the-mega-banks-most-devious-scam-yet-20140212.

Chapter 20 | More Platform Projects

The lack of a connection between universities and the financial sector is unfortunate. Various smart academics work in finance, and a wealth of market knowledge could flow back to universities if they began engaging those individuals. Just like inviting potential joint venture partners and investors to a demo day, wealthy individuals and their advisors can be an excellent addition to a university's network. Ultra-high-net-worth individuals (UHNWIs) are generally curious about research and science and often support projects without an immediate financial return. They are strong allies to raise unconventional financing even for slightly crazy endeavors such as asteroid mining[12] and private space travel.[13]

Some universities are in ideal positions at the intersection of research, public policy, and finance. Singapore, for example, is a melting pot of the world's wealthiest people. Yet there exists a gulf between many of Singapore's universities and the bustling financial sector of the city state. Nonetheless, finance professionals and wealthy individuals are open to learning about what is going on at universities. Knowledge is power, and UHNWIs very much want to have an edge over the next guy. Their curiosity could be the spark to ignite their engagement in a university's startup track. They could be ideal candidates to ask for feedback about products and business models. Not only do they bring financial firepower to the table, but their experiences and networks are also attractive for startups. With clearer deliverables for investible, validated startups, universities can take a leadership role in bridging the gap with the financial community.

Whenever I bring this up with startup teams, they say they will get financial connections later, when they need funding. However, that misses the point entirely. Entrepreneurs should have a robust network before they ever need anything. They can engage the financial community today as a sounding board for their business and financial model and collect feedback from them along the way. When the entrepreneurs need funding down the road, they can approach those members of the financial community as existing contacts. Asking for an introduction to a venture capital firm will be easier then.

Few people have a deca-millionaire in their group of friends, let alone a billionaire. When they finally meet one, they are surprised how normal and likable that person is. Of course they are (most of them); how else could they have interested enough people to buy their products or services, which made them rich in the first place?

But what about the evil private equity funds, the *vampire squids*, the arrogant hedge-fund managers, and the insensitive venture capitalists? Surely you don't want to deal with them? Granted, there may be unpleasant characters at certain financial outfits. Some of them, usually lower-level employees, can be

---

[12]Planetary Resources, www.planetaryresources.com.
[13]Virgin Galactic, www.virgingalactic.com.

summed up as having "one inch of power": this means they have climbed the ladder just high enough to have an inflated ego. This is hardly who you want to do business with. As soon as you get higher up the chain of command at funds and financial institutions, things get interesting. Believe it or not, getting to the top in finance requires entrepreneurial thinking. Decision-makers at funds and financial institutions feel at ease with other entrepreneurial, unconventional types. Many of their investments are bets on special situations, unexpected economic developments, market shifts, and geopolitical changes that influence the product line of startups. They can contribute considerable pragmatic advice to startup teams and their evolution.

Stop thinking about an investment fund as a casino, and see it as an entrepreneurial think tank. Stop thinking about wealthy individuals as people who deprived someone else of their fair share, and view them as hard-working folks who once were and still may be entrepreneurs. UHNWIs live a life of very few constraints. That opens up the mind. Stop thinking in terms of entitlement—it is not the duty of wealthy people to give you money. Assume responsibility for all your actions, because nobody owes you anything. The sooner you adopt this mindset, the better. A new world will open up to you. A startup may be the vehicle that will shift your thinking in this direction.

By now, you may have noticed that all these platform initiatives involve the same deliverables: creating benefit-centered, investible startups; validating hypotheses about products and the market; adapting communications to be more inclusive for non-academics; and engaging third parties with actionable next steps. All of these should be at the top of the agenda for universities and their startups. You may have also noticed that these initiatives require the same effort on the part of the university and the startup: keeping an open mind, engaging third parties early, asking them for feedback about your products and processes, and including them in your entrepreneurial network.

Once universities have adopted platform thinking as a whole, many startup initiatives can launch with little extra effort, because they build on each other. The key is to take the first step and look for leverage. After you have carried out the first platform project, the next one will be much easier. With platform projects, your university has the opportunity to transform itself. It just has not tried hard enough yet.

An Investment Fund as the Master Platform

A final idea is creating a university-led investment fund. I know, red flags go up immediately. The university is no investment bank, and certainly it is not a hedge fund. It does not have any interest in short-term gains; only long-term scientific excellence matters. I have heard all these objections before. I understand them and agree with them. However, they largely stem from misunderstanding the intentions behind the recommendations in this part of the book.

Chapter 20 | More Platform Projects

If you take these ideas out of context, I admit that some of them may sound strange. It is the underlying logic that makes the difference. Universities should keep an open mind and look for unorthodox ways to build and strengthen their entrepreneurial platform. They should reach out to as many companies as possible to enable entrepreneurial knowledge transfer back to the university. Invariably, this includes some unconventional ideas. If you can be enterprising and receptive, you will make the most of this book.

Ideas about finance are sometimes difficult to understand and often downright scary for those outside the financial sector. Besides, embracing capitalism is rarely a strong point of academics. Whatever your personal convictions, nobody asks you to convert to capitalism. This is about launching projects to engage third parties for the good of a university's startup program. Financial institutions are such third parties. So are UHNWIs, insurance companies, and IGOs such as the World Bank and the Asian Development Bank. If interaction with those financial stakeholders makes sense, then an investment fund could be the master vehicle to unify all the platform projects described in this chapter. Let's examine how universities can do this.

A team around Professor Andrew Lo of MIT popularized the idea of a *mega fund* to commercialize research. They published a paper in *Nature Biotechnology* that suggested pooling several biomedical research projects aimed at healing cancer into a multibillion-dollar investment fund.[14] Without going into too much detail, the following paragraph describes how this works.

The risk of investing in an individual biomedical research project is high. The entire investment can be lost. But if the project proves to be successful, its payoff is enormous, perhaps 100 times the investment or more. A diversified stock portfolio invested in several stocks is less risky than investing all your money in one stock. With the same logic, building a mega fund that invests in several biomedical research projects is safer than one large investment in an individual project. With relatively simple financial engineering, Lo showed that a mega fund could achieve returns of 5% or more with relatively low risk. The individual projects did not change, just the way the fund structured them and made them investible.

This approach has the power to attract a large group of institutional and private investors who would never dream of investing in individual drug-discovery projects. However, because the fund diversifies away much of the risk, they may be open to investing in a mega fund if it existed. Put another way, such a fund is comparable to investments they already know and invest in

---

[14]Jose-Maria Fernandez, Roger M. Steinl and Andrew W. Lo, "Commercializing Biomedical Research through Securitization Techniques," *Nature Biotechnology* 30, no. 10 (2012).

University Startups and Spin-Offs

with good results. With this reasoning, an ocean of new capital would become available to finance biomedical research, and the extra capital could speed up discovery of new drugs.

This sounds intriguing. The same approach could work for research projects and university startups in general. However, most universities oppose ideas along those lines. Financial engineering is anathema for many academics and public servants. Yet private and institutional investors are allocating billions of dollars to comparable investments and often struggle to find a market deep enough to absorb all the liquidity available. Market demand from financial investors exists. With relatively low risk, a university could take the lead and spearhead the first investment fund made up of research projects and promising startups.

Of course, this would not be a slush fund to finance university overhead. It would not be "free money" like the government funding and donations that many universities receive now. Nevertheless, it would compare to a venture capital investment in exchange for equity or debt in a startup. In this light, it becomes obvious that little would change for the startups and the university. The upside is the fact that they would have a source of funding available from inside the university. Other than purely monetary benefits, the fund would serve as a master platform with network effects for all parties. As an interdisciplinary vehicle, it would occupy a position at the intersection of science, international business, and finance. Because it would be a market-oriented investment fund (not a think tank), interactions and communications on this platform would have urgency and would need to be action-oriented. This would break the habit of endless deliberation before making moves in the real world. An investment fund could be rocket fuel for university startups.

Example: Venture Capital vs. Mega Fund

Suppose a university has the five startups mentioned earlier. Their areas of expertise are biodegradable batteries, prediction of seismic activity, robotic manufacturing, an electric scooter, and a glue for construction. Assume that these startups have progressed through their MVP testing and launched a first product in the market with good feedback. Each startup has landed a joint venture partner that holds 51% of the venture; 44% is held by the research team and 5% by the university. The joint venture partner covers all overhead of the startup, so there is no immediate need to raise capital to make ends meet. The joint ventures have validated their products and are now refining production to cut costs. Several venture capital firms have approached each startup, offering $1 million to buy a 20% stake in the company (each company is valued at $5 million). Let's see what happens if the startups take that offer. The capitalization table of the startup changes as shown in Table 20-1.

Chapter 20 | More Platform Projects

Table 20-1. Capitalization Before and After Investment

	Before Investment	After Investment
University	5.0%	4.0%
Research team	44.0%	35.2%
Joint venture partner	51.0%	40.8%
Venture capital firm	-	20.0%
	100.0%	100.0%

As you learned previously, venture capital looks great on paper, but it comes with strings attached. The relationship is a tradeoff. The startup receives cash and access to the resources and know-how of the VC firm. But it also has to consider the corporate interests of the new investor, which may conflict with those of the startup and the university when they have to meet certain milestones. VCs can and do veto startup team decisions. They invest other people's money, so they have to answer to their shareholders. These may complain if returns from the investment in this particular joint venture fall short of expectations. And that is where the trouble starts.

A venture capitalist is a bit like a rich uncle who funds your college tuition, only to feel entitled later to meddle in every decision of your life. When startups need funds, venture capital may be grand. However, if a startup has another source of funding available, that may be even better. Who or what could this other source be? No bank will invest a million dollars in a company with little or no revenue, regardless of its joint venture partner. But if you had 100 companies, the story might be different. Just as with the mega fund, investing in many diverse assets is less risky than investing a large sum in a single asset. If universities structured their startup companies this way, the investment risk would decrease, and they might gain access to additional sources to raise capital.

In Table 20-1, you see that an investment in a company is a straightforward transaction. Where the investment comes from has no impact on the transaction. I said it before: investment in a startup is not a question of money alone. If a venture capital firm supports a startup with positive synergies, it can add a lot. But if it begins pushing the startup in a direction the entrepreneurs dislike, then other sources of capital would have been a better choice.

Impact Investment

Before I discuss how to put together such a fund, let's first look at a recent trend in finance called *impact investment*.[15] (This differs from the slightly more settled *socially responsible investment [SRI]*, which seeks to minimize negative effects rather than proactively create positive social change or environmental impact.) Investors forgo a small portion of returns to ensure that the projects they invest in make a difference. They should have a positive social impact or must be good for the environment. An example may be micro loans made by a bank in a developing country, which could raise $100 million from impact investors. The loan fund is rated by a renowned rating agency and syndicated on commercial terms among institutional investors, such as pension funds, in Europe and the United States. This investment yields financial returns and has a positive impact on society by making micro loans available for entrepreneurs in a developing country. However, impact investments also make sense in the developed world. For example, they may focus on sustainable energy or social causes.

Such investments produce an acceptable return, but it may be slightly lower than that of a conventional financial product like a corporate bond. Other popular applications of impact investing are clean technology, public health, job creation, community development, and more. J.P. Morgan predicts that the impact investing market has the potential to reach $1 trillion of invested capital by 2020, with profits of up to $667 billion.[16] This is not a blip on the radar, but a trend on the horizon.

Let's go back to our five university startups. Would investments in these startups qualify as impact investments? Possibly, if they are businesses with the intent of making a positive social or environmental impact. The emphasis is on *business*, meaning a startup cannot simply be a PhD project with no other goal than the PhD getting tenure at a university. These must be serious companies with proven market demand for their products. It must be credible that they will earn revenues sometime in the future. And their teams must have the motivation to go the distance.

To clarify, imagine the following fictitious example. The electric scooter startup has devised a socially responsible business model. Factories of a joint venture partner located in rural communities in a developing country produce the scooters from recycled material. The scooters sell for a high price in developed countries. This allows the company to pay employees a higher wage and offer free education and entrepreneurship workshops for their families.

---

[15] Jessica Freireich and Katherine Fulton, "Investing for Social & Environmental Impact," Monitor Institute (2009), http://monitorinstitute.com/downloads/what-we-think/impact-investing/Impact_Investing.pdf.
[16] J.P. Morgan Global Research, *Impact Investments: An Emerging Asset Class* (2010), www.jpmorgan.com/directdoc/impact_investments_nov2010.pdf.

The Asian Development Bank has decided the startup is in line with its *Strategy 2020*, aimed at reducing poverty in Asia.[17] It has therefore invested on generous terms that allow the startup to build several schools in the community. To open factories in additional communities, the startup is now raising more capital from impact investors. Because it makes a positive impact in the communities and is a force for social change, it qualifies as an impact investment.

When you get into the complexity associated with platform thinking, it should be clear that it makes sense only for serious, honest efforts of dedicated, motivated entrepreneurs. When startups have gone through the process of lean development and have identified strong demand for their product, they have taken the first step. As soon as they have attracted a joint venture partner with a mutually beneficial value proposition, they are one step further. Once they have revenue and a credible growth strategy, they are respectable businesses that could qualify as an investment by a fund.

Benefits of an Investment Fund

Within this investment fund, all the platform projects described in this chapter come together. The entrepreneur-in-residence program now takes place on the level of the fund. An EIR works with portfolio companies and is in contact with interesting stakeholders on the fund platform. Demo days showcase not only individual startups, but also portfolio companies and their potential projects, to attract new investors to the fund. IGOs may also take part on a larger scale; an impact investment fund is a more promising vehicle for them than an individual small project. And finally, the discussion with the financial sector takes place on equal footing. The financial community is no longer a donor but an investor.

This new model of knowledge exchange and interaction has many benefits:

- Action-oriented knowledge exchange with SMEs and multinational corporations
- Action-oriented knowledge exchange with large organizations such as IGOs, governments, NGOs, and industry organizations
- Better chance for startups to enter into equal joint ventures with companies
- Potential access to investment capital, if startups and spin-offs pass due diligence
- Being part of a bold initiative to enable research to make a bigger measurable impact

---

[17] Asian Development Bank, *Strategy 2020*.

This fund would be the ideal master platform for a university to fully engage all available synergies. It could effectively channel energy into launching startups. When this happens, those startups have the power to reach escape velocity much faster.

In theory, this approach holds much promise for university startups. My personal discussions with investment bankers and private equity firms have shown that interest from the financial sector exists for such an instrument. Given that sustainable investment and impact investment are growing in importance each year, many university startups align with the goals of investors once they achieve traction in the market. These are all favorable developments that make the case that such a fund could take off.

However, in reality, setting up a fund in the current university structure would not be a cakewalk. Universities are unprepared to deal with investment capital, because they are not-for-profit entities, funded by the government. As with all entrepreneurship initiatives, many incumbents at the university would fear the changes that these new ideas bring to their doorstep. The terms "structured finance" and "financial engineering" scare and upset them, and they have no interest in working with private equity firms and investment bankers. There would be major debates about the principles necessary before a new entity within the university could start setting up the fund. The university would have to hire financial staff to put together the fund and manage its assets. Questions about liability and reputation risk would need answers. All this takes patience and time.

Of course, no university wants to be the first to launch a fund with the risk of a total loss for all investors a few years down the road. But when somebody cracks these issues and launches the first successful research-backed investment fund, it will open the door for universities to follow. They will be able to access large new sources of financing that infuse their startups with rocket fuel. Network effects will kick in. Students and researchers will realize early in their university career that a startup is an alternative. They will see that it is possible because many before them have launched startups that made an impact in the real world. Young founders will tap into the new entrepreneurial ecosystem of their university, their startup alumni networks, mentors, and platform projects. It will be a brave new world for startup entrepreneurship. Until that happens, much work is necessary.

There is a silver lining on the horizon, and universities have started to take the first steps. I wish them the courage to keep going and to realize their own entrepreneurial ambitions and those of their students and researchers.

APPENDIX A

Additional Considerations

The following articles and resources are related to startup entrepreneurship but go beyond the practical steps presented in this book so far. Sometimes a single sentence can bring about the solution to a specific problem you are wrestling with. Who knows? Perhaps you'll find this sentence somewhere in this appendix.

How Your Startup Could Make a Billion Dollars

Most entrepreneurs say money is not a motivation for them. I believe this is true. Financial reward alone is insufficient to instill in you the entrepreneurial fire that will push you forward in rough times. A paycheck will motivate you enough to complete a certain task and then leave the office at five o'clock, but you will rarely compete on a global scale this way. At the same time, it would be nice if your entrepreneurial efforts paid off as well. If you have been working 100-hour weeks for several years without much to show for it, you will undoubtedly ask yourself if this is worth doing. If you have a PhD, you will wonder whether your friends who took cushy jobs at a university or consultancy made the better choice. In such cases, you may briefly think of other entrepreneurs for whom such toil paid off handsomely. The prime example is Mark Zuckerberg, who is now worth about $28 billion.[1] Many others exist, and not only in the tech space. How did they get there? Which forces did they leverage to attract such massive wealth? Here is an attempt at an explanation.

Overcome Social Norms

Mark Zuckerberg earned about $3 billion on average each year over the last ten years. Is this possible by playing nice, obeying all the rules, and making many friends along the way? Author Martin Fridson finds that the two primary obstacles to amassing a billion-dollar fortune are the menace of competition and the obstacle of social conventions. To enter the billion-dollar club, entrepreneurs must overcome market forces and conventional wisdom. Walmart founder Sam Walton violated the age-old convention of cordial relationships with sellers. He went around the wholesalers and bought directly from manufacturers. Not only this, but Walton publicly stated that he stole all his good ideas from competitors. He broke the social norms expected of a business person, and Walmart pulled away from the pack.[2]

Social conventions come in many forms. They often brand becoming wealthy as a crime. Ask anyone if they believe it is ethical to travel by private jet. They may consider this snobbish and wasteful, which is the expected answer that most people are comfortable with. But will being compatible with the majority help you if your goal is a billion-dollar company? You will never be able to attract this kind of money with conventional wisdom. This is by no means a value judgment about people's personal opinions, just a simple statement of the mindset needed to earn a massive fortune.

Do Something Old, and Do It Better

Many startup entrepreneurs think they have to do something no one else has ever done before. They believe that success comes down to creating an entirely new product that serves a new market. Coming up with a disruptive invention may be one path to a billion-dollar company. But Twitter founder Evan Williams disagrees. He believes that success comes down to fulfilling age-old needs, but in a better way. In a speech, he mentioned the example

---

[1] Forbes, *The World's Billionaires: Mark Zuckerberg Profile*, www.forbes.com/profile/mark-zuckerberg.
[2] Martin S. Fridson, *How to Be a Billionaire: Proven Strategies from the Titans of Wealth* (New York: Wiley, 2009).

of car-sharing service Uber, which is valued at $18 billion at the time of this writing.[3] The need to get from A to B is by no means original, yet the popular app manages to connect passengers and drivers more effectively. Compared to hailing a cab the old-fashioned way, Uber took out several steps in the process and streamlined the experience. In Williams' view, the Internet is just a machine that gives people what they want. Instead of a utopian world, it is simply a tool to do old things in a better way.[4]

Create Frictionless Markets

Software, technology, and automation have removed much friction from processes that were previously cumbersome. Authors Eric Brynjolffson and Andrew McAfee find that the most radical progress in robotics and 3D printing happened in the last few years, after a frustratingly long period of slow development. The advances are opening the door to near-frictionless markets in various applications that were previously safe from automation. The authors point toward middle-class jobs like medical diagnostics and low-skilled manual labor like picking fruit, which computers and robots could soon automate away.[5] Technology reduces inefficiencies and cost, and increases transparency. The same goes for the rapid digitization that is taking place today. Sharing digital files is much easier than distributing physical product. This happens online, where file sharing disrupted the music industry to the core. The communication industry also took a hit: worldwide video conferencing is now freely available to anyone through Skype. When technology takes over, network effects kick in, and change speeds up even more. This allows the newly emerging frictionless market to produce more profits than the market it replaced (see Figure A-1).

---

[3]Andrew Ross Sorkin, "Why Uber Might Well Be Worth $18 Billion," *New York Times Dealbook*, June 9, 2014, http://dealbook.nytimes.com/2014/06/09/how-uber-pulls-in-billions-all-via-iphone.
[4]Ryan Tate, "Twitter Founder Reveals Secret Formula for Getting Rich Online," *Wired*, September 30, 2013, www.wired.com/2013/09/ev-williams-xoxo.
[5]Eric Brynjolffson and Andrew McAfee, *The Second Machine Age: Work, Progress, and Prosperity in a Time of Brilliant Technologies* (New York: W. W. Norton & Company, 2014).

Appendix A | Additional Considerations

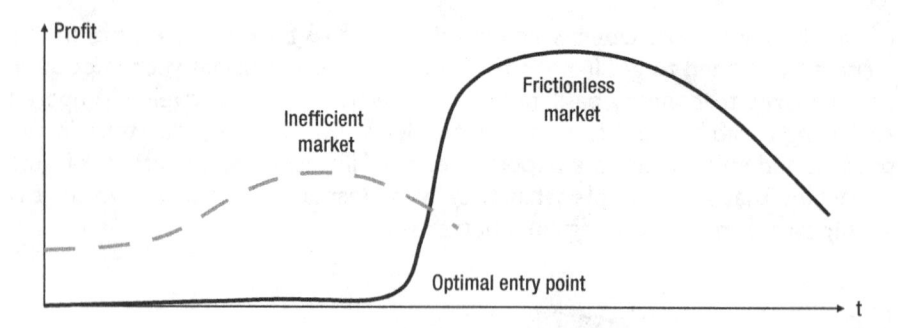

Figure A-1. Higher profits in technology-enabled frictionless markets

If your company replaces established processes with new technology, it could potentially earn billion-dollar revenues. Timing is obviously crucial, because the old market may be too powerful to suppress the new technology, or people may be unwilling to give up their established habits. The technology may also still be on the flat part of the curve, not yet ready to deliver the promised gains in efficiency. But when you hit the right entry point to launch a disruptive product in the market just where the exponential curve takes off, then chances are high you will succeed. Hitting this ideal entry point is probably more an art than a science, and it is easy to spot in hindsight.

Ride the Market Expansion in a Subsector

Addressing an existing market and riding its current growth rate has a small chance of making you a billion dollars over night. It may allow your company to become profitable over a long period of time. But unconventional returns require massive leverage. Author and venture capitalist Damir Perge reminds us that in certain *subsectors* of an existing market, the rate of change is much higher than in the main market. Just like in frictionless markets, if you catch the right entry point, your company can surf a large expansion of that subsector, which happens very quickly.

Compare the social media sector with the *mobile* social media sector, which has witnessed an explosion in the past two years. Social media grew rapidly, but the newly emerging subsector grew much faster.[6] An example is the mobile social messaging app WhatsApp, which Facebook bought in 2012 for $19 billion in cash and stock.[7]

---

[6] Damir Perge, "Build a Billion Dollar Startup Almost Overnight," video series, *entrepreneurdex*, July 25, 2013, www.entrepreneurdex.com/video/how-to-build-a-billion-dollar-startup-almost-overnight-pt-1.
[7] Facebook, "Facebook to Acquire WhatsApp," *Facebook Newsroom*, February 19, 2014, http://newsroom.fb.com/news/2014/02/facebook-to-acquire-whatsapp.

Tesla Motors is another example. After becoming an innovator in the hybrid automobile sector, a subsector of the automobile industry, the company went public and now has a market cap of close to $30 billion (Q3, 2014).[8] Riding the market expansion in a subsector looks something like Figure A-2.

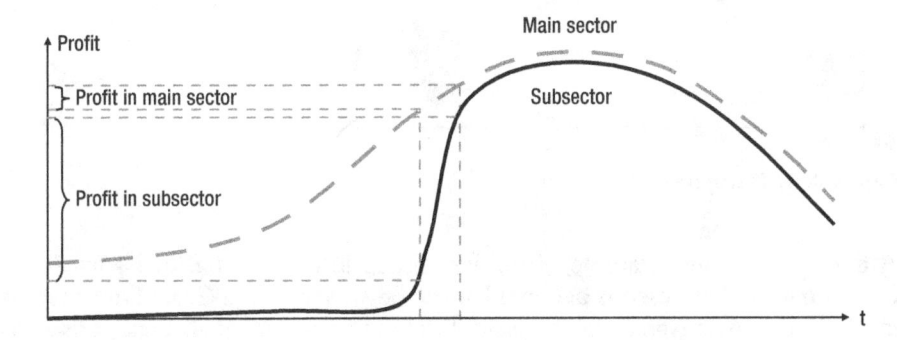

Figure A-2. Comparison of profit in the main sector and a subsector

If your product exists in an established market but serves a newly emerging subcategory of the existing base of customers, then explosive growth is possible. This is incredibly hard to engineer and plan but always easy to explain in retrospect. One thing is certain, though: if you find out your product serves a declining established market, then the chance for explosive growth is small.

Take Advantage of Disruption

A common case of market disruption takes place when governments privatize certain sectors. After the Cold War, the energy industry in Russia underwent rapid privatization, in the process minting many billionaires. Legitimate or not, the privatization process explains how immense wealth can flow to a single person. Whenever a legacy market becomes stale and inefficient, after a sustained decline in profitability, new players come in through deregulation or privatization. These new players introduce free-market thinking into the former state-owned enterprise and bring it back up to speed. The following recovery of the market is profitable. Market A in Figure A-3 serves as an example.

---

[8]Yahoo Finance, "Tesla Motors, Inc. (TSLA)", http://finance.yahoo.com/q?s=TSLA.

Appendix A | Additional Considerations

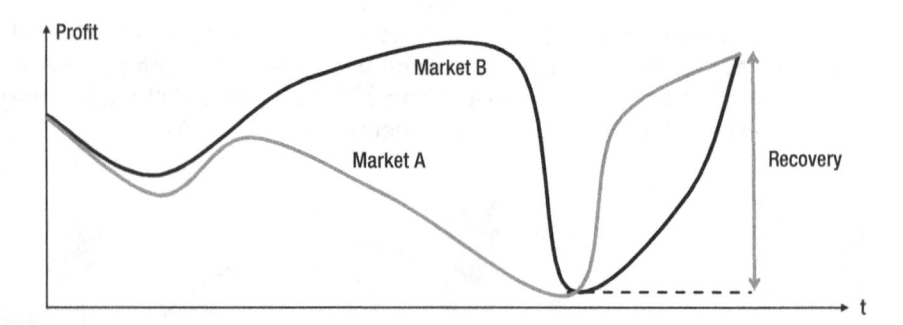

Figure A-3. Disruptions of a market

A crash is another example of market disruption (market B in Figure A-3). Prominent market crashes occurred at the beginning of the Great Depression in 1929, the Asian financial crisis in 1997, and the global financial crisis in 2007/8. In a market crash, a fire sale of distressed assets takes place. Newly available assets often look unattractive at first sight, because they are run-down, deep in debt, or otherwise considered worthless. However, what could be easier than buying an asset that nobody wants, and later selling it when everybody is clamoring for it? Not every disruption scheme ends in billion-dollar success. But it is a mechanism that has enough leverage to enable it. Anyone with sufficient courage and liquid funds can potentially buy low and sell high when a market crash occurs. If they pick the right assets and play it smart, they make headlines and the Forbes list a few years later.

Launching a startup in times of crisis is a good strategy. If the venture is agile, it can take advantage of market disruption and inexpensive assets in the crash. While everybody else is scrambling to keep their existing operations running, startup entrepreneurs can build theirs from the ground up. They can incorporate lean principles and low overhead into the company from day one. When the economy inevitably picks up again, they are in an ideal position to reap the rewards with high profit margins.

These concepts explain only a few of the mechanics that underlie billionaire wealth. It is obvious that becoming a billionaire is no small feat. These examples make it apparent that there is much more to it than working hard and paying your dues. Most of all, achieving massive success forces you to become an extreme individual. A group thinker has never achieved great wealth. Nor has someone too concerned with what others think about them. Making up your mind to become successful and super-rich subordinates all else. Whether this is advisable is another question. It requires intense focus that dominates your entire life. This will inevitably alienate some of your old friends, and it will make you a target for envy and ridicule—until, of course, you have achieved your goal.

Where Does Entrepreneurial Success Come From?

What primes startups for success is a matter of heated debate. There is obviously no sure-fire recipe, no ten-step plan that makes a fledgling venture the next Google. Here are some thoughts about what may cause a startup to gravitate toward success or failure. This may be helpful for entrepreneurs, universities, and investors alike.

On their journey, successful entrepreneurs need three main ingredients as fuel in their tank: a wild idea, bold execution, and persistence. These three ingredients combined make or break the project. By a wild idea, I mean a slightly controversial hypothesis. If the idea is so mainstream that everyone will accept it, then chances are high that someone else is already working on it. As explained by author Derek Sivers, a brilliant idea with weak execution may still yield profits, as may a weak idea with strong execution.[9] To find a superstar, all three ingredients have to be of top pedigree. The quality of execution and persistence are in turn influenced by an entrepreneur's decisions about how to approach them. As illustrated in Figure A-4, these decisions can be good (light gray dots) or bad (black dots), and they influence execution and persistence.

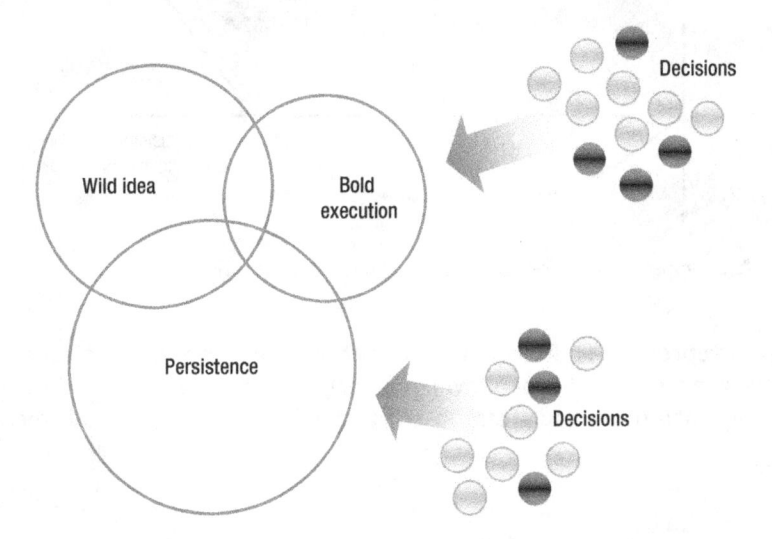

Figure A-4. Main ingredients of a startup and forces that influence them

---

[9]Derek Sivers, *Anything You Want: 40 Lessons for a New Kind of Entrepreneur* (The Domino Project, 2011).

Appendix A | Additional Considerations

Once an entrepreneur has an idea, they must transform it into reality. This is where execution and persistence come in. Startup success often boils down to *why* and *how* founders do something, rather than *what* they are doing. This book has addressed the *what* sufficiently up to this point. Instead of locking onto the words *execution* and *persistence*, let's examine the forces that influence them (the *how* and *why*).

Success Parameters

Startups move along a so-called J-curve, where we expect a return on investment down the road after early losses. The pace at which they move along the x-axis depends on a tug-of-war between the entrepreneurs' good and bad decisions (along the large arrows in Figure A-5). As described by author Jeff Olson, a series of small good decisions, followed up persistently, will yield good results in the long term, whereas small bad decisions, followed up persistently, will yield weak results.[10]

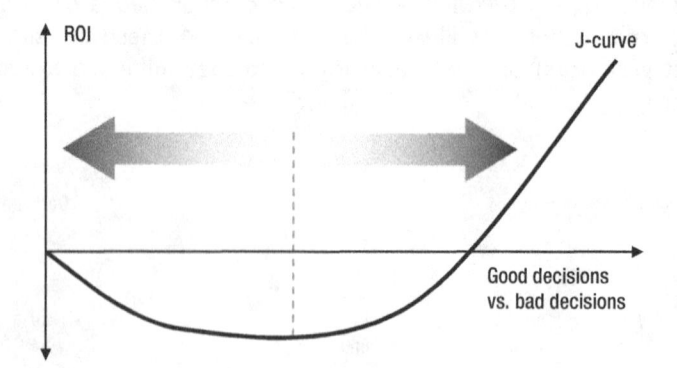

Figure A-5. Impact of decisions on return on investment (ROI)

Every entrepreneur and investor will of course prefer good decisions, which I believe are a result of the following underlying factors: strong intrinsic motivation, an open mind, and a can-do attitude. What exactly does this mean?

---

[10]Jeff Olson, *The Slight Edge: Turning Simple Disciplines into Massive Success and Happiness* (Atlanta: Success Books, 2005).

Strong Intrinsic Motivation

In contrast to extrinsic motivation, where external factors like reward and punishment are the driving forces behind taking action, intrinsic motivation comes from within a person. It is a burning desire to reach a goal, no matter what it takes. There is a difference between *wanting* to succeed and *committing* yourself to success. If you have the motivation to achieve a goal, there is no reason you cannot make it happen. A desire to prove yourself or a competitive drive for excellence may push you to aim for the gold. Entrepreneurs give themselves every reason to get up in the morning. The desire to do and achieve always trumps a feeling of obligation or fear.

An Open Mind

Invariably, a startup will encounter roadblocks. The technology on which the main idea builds may flounder. There may be legal hassles, or blatant flaws in the original business model may emerge after you work on your startup for a while. To admit you were wrong and to change your mind is easier said than done, because most humans feel they must be consistent with whatever rules they have set up for themselves. But this is definitely not the case for a successful entrepreneur: if the entrepreneur has a change of heart, pivoting will move the startup forward. Resisting the pivot will set the startup on a negative trajectory. Keeping an open mind will allow you to look past conventions and strict rules. You will see what others don't. If you can only get there with a pivot, then embrace it despite conventions or prior commitments.

Can-Do Attitude

This is the entrepreneur's hallmark. Strongly related to keeping an open mind, the can-do attitude takes it one step further. Suppose an employee has volunteered to do a task over the weekend and shows up on Monday with the task uncompleted. The excuse is that he really *tried* but simply could not finish. This is such a normal event in most organizations that it may not even register. However, this mindset is incompatible with startups and entrepreneurship. "No" means "maybe," and "maybe" means "yes": that is the way entrepreneurs approach things. If you have been an employee, then this shift may not come naturally. You must take full responsibility for all your actions. Henry Ford knew that "Whether you think you can, or you think you can't—you're right." You are thinking anyway, so it is better to think you can.

Some of these success factors may seem impractical to you on first sight. Nevertheless, be aware that entrepreneurs compete with other entrepreneurs, not with other employees, and not with other university students or researchers. The two worlds require different mindsets to succeed.

Regardless, even if you follow the recommendations for the three success factors, there are still roadblocks that can prevent success from taking place. You must avoid those. What puts the brakes on startup success? Financial desperation, analysis paralysis, and a can't-do attitude.

Financial Desperation

As you already know, intrinsic motivation always trumps extrinsic motivation. If you desperately need to earn an income fast, this may be to the disadvantage of your startup. When you have heavy impending overhead or debt payments, you should find a high-paying job and follow entrepreneurship on the side. The same goes for partnering with co-founders: if one of them has money woes, stay clear. This advice may not sound sensible, but ignoring it has led to trouble for many founders.

A startup needs considerable goodwill along the way to succeed. There is of course nothing wrong with following a profitable idea just for the sake of profit. But if a founder displays money-mindedness as their leading motivation, this will alienate honest backers and attract people with questionable motives. Here is a simple rule: only if you would trade places with somebody, ask them for advice or work with them. Those with money woes will automatically fall through this screen.

Analysis Paralysis

Especially in academic circles, analysis paralysis runs rampant. Have you already spent so much time analyzing a situation that you have lost sight of what to do next? How many more PowerPoint presentations and data visualizations do you need to convince yourself and take action? Academics often confuse a startup with a thought experiment. However, entrepreneurship has little to do with writing an academic paper, where at the end of the process a group of experts either approvingly nod or reject the idea. Startups are often irrational endeavors whose fate is decided by volatile market forces, not all-knowing gatekeepers.

Most worthwhile ideas were at some point rejected by experts. If you must convince others, then let them be people on the same wavelength as you. If you lack conviction and feel you must convince yourself to the degree that it hampers your ability to take action, then check whether you are really on board with the idea. You may find that you hold doubts about it that prevent you from moving along. However, if your environment has dragged you into a negative feedback loop, read the next point.

Can't-Do Attitude

If you think it cannot be done, then you will prove yourself and your peers right. This belief may have grown in you over the years. Be aware that it is hard to thrive as an entrepreneur in an unsupportive environment. Influence is a subtle process: peers are rarely outright hostile. Slight criticism, a raised eyebrow, or a smug remark here and there when you speak about your ideas can have enough cumulative abrasive force over the years to grind away your entrepreneurial spirit. This happens without your knowing it. Be selective about your associations, and make sure they are encouraging and positive.

If a startup begins working on a wild idea and follows up with strong execution and dogged persistence, the main ingredients for success are in place. If an entrepreneur repeatedly makes good decisions, the gears are set in motion to reach escape velocity. To understand how the entrepreneur is thinking, find out whether they display a strong intrinsic motivation to make the idea succeed, an open mind to pivot when necessary, and a can-do attitude to combat adversity. Look at factors that may hamper success: whether there are extrinsic motivators that are misaligned with entrepreneurship, a lack of conviction to run with the idea, or a negative attitude that turns the entrepreneur into their own worst enemy.

Use this checklist to assess your own situation. Also be aware that venture capitalists look at similar factors to assess you and your idea. Of course, making better decisions is desirable for more than just startup success. If you can enable positive forces in your life that automatically guide you toward making better decisions, both you and your startup will be happier.

Stop Pitching Ideas

In the past, I have heard pitches of "the next big disruptive idea," "the future of social networking," and an idea "ten times better than Facebook" (seriously, I am not making this up). Entrepreneurs seek to attract capital with these claims (venture capital or angel funding), to make their projects reality. The point they often miss is that pitching ideas is a waste of time and a huge turnoff to experienced investors. Pitches may be amusing, but they can shut investors' doors before the first MVP has been tested.

By *pitching ideas* I do not mean talking about a fresh idea with a friend and asking for their feedback. I mean the belief that an idea alone is enough to attract investment. You learned throughout this book what it takes to engage third parties with confirmed value propositions. If you stick to what this book suggests you do, you will never feel compelled to pitch ideas.

During the dot.com boom ten years ago, the story was a little different: getting an online presence required making an upfront investment in server infrastructure, paying database license fees, and hiring an experienced staff that was hard to find. The initial costs of an Internet startup could amount to $1 million. Luckily, we face an entirely different reality today: cloud and scalable VPS hosting, even designated servers, can be had for less than $100 per month. CMSs and databases are a dime a dozen; most businesses can pick from a wide offering of free open source or inexpensive solutions. Relevant experience is also much easier to find: basic coding and front-end user experience are simple with WYSIWYG and widget programming. Job fairs like elance.com and odesk.com offer competitive skills for hire. Rapid prototyping is quickly becoming the norm, with workable prototypes available for less than $50.

We talked about the importance of the minimum viable product throughout this book. If you are an entrepreneur, you need a prototype today. If you are still pitching ideas to attract investment, no matter how sophisticated your pitch deck and the financials look, it will be hard to obtain funding. More important than putting together that killer presentation is getting started and leaving the building to test your hypothesis in the market. Once you have a couple of prospective clients for your product, you can begin to iterate, tweak, and jumpstart grassroots marketing efforts. It is not rocket science to put an idea on the ground and test it, and investors want to see entrepreneurs do exactly that.

Expertise Is the New Venture Capital

Because almost no investment is required to found a startup, it has become more critical for young companies to focus on finding advice about product development, scalability, and marketing. An experienced entrepreneur or investor can provide you with a professional network. This is usually more important than funding. If your MVP shows initial traction, you have much more leverage to attract qualified advice. To come across as a doer, not a talker, you must prove you can deliver. And when you do that, you are no longer pitching ideas. Only then can you engage others to get on board with you who can help your startup.

Why You Cannot Replicate Silicon Valley

Silicon Valley is the nickname for Santa Clara Valley, the South Bay portion of the San Francisco Bay area in northern California. In the last years, the term has become a synonym for innovation. Research parks often dream out loud of copying Silicon Valley. Occasionally, someone makes the mistake of publicly declaring that they will take it on head to head, only to silently fade into oblivion a few short years later. Moscow's Skolkovo innovation center is a legendary example. Billions of rubles flowed into an entrepreneurship and research hub dubbed the "Silicon Valley of Moscow," with little certainty of success.[11]

Even the residents of Silicon Valley struggle to explain how its success came about. According to author Deborah Perry Piscione, we have to go back to the year 1884, when Leland Stanford thought about what a university in his son's honor could look like. Piscione goes on to explain several ingredients of the success story that is Silicon Valley.[12] Let's look at some of them and examine the three main building blocks that made Silicon Valley what it is today.

Stanford University, the "MIT of the West"

Stanford University, located in the north part of the valley, has been one of its defining elements. Its founder, Leland Stanford, insisted that "science provide direct usefulness in life," which put the university in a league of its own. Stanford now runs its own industrial park, which over 150 companies call home. Most other universities ignored the relevance of science at the time, and, unfortunately, not much has changed in the meantime.

After World War I, the U.S. military granted $450 million (in 1945 dollars) to weapons R&D. Several universities on the East Coast (such as Harvard and MIT) shared this money. But only $50,000 found its way to Stanford University, which at the time lacked the reputation of being a credible research center. Frederick Terman, then Stanford's chair of engineering, felt so personally offended that he vowed to recruit away from East Coast universities the best research talent available. He transformed Stanford into the "MIT of the West," as author Steve Blank puts it. When the Cold War intensified after 1950, Stanford University became a full partner with the military, the CIA, and the NSA.

Stanford researchers routinely work with industry as paid consultants. This not only ensures that the latest technological know-how finds its way into the market, but also channels insight about business and industry trends back to students and researchers. So far, the university has spawned more than 6,000 companies.[13] Some of them include Charles Schwab & Company, Cisco Systems, Dolby Laboratories, eBay, E*Trade, Electronic Arts, Gap, Google, Hewlett-Packard, IDEO, Intuit, LinkedIn, Logitech, MathWorks, Netflix, Nike, NVIDIA, Odwalla, Orbitz, Rambus, Silicon Graphics, Sun Microsystems, Tesla Motors, Varian, VMware, Yahoo!, Zillow, and Instagram. Together they amount to hundreds of billions of dollars of market capitalization.

---

[11]Isabel Gorst, "Massive Funds for a 'Silicon Valley' Lookalike, *Financial Times*; October 18, 2012, www.ft.com/intl/cms/s/0/67850d9c-1480-11e2-8cf2-00144feabdc0.html.
[12]Deborah Perry Piscione, *Secrets of Silicon Valley: What Everyone Else Can Learn from the Innovation Capital of the World* (New York: Palgrave Macmillan, 2013).
[13]Stanford University, *Wellspring of Innovation*, www.stanford.edu/group/wellspring.

U.S. Military Funding Started a Chain Reaction

Most people believe the United States is leading the technology sector because of fiercely independent entrepreneurial minds. In reality, the government created all these sectors with a heavy hand that had a big influence on the destiny of Silicon Valley. By transforming hundreds of acres of farmland into a hub of cutting-edge military technology, the U.S. Navy built Moffett Federal Airfield at the southern tip of San Francisco Bay in the 1930s. Large-scale subsidies from the military enabled the thriving electronics and semiconductor industry. The Internet emerged from a military research project. Heavy military funding started a chain reaction that led to the Silicon Valley we know today.

The electronics industry transformed the valley into a hotbed of innovation with Hewlett-Packard (HP) and Varian as its biggest success stories. They went public in 1956 and 1957 as the first Silicon Valley companies in history. Shockley Labs, set up in the heart of the valley, was the first company to work on silicon semiconductor devices and gave the region the nickname Silicon Valley. Its eight leading scientists later left Shockley together to create a joint venture with Fairchild Semiconductor, which revolutionized the chip-manufacturing industry. Many of the original founders of Fairchild Semiconductor set out to start their own companies in Silicon Valley: for example, Robert Noyce and Gordon Moore started Intel, and Jerry Sanders and John Carey started Advanced Micro Devices (AMD). These new companies had inclusive cultures with flat hierarchies and in many ways created a new generation of companies.

The Growth and Profitability of Venture Capital

Wealthy investors became interested in Silicon Valley after the first successful IPOs in the electronics and semiconductor industry. The passage of the Small Business Investment Act in 1958 enabled the large-scale financing of small entrepreneurial businesses in America. Another milestone was the establishment of the limited partnership as a business structure in the 1970s. This provided an opportunity for general partners of venture capital funds to legally charge a 1–2.5% management fee of the investment capital raised. In addition, they charged a 20% fee on all profits of the fund. This is the venture capital model still in existence today.

It becomes apparent that the birth of Silicon Valley was not an overnight affair. In fact, it took more than 100 years to transform an area of farmland into the epicenter of innovation we know today. Not only were large-scale military funding and government protectionism a big part of it, but much luck and serendipity played into this success story. When a government announces that it will build "the Silicon Valley of XYZ," then we must assume they turn a blind eye on history. Many puzzle pieces fell into place over decades to make it happen. None of them would have worked out of context in a different environment to quickly force the same ecosystem into existence.

If you have ever been in Mountain View, you notice that there is a certain energy in the air. A few millions, even billions, cannot buy this energy. It cannot be summoned by willpower. No government can legislate it into existence. And no university can just say it would *like* to have this energy and make it magically appear.

Forget about comparing universities or research parks with Silicon Valley. By aiming at the Sun, you may end up on the Moon, this is true. But there are other proven ways to make startup entrepreneurship work. Simple, practical steps have led to success in hundreds of startups, and some of them are outlined in this book. Begin applying them one by one, without trying to reinvent the wheel. Then your university and your startups will succeed.

I

Index

A

Accelerators
    alumni and founder networks, 135
    B-grade companies, 134
    business incubators, 132
    creating bubbles, 134
    focus on smaller companies, 134
    hardware startups, 133
    profit versions of incubators, 132
    software and technology startups, 133
    startup founders, 134
    startup schools, 135
    universities benefit, 135
    useful companies, 134
    venture capital firms, 133
    Y Combinator, 133

Angel investors
    and universities, 128
    and venture capitalists, 127
    celebrities, 127
    description, 127
    FFF round, 128
    profitability, 128
    Ramen profitability, 128
    tech hubs, 128

Asian Development Banks (ADBs), 192–193

B

Bazaar approach, 154

Benefits *vs.* features
    academic entrepreneurs, 61
    checklist, 66
    listen and learn, 65–66
    MVPs, 66
    SPIN technique, 62–65
    venture capitalist, 61

Big Battery Corporation (BBC), 105

Burn rate, 81

Business cards, 112

Business lunch, 113–115

Business model canvas, 167–168

Business model canvas/lean canvas, 111

C

Chief executive officer (CEO)
    and CIO, 113
    Big Battery Corporation (BBC), 105
    The Business Post, 105
    feedback, early-stage product, 115
    full presentation, 114
    LinkedIn group, 116
    R&D, 106

D

Demo days, 189–191

E

Economic theory
    and business school knowledge, 91
    corporate finance, 88
    description, 90
    disadvantage, 88
    high-price environment, 90

Index

Economic theory (cont.)
  London School of Economics, 90
  low-price environment, 90
  macroeconomics, 88
  MBA, 90
  microeconomics, 88
  real-estate boom, 89
  supply-and-demand model, 88–89
Electric scooter startup, 22–23
Elevator pitch, 103–106
Engaging others with actionable next steps
  checklist, 60
  interaction, 55
  MVPs, 56
  NDA, 55
  one-page proposal, 57–60
  public university, 56
  with actionable next steps, 56
Entrepreneur alumni networks, 174
Entrepreneur-in-residence (EIR)
      program, 160
  business schools, 188
  definitions, 188
  entrepreneurial, 188
  intrapreneur, 188
  modules, 188–189
  multinationals and governments, 188
  source of excellent media coverage, 189
Entrepreneurship, learning, 173

F

Failing fast, 129–130
Financial business model
  assumptions, 83
  checklist, 91–92
  costs, 83
  economic theory, 88–91
  existing market, 85–86
  financial accounting, 83
  hockey-stick growth, 86
  investing, 84–85
  investor, 87
  market size and share, 87
  MVP testing, 87
  new market, 86
  potential partners, 87
  product/market fit, 86
  profit projections, 83
  projected future cash flows, 84
  real-estate investment, 87
  re-segmented market, 86
  revenue, 83
  serving, 87
  specialists, 91–92
  venture capitalists, 84
Financial business models
  and projections, 82
  burn rate, 81
  corporate finance, 82
  costs, 83
  investors, 81
  potential market, 81
  profit, 83
  profit margin, 83
  revenue, 82
  spreadsheet software, 81
  venture capitalist, 82
Financial model, 111
Fundraising materials
  demo or prototype, 142
  due-diligence materials, 142
  financial model, 141
  lean canvas, 141
  PPC, 142

G

Government visits, 179–180

H

High-net-worth individuals
      (HNWIs), 56, 126

I

Ikiru, 53
Impact investment, 199–200
Incremental product development
  description, 17
  MVP, 17
Incubators
  acceptance criteria, 132
  business support programs, 132
  economic development
      organizations, 132

Index

government entities, 132
research and technology parks house incubation programs, 131
startup stage, 131
venture capital firms, 131

Industry links, 174

Industry visit
commercializing technology, 181
feedback, 182
intellectual property, 182
leveraged approach, 182
multinational corporations, 181
multinational industry, 182
multinational industry giant, 181
MVP testing, 182
R&D operations, 182–183
real partnerships, 181
small and medium enterprises (SMEs), 181, 183
technology transfer/licensing office (TTO/TLO), 181

Initial public offering (IPO), 126, 143

Intergovernmental organizations (IGOs)
Asian Development Bank (ADB), 192
biodegradable battery technology, 193
channeling, 193
economic scale and momentum, 192
electric scooter, 193
funding requests, 192
global organizations, 191 mission, 192
prediction of seismic activity, 193
robotic manufacturing, 193
STI, 192

International Monetary Fund (IMF), 192

Intrapreneur, 188

Investment fund
benefits, 200–201
master platform, 195–197

Investor visit, 183–185

IPO. See Initial public offering (IPO)

J

Joint venture
chemistry and mutual trust, 139
company and university research team, collaboration, 139
MVP testing, 139
partners, 139
SMEs, 138
startups and industry, 138

K

Kamikaze-style, 32

Key performance indicators (KPIs), 9, 147–148, 153

L

Lean product development, 22

The Lean Startup
business plan, 25
description, 15
incremental product development (see Incremental product development)
lean canvas and financial model, 27
startup coach, 24

Li-ion battery technology, 96

Limited liability company (LLC), 95

M

Macroeconomics, 88

Meetings and communication skills
business cards, 112
business lunch, 113, 115
business model canvas/lean canvas, 111
checklist, 118
confidentiality, 109–110
elevator pitch, 103–106
financial model, 111
micro-scripts, 103–106
MVP testing, 107
NDAs, 109–110
one-page proposal, 111
photographs, 112
points to discuss, 110–111
Powerpoint, 99
10/20/30 rule, 100–103
    backup plan, 103
    call to action, 101
    large font size, 101
    potential project, 103

Index

Meetings and communication skills (cont.)
    PowerPoint slide before
        applying, 101–102
    Silicon Valley, 100
    SPIN technique, 103
    third parties, 100
  sketches, 112
  SPIN, 107
  technical drawings, 112
  unexpected situations, 108–109
  well-researched requests, 115–118
Microeconomics, 88
Micro-script rules, 103–106
Millennium Development Goals (MDGs), 180
Mind maps, 74–75
Mind storming, 72–73
Minimum viable product (MVP), 17, 56, 68, 167–168
  checklist, 19
  electric scooter, 24
  growth hypothesis, 18
  testing, 104
  process, 18
  value hypothesis, 18

N

Non-disclosure agreement (NDA), 109–110
North-American Free Trade Agreement (NAFTA), 191

O

One-page proposal
  action, 58
  description, 57
  financial, 58
  name and date, 58
  preparation, 60
  rationale, 58
  sample, 59
  secondary targets, 58
  status, 58
  target, 57
  title, 57
Open IP
  bazaar approach, 154
  intellectual property, 155

  NSF, 155
  ownership of projects, 155
  PCT, 155
  WIPO, 155
Optimization approach, 178

P, Q

Parkinson's Law, 70–71
Patents and technology transfer
  Brookings Institution, 154
  KPIs, 153
  positive grant system, 154
  revenue, 153
  TLO, 152–153
  TTO, 152, 154
  universities, 152
Platform projects
  banks, 193–195
  communication, 187
  demo days, 189–191
  entrepreneur-in-residence (EIR) program, 188–189
  feedback and two-way knowledge exchange, 187
  funds, 193–195
  IGOs, 191–192
  impact investment, 199–200
  investment fund, 195–197, 200–201
  MVP, 187
  presentations for investors, 193–195
  venture capital vs. mega fund, 197–198
Platform-thinking approach
  active exchange of ideas, 178
  business model and financial model, 177
  communication, 177
  financial matching scheme, 177
  government visits, 179–180
  industry visit, 181–183
  innovation and growth, 178
  intergovernmental organizations, 178
  internal efforts, 186
  investor visit, 183–185
  key performance indicators (KPIs), 177
  optimization approach, 178
  self-sustaining entities, 178
  stuff approach, 178
  university ecosystem, 179

Powerpoint, 99
PPC. *See* Private placement memorandum (PPC)
Price differentiation, 46
Private placement memorandum (PPC), 142
Product/market fit, 86

R

Return on investment (ROI), 127

S

Seismic Software, 108
SensorX sensors, 109
Simple strategies
    business approach, researchers and entrepreneurs, 69
    deadlines, 70–71
    mastermind groups, 71
    mind maps, 74–75
    mind storming, 72–73
    murky waters, entrepreneurship, 67
    one action per day, 69–70
    spend just ten more minutes, 75
    taking action, 68–69
    think on paper, 73–74
    to think, 72
    visualization, 76
Situation problem implication need-payoff (SPIN) technique, 62–65
Small and medium enterprises (SMEs), 138, 169, 172
Smartphone battery technology, 20–21
Socially responsible investment (SRI), 199
Startup
    attorney, 96
    business, 93
    checklist, 98
    clarity about ownership, 95
    corporations, 95
    ease of investment, 95
    interest, 93
    investible, 96
    investor/venture capitalist knocks, 93
    limited liability company (LLC), 95
    never spend money to make money, 97–98
    ownership, 96
    partnership, 95
    sole proprietorship, 94
Startup entrepreneurship
    advice, 51
    and stockbroker, 53
    big numbers, 45–46
    bootstrapping, 36–37
    business abroad, 39–40
    checklist, 54
    comfort zone, 41, 43
    creativity, 30–31
    dedicating time and resources, 30
    20% generalist, 47–48
    global stage, 30
    good first impression, 37–39
    hollywood version, 53
    Ikiru, 53
    launching own company, 52
    learning, 49–50
    management, 30–31
    mindset, 40–41
    mission and purpose, 52
    motivations, 29
    persistent movement, 30
    read and improve, 43–45
    scratching and clawing, 30
    80% specialist, 47–48
    stop being late, 35
    teaching, 52
    time management, 32–35
    turtle-style, 32
    willpower *vs.* self-confidence, 32
    working, 52
Startup grants
    advisors, 122–123
    early funding, 120
    entrepreneurs, 119
    funding, 123–124
    government programs, 121–122
    investment, 120
    investors, 122–123
    money and entrepreneurship, 122
    network effects, 121–122
    universities, 119
    writing proposals and business plans, 120

Index

Startup launch process
    companies and financial sector, 14
    motivation and freedom, 11
    network effects, 11
    practical strategies, 14
    roadblocks, 12
    sequence, 10
    synergies and ecosystem, 11

Startup stage
    entrepreneurship, stages, 137–138
    joint venture deal, 138
    MVP testing mode, 137
    toolkit, analytical tools, 137

Stuff approach, 178

Sustainable transport initiative (STI), 192–193

T

Technology licensing office (TLO), 148, 152–153, 173

Technology transfer/licensing office (TTO/TLO), 51

Thriving business, 4

Time management, 32–35

Troubleshooting
    bankruptcy, 79
    "build, measure learn", 78
    checklist, 80
    conflicts, 77
    entrepreneurial experience, 79
    interim CEO, 79
    joint venture plans, 78
    money, 78
    network and entrepreneurs, 78
    open communication, 78
    priority, team, 77
    problem-solving, 79
    product and business model, 79
    quiet moment, 78
    stakeholders, 78
    startup teams, 79
    team lost, 78

Turtle-style, 32

Twenty idea method, 72–73

U

Ultra-high-net-worth clients (UHNWI), 184–185

Ultra-high-net-worth individuals (UHNWIs), 194

United Nations (UN), 191

Universities
    academia, 8
    American counterparts, 148
    Asian campuses, 148
    commercial ideas, 148
    communicate ideas, 145
    ecosystem, 7
    entrepreneurial experience, 145
    entrepreneurship, 6
    entrepreneurship program, 145
    entrepreneurship work, 147
    Europe, 148
    incomplete launch pad, 9
    individual experiences and feedback, 145
    institutions approach, 9
    integrating entrepreneurship, 146
    key performance indicators (KPIs), 9, 147
    launching startups, 146
    magnets for smart people, 145
    network building and cooperations, 6–7
    privileged position, 146
    startup success, 147–149
    students and researchers, 5
    synergistic interaction, 9
    vanity metrics, 146

Universities, support for startups
    fail smart and collect data, 170
    guidelines, 166
    industry networking, 169–170
    management activities, 168–169
    mentors vs. workshops, 166–168
    new ideas, 165
    sweeping changes, 165

University, measurable impact
    Facebook, 152
    open IP, 154–155
    patents and tech transfer, 152–154
    performance metrics, 152

University startup entrepreneurs
   characteristics, 4
   conventional advice, 2
   desktop computer, 3
   external parties, 1
   fail-safe system, 1
   media stories, 4
   own business, 2
   paid project, 3
   part-time work, 2
   trial phase, 3
   venture capital, 4
   will and common sense, 4

University startups
   entrepreneurship networks, 160
   grants and workshops, entrepreneurship, 157
   hands-off approach, 160
   job, entrepreneurship, 163–164
   knowledge exchange entrepreneurship
      initiatives, 159
      joint venture partners, 158–159
      university research, 158–159
   opportunity cost, 158
   standardization, 162
   startup experts, 161

V

Venture capitalists (VCs)
   firm invests, 125
   HNWIs and institutional investors, 126
   IPO, 126
   lack of business and financial models, 126
   ROI, 127
   sound track record, 127
   students and researchers, 126
   winners, 127
   World War II, 126

Venture capital (VC)
   amount of capital, 141
   best VCs, 142
   fundraising materials, 141–142
   IPO, 143
   startup entrepreneurs, 140–141
   startup investigation, 142–143
   term sheet, 143

Venture capital *vs.* mega fund, 197–198

Volcanic-eruption module, 108

W, X, Y, Z

World Trade Organization (WTO), 191

Get the eBook for only $10!

Now you can take the weightless companion with you anywhere, anytime. Your purchase of this book entitles you to 3 electronic versions for only $10.

This Apress title will prove so indispensible that you'll want to carry it with you everywhere, which is why we are offering the eBook in 3 formats for only $10 if you have already purchased the print book.

Convenient and fully searchable, the PDF version enables you to easily find and copy code—or perform examples by quickly toggling between instructions and applications. The MOBI format is ideal for your Kindle, while the ePUB can be utilized on a variety of mobile devices.

Go to www.apress.com/promo/tendollars to purchase your companion eBook.

Apress®
THE EXPERT'S VOICE™

All Apress eBooks are subject to copyright. All rights are reserved by the Publisher, whether the whole or part of the material is concerned, specifically the rights of translation, reprinting, reuse of illustrations, recitation, broadcasting, reproduction on microfilms or in any other physical way, and transmission or information storage and retrieval, electronic adaptation, computer software, or by similar or dissimilar methodology now known or hereafter developed. Exempted from this legal reservation are brief excerpts in connection with reviews or scholarly analysis or material supplied specifically for the purpose of being entered and executed on a computer system, for exclusive use by the purchaser of the work. Duplication of this publication or parts thereof is permitted only under the provisions of the Copyright Law of the Publisher's location, in its current version, and permission for use must always be obtained from Springer. Permissions for use may be obtained through RightsLink at the Copyright Clearance Center. Violations are liable to prosecution under the respective Copyright Law.

Other Apress Business Titles You Will Find Useful

Why Startups Fail
Feinleib
978-1-4302-4140-9

How to Create the Next Facebook
Taulli
978-1-4302-4647-3

Startup
Ready
978-1-4302-4218-5

Founders at Work
Livingston
978-1-4302-1078-8

Venture Capitalists at Work
Shah/Shah
978-1-4302-3837-9

Inventors at Work
Stern
978-1-4302-4506-3

The JOBS Act
Cunningham
978-1-4302-4755-5

Design Thinking for Entrepreneurs and Small Businesses
Ingle
978-1-4302-6181-0

Financial Modeling for Business Owners and Entrepreneurs
Sawyer
978-1-4842-0371-2

Available at www.apress.com

CPSIA information can be obtained
at www.ICGtesting.com
Printed in the USA
LVHW090758230920
666787LV00029B/155